# PHOTOGRAPI

ROCKPORT

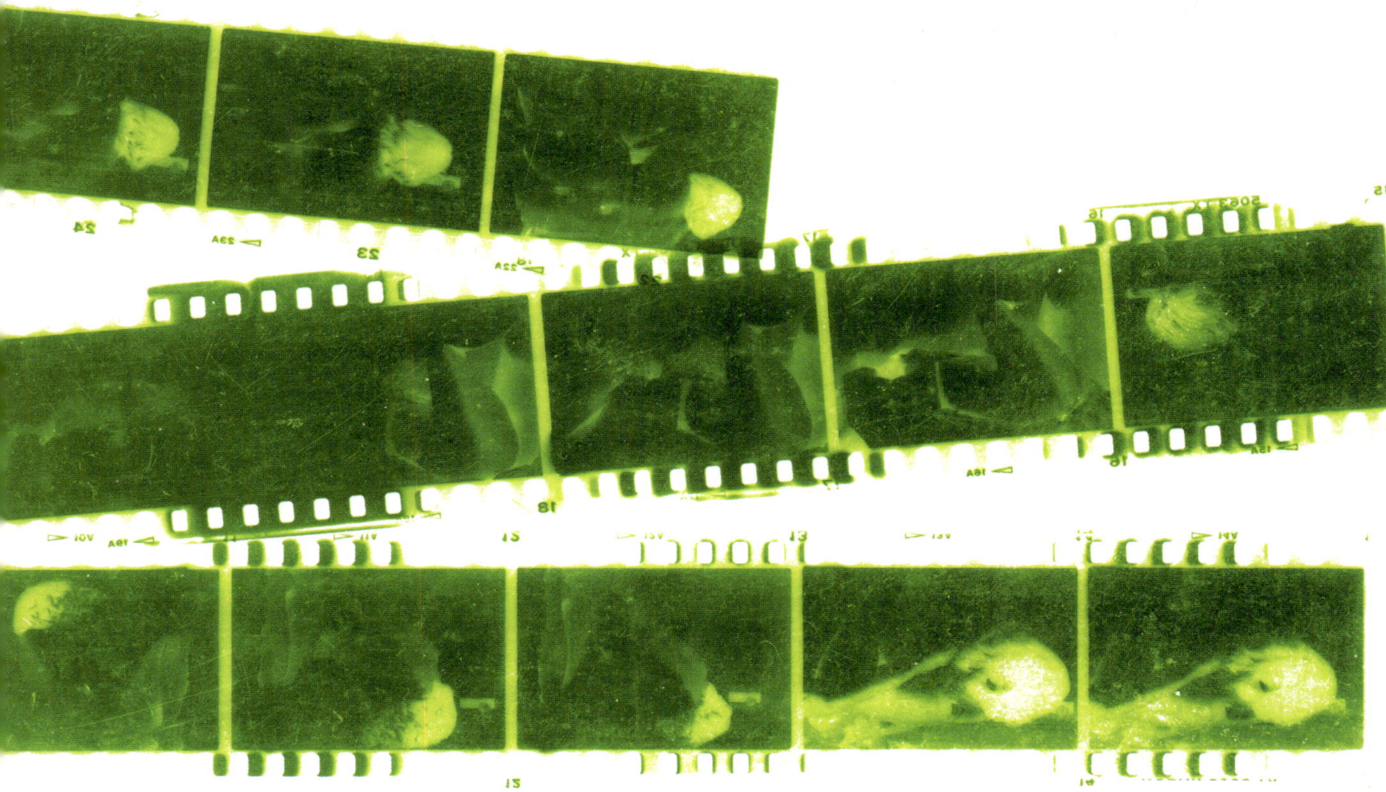

First published in the United States of America by
Rockport Publishers, Inc.
33 Commercial Street
Gloucester, Massachusetts 01930-5089
Telephone: (978) 282-9590
Facsimile: (978) 283-2742

Distributed to the book trade and art trade in the United States by
North Light Books, an imprint of
F & W Publications
1507 Dana Avenue
Cincinnati, Ohio 45207
Telephone: (800) 289-0963

Other distribution by
Rockport Publishers, Inc.
Gloucester, Massachusetts 01930-5089

ISBN 1-56496-597-X

10 9 8 7 6 5 4 3 2 1

Design: Stoltze Design
Cover Image: Brian Azer
Cover Photography: Christine Navin and Brian Azer

Printed in China.

# PHOTOGRAPHY

*Creating Effective Graphic Design with Photography*

*Cheryl Cullen*

graphicIDEA resource

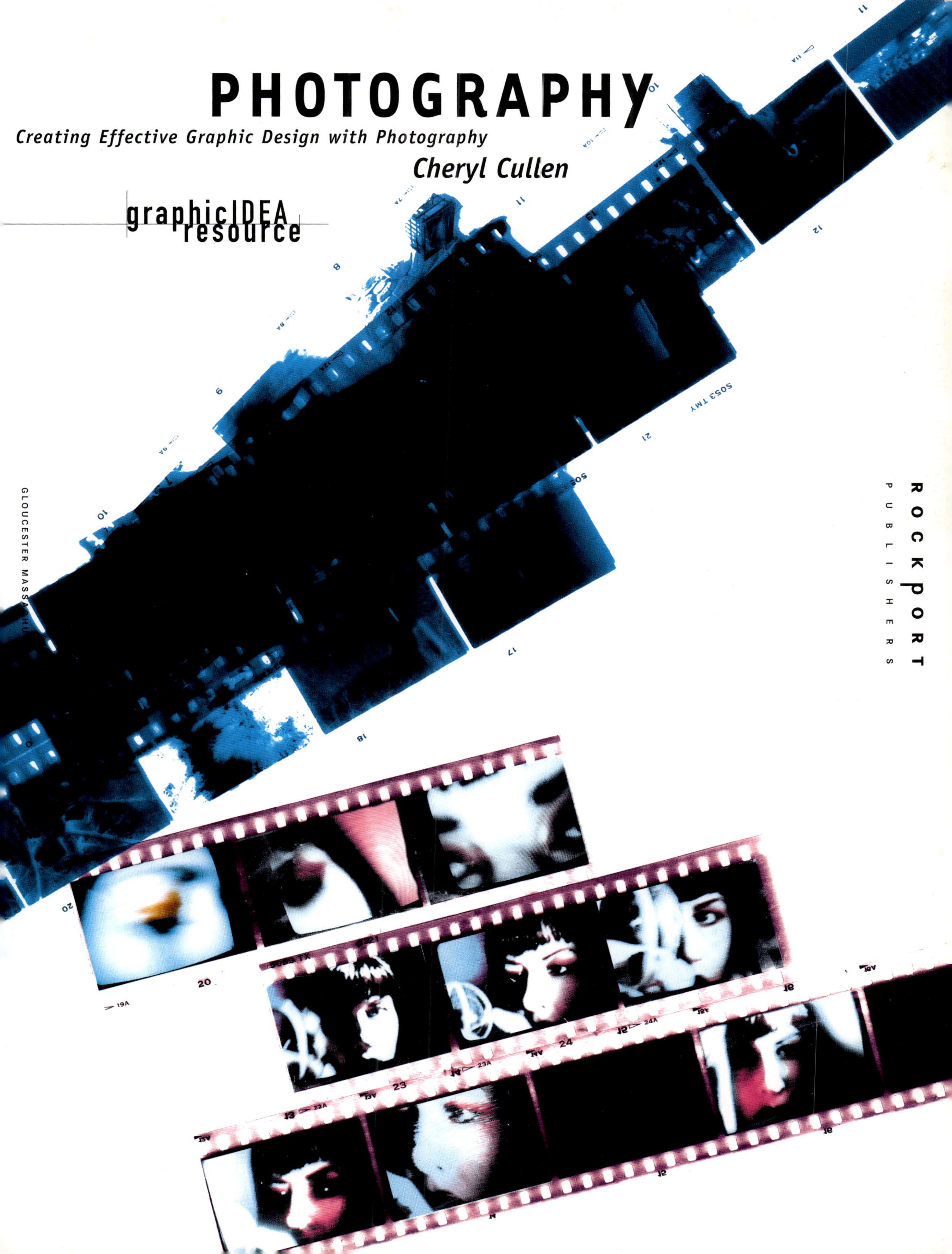

ROCKPORT PUBLISHERS

GLOUCESTER MASSA

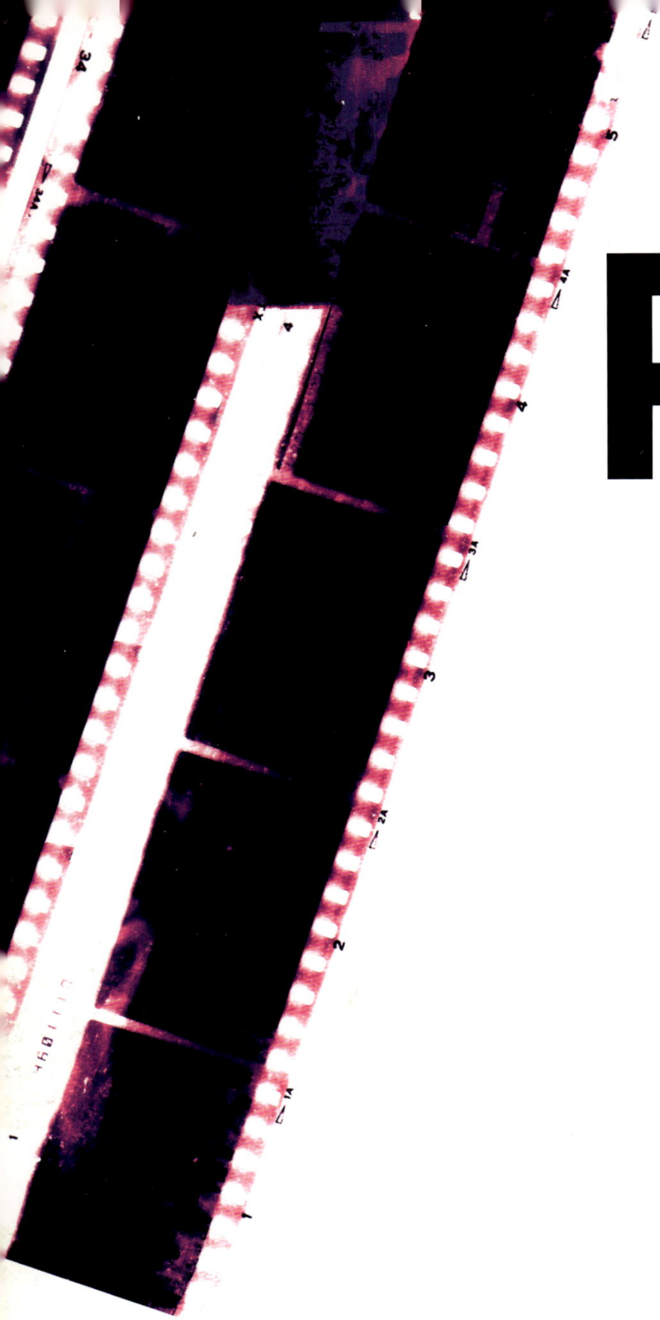

# PHOTO

# GRAPHY

Since its inception in the early nineteenth century in the form of daguerreotypes and tintypes, photography has always been a treasured, creative art form. Now, as then, we are amazed by how a photographer can convey even the most subtle message through shadows and light and black and white or color. Every decision the photographer makes, from the choice of film speed and exposure to secret formulations in the darkroom, can and does affect the ultimate outcome.

Before the advent of computer technology, the photographer retained much of the creative control for how a photo reproduced in graphic design. But, now with the technological resources available to the designer, the final form an image takes is no longer the sole domain of the photographer.

Today, designers have as much say about the final outcome of a photographic image as the photographer. Together, they are raising photography in graphic design to an entirely new level of art form. Photo-imaging software allows designers and photographers to tweak images to the *n*th degree. With an infinite variety of filters, photos can now be pixilated, masked, reversed, and manipulated, in ways never dreamed possible.

As we approach the twenty-first century, we have more choices than ever before and more technological resources available with which to experiment. We can peruse volumes upon volumes of stock photo images, scan a multitude of images online, carefully set and stage original photography, or seek out candid shots. The adage, rules were meant to be broken, applies more than ever to using photography in graphic design.

In fact, there are no more rules, for photography and the methods of manipulating the captured image have evolved into a medium without boundaries. In this collection of photography in graphic design, you will see everything from white type on a white background to entire photographic images that have been blurred save for one small area.

Photography and its use in design have traveled a long road since the days of daguerreotypes, which, for all of their inventiveness at the time, look overly simplistic by today's standards. Perhaps that explains the resurgence in popularity of early photographic art forms as highly valued collectibles—they provide a tangible link to the past that reminds us of how far photography has come and how much further it can be taken.

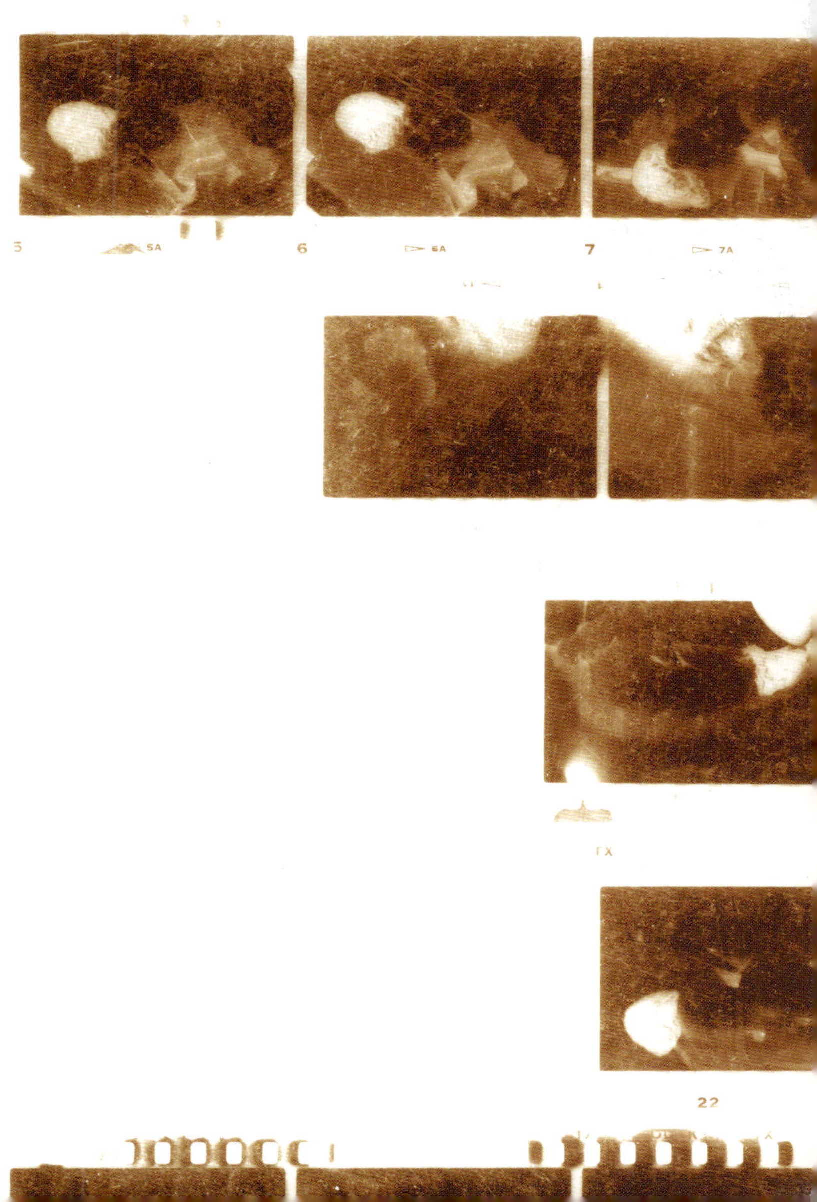

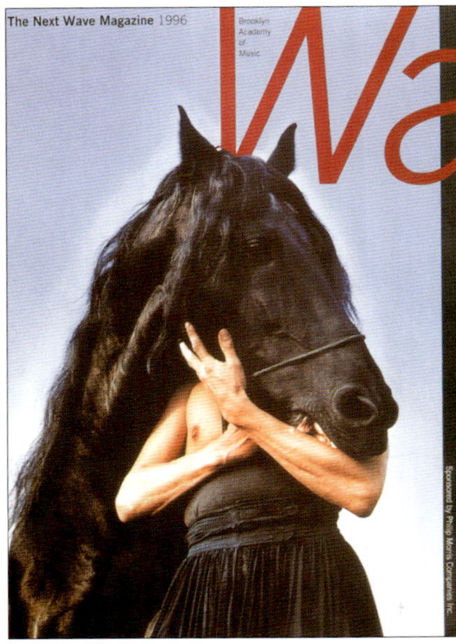


## BROOKLYN ACADEMY OF MUSIC *THE NEXT WAVE* MAGAZINE

**Design Firm** *BAMdesign*
**Design Consultant** *Michael Bierut*
**Art Director** *Rafael Weil*
**Designer** *Jason Ring*
**Photographer** *Brigitte Lacombe*

The photograph in this promotion for the Brooklyn Academy of Music's Next Wave Festival grabs the casual reader's attention and demands they take a second look. All of which works for the institution, whose goal is that the public do exactly that.

## BROOKLYN ACADEMY OF MUSIC ZINGARO BROCHURE

**Design Firm** *BAMdesign*
**Design Consultant** *Michael Bierut*
**Art Director** *Rafael Weil*
**Designer** *Jason Ring*

To promote an equestrian event, this direct mailer cuts to the chase and spotlights the topic in strong images that leap from the page. The mailing helped the Brooklyn Academy of Music exceed its overall sales goal.

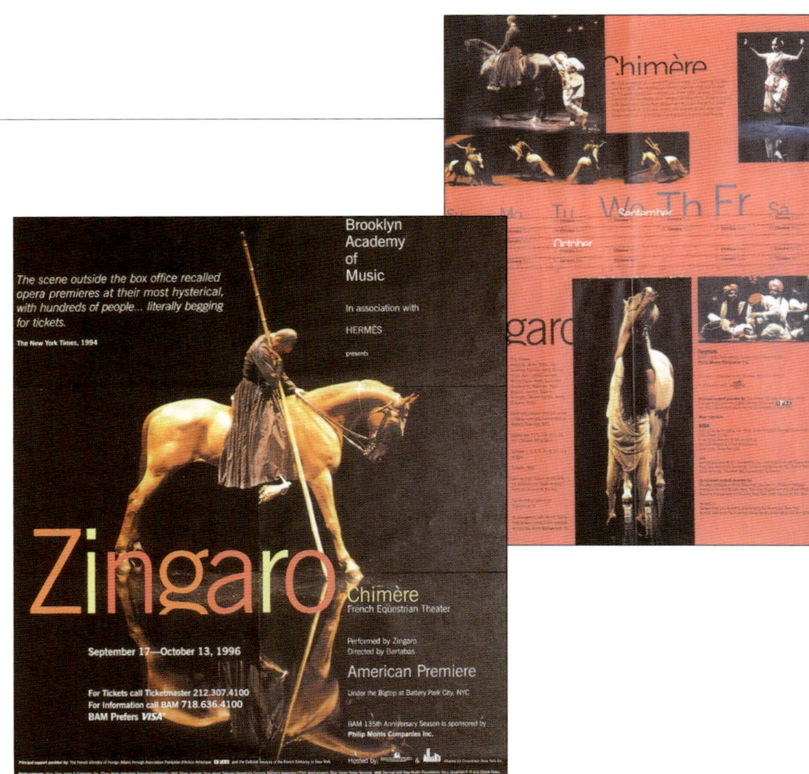

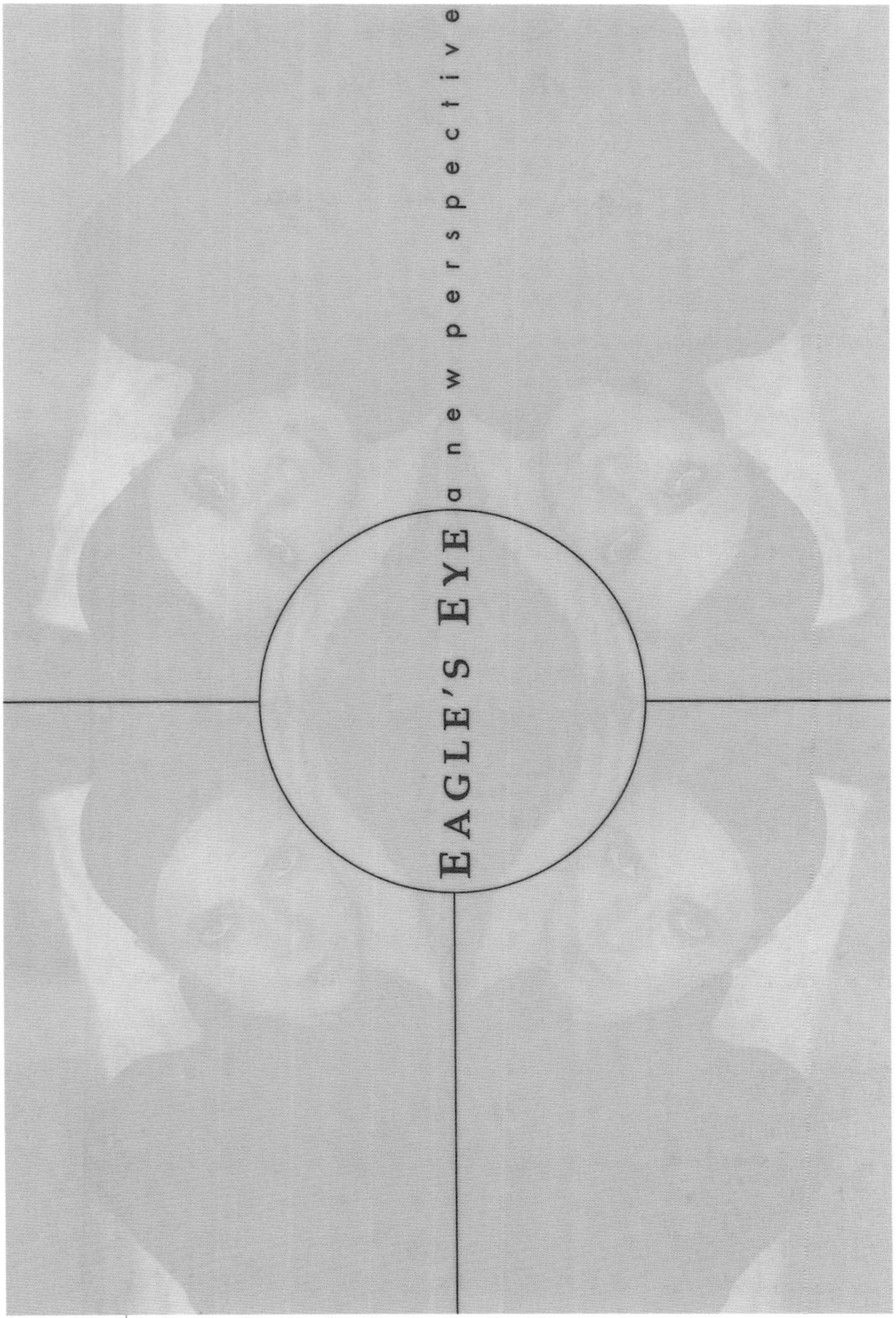


**EAGLE'S EYE IMAGE BOOK**

**Design Firm** *Socio X*
**Creative Director** *Deborah Moses*
**Art Director** *Bridget de Socio*
**Designer** *Albert Lin*
**Photographer** *Ruven Afanador*
**Digital Images** *Ninja von Oertzen*

Designed to transition Eagle's Eye apparel from manufacturer to brand name, this image book implies that the company is more than meets the "eye" by interspersing color and black-and-white photography with transparent pages. A thick mylar cover, which shades the underlying mirrored-image photo, communicates this message at first glance.

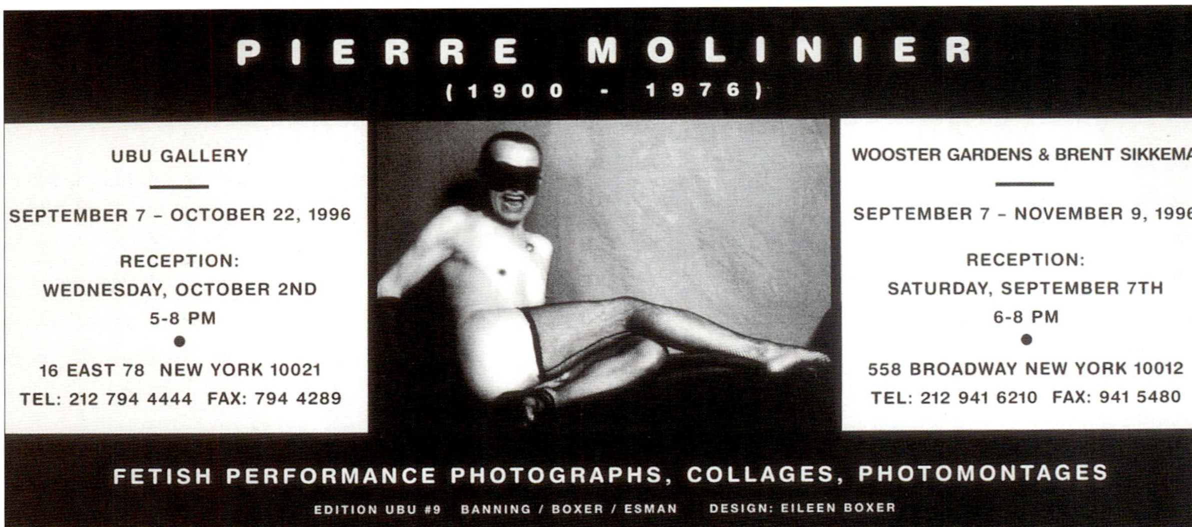


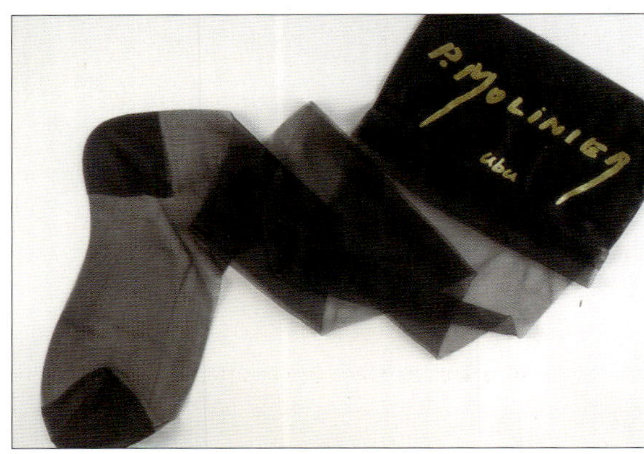


**UBU GALLERY PIERRE MOLINIER INVITATION**

**Design Firm** *Boxer Design*
**Art Director** *Eileen Boxer*
**Designer** *Eileen Boxer*
**Consultants** *Jack Banning, Adam Boxer, Rosa Esman*

This invitation to a showing of the photographic works of Pierre Molinier was intentionally under designed so as not to detract from the central photo, which is suggestive, yet appropriate for the style of art. An actual black silk stocking with the artist's name printed in gold accompanied the mailer.

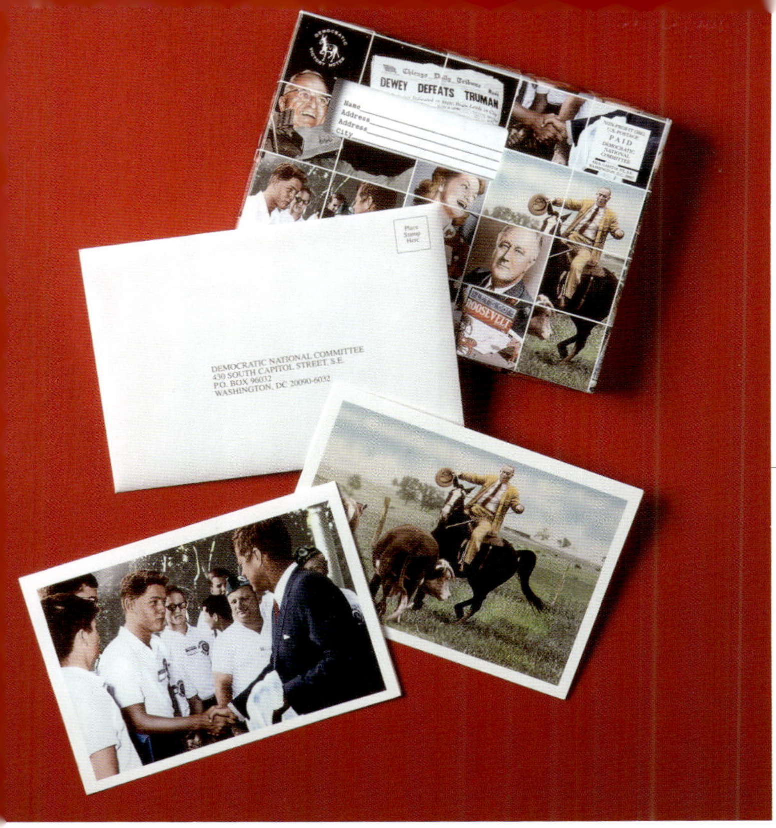


## DEMOCRATIC NATIONAL COMMITTEE NOTE CARDS

**Design Firm** *Thomas Drymon Design*
**Art Director** *Tom Drymon*
**Designer** *Tom Drymon*
**Copywriter** *Malchow Adams & Hussey–Lisa Selner*

By hand-coloring the photographs of historical events depicted on these note cards, this fundraising appeal, targeted primarily at senior citizens, conjured up a wave of nostalgia that resulted in a response rate 281 percent higher than the average rate for all appeals to the DNC in the previous year.

## UNITED STATES HOLOCAUST MEMORIAL MUSEUM MAILING

**Design Firm** *Lautman & Company*
**Art Director** *B & G, Inc.*
**Designer** *B & G, Inc.*

Simulated snapshots from 1945 of concentration-camp victims following the liberation allow us to put faces on the personal testimonials from American holocaust liberators.

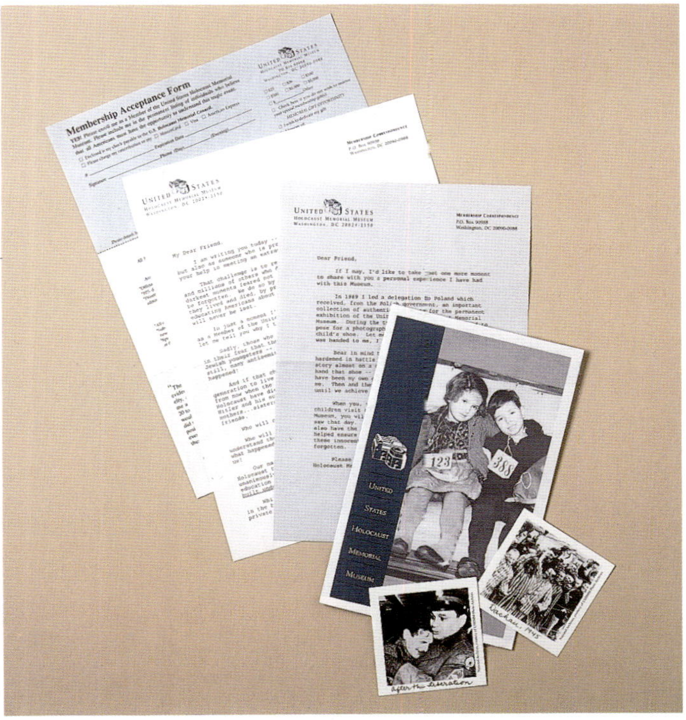

**RON ET NORMAND FASHION CATALOGS**

**Design Firm** *Moondog Studios, Inc.*
**Art Director** *Odette Hidalgo*
**Designer** *Derek von Essen*
**Photographer** *Cindy Sommerfield*

The full-color cover photo is seemingly larger than life, distinguishing Ron et Normand's catalog from the competition. The stark white background lets the reader focus on the clothing. Inside, the photos are black and white, again drawing attention to the product.

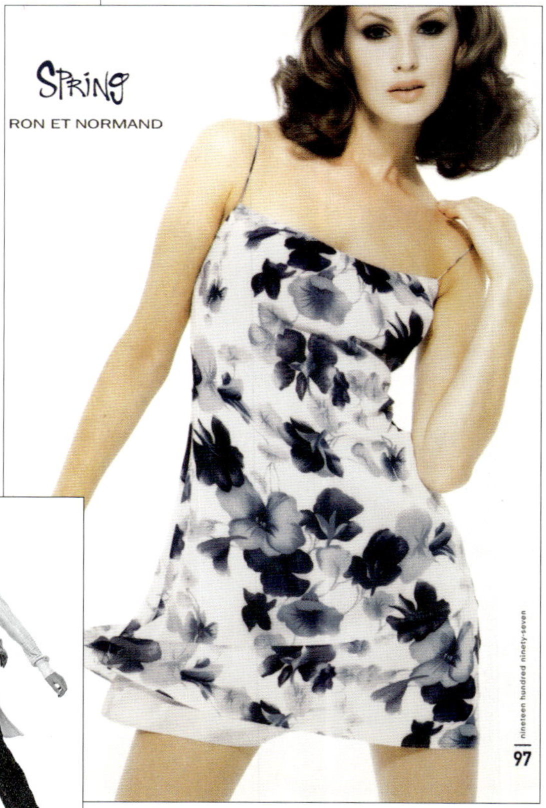


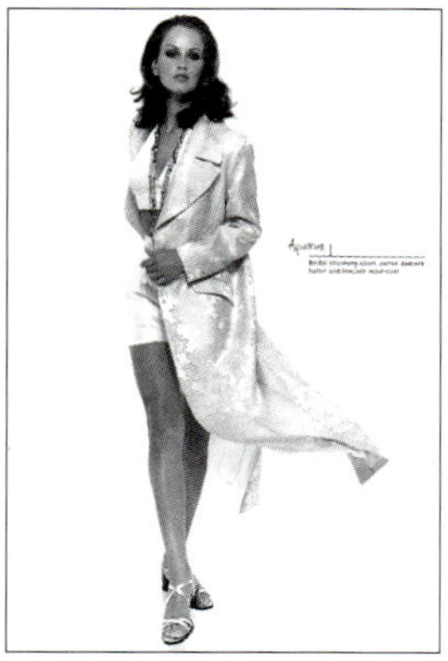

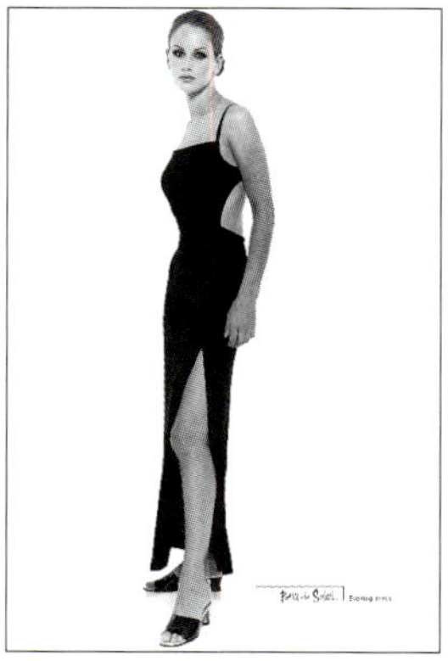

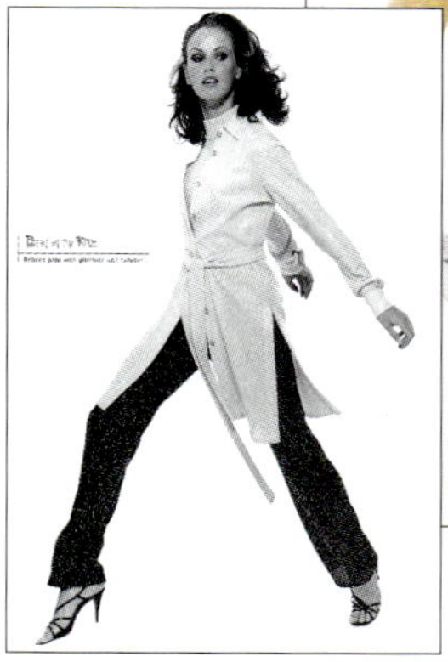

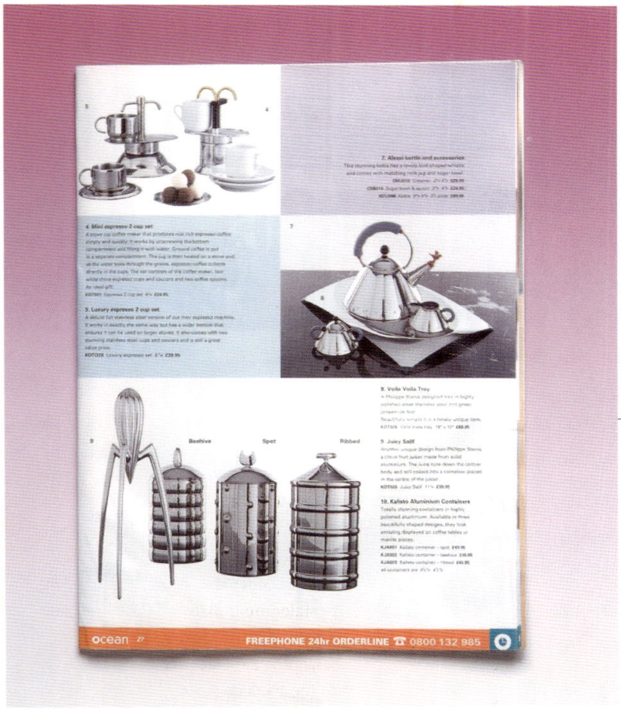


**OCEAN HOME SHOPPING LTD. CATALOG**

| | |
|---|---|
| **Design Firm** | *Gavin Joule Design* |
| **Creative Director** | *Aamir Ahmad* |
| **Art Director** | *Sean Galligan* |
| **Designer** | *Gavin Joule* |
| **Copywriter** | *Michael Harvey* |

Neutral-toned photographs of aluminum and steel objects are offset with color blocks that highlight product information without detracting from the products themselves. The clean, uncluttered look of the photos appeals to the high-tech kitchen-gadget lover.

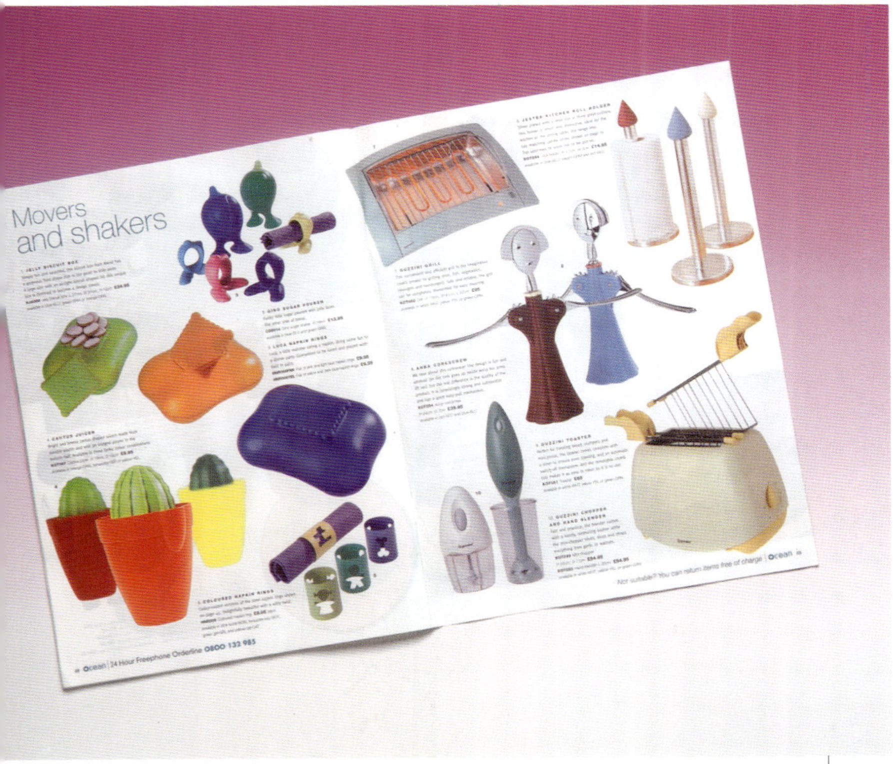


**OCEAN HOME SHOPPING LTD. CATALOG**

| | |
|---|---|
| **Design Firm** | *Gavin Joule Design* |
| **Creative Director** | *Aamir Ahmad* |
| **Art Director** | *Sean Galligan* |
| **Designer** | *Gavin Joule* |
| **Copywriter** | *Michael Harvey* |

This spread in the Ocean catalog, aptly titled, Movers and Shakers, entices the impulse buyer to choose from a virtual rainbow of products at an equally wide spectrum of price points.

## TAKASHIMAYA NEW YORK HOLIDAY CATALOG

**Design Firm** *Design: M/W, NYC*
**Art Directors** *Allison Muench Williams, J. Phillips Williams*
**Designers** *Allison Muench Williams, J. Phillips Williams*
**Copywriter** *Laura Silverman*
**Photographer** *Carlton Davis*

This innovative East/West department store deviates from the traditional seasonal catalog with a streamlined layout that uses its photography to lend an element of surprise to each page.

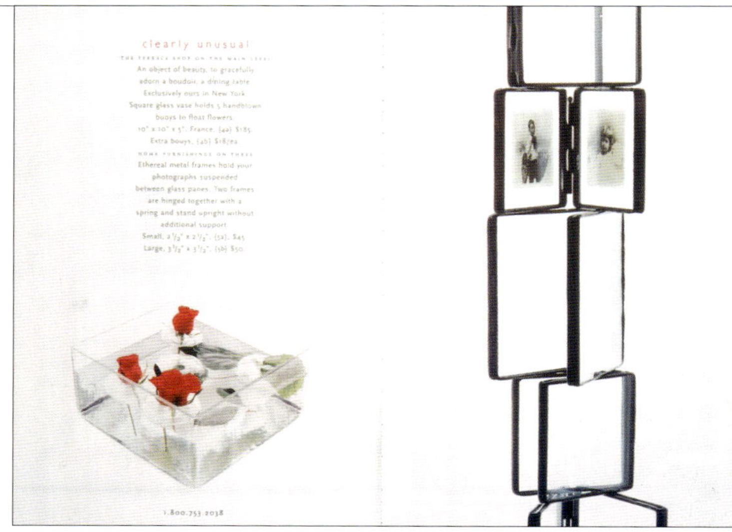


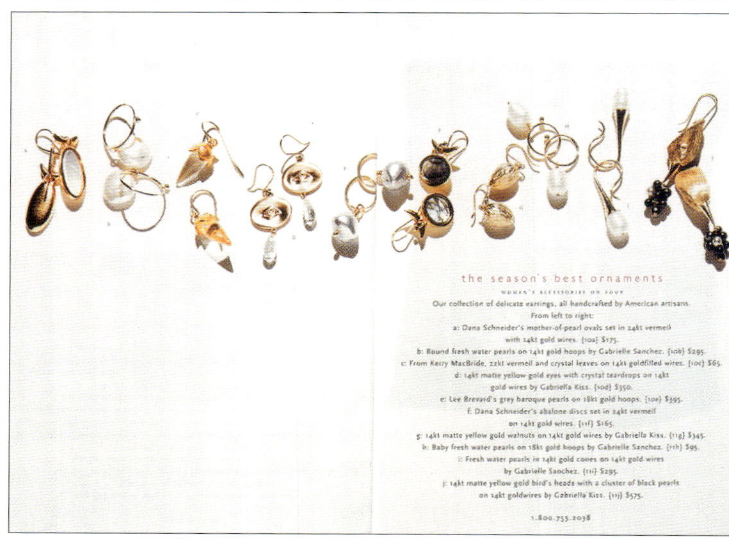


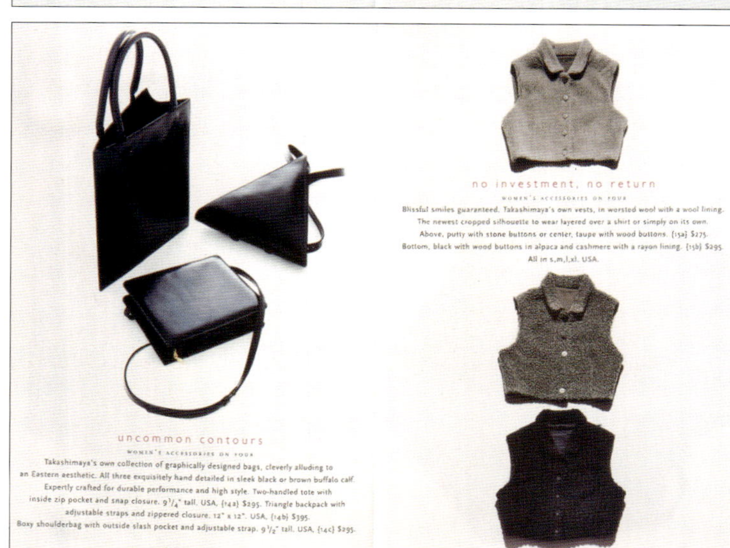

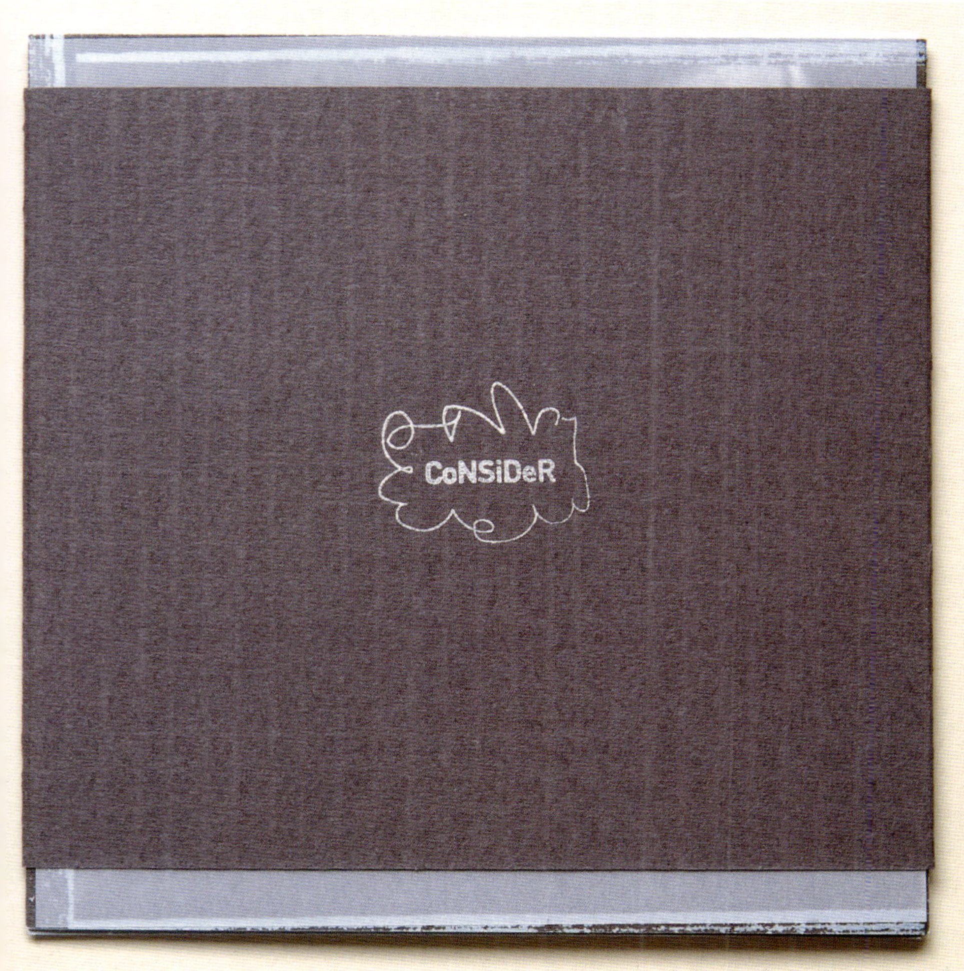


**STEWART MONDERER DESIGN, INC.**
**SELF-PROMOTION BROCHURE**

| | |
|---|---|
| **Design Firm** | *Stewart Monderer Design, Inc.* |
| **Art Director** | *Stewart Monderer* |
| **Designer** | *Aime Lecuscy* |
| **Photographer** | *Keller & Keller* |

Photos shot from unique perspectives and coupled with thought-provoking copy make the reader "Consider" the possibilities. Printed in three PMS colors, photos invite the readers to "Remember when..." and then lead them through a series of images that bring the message to fruition.

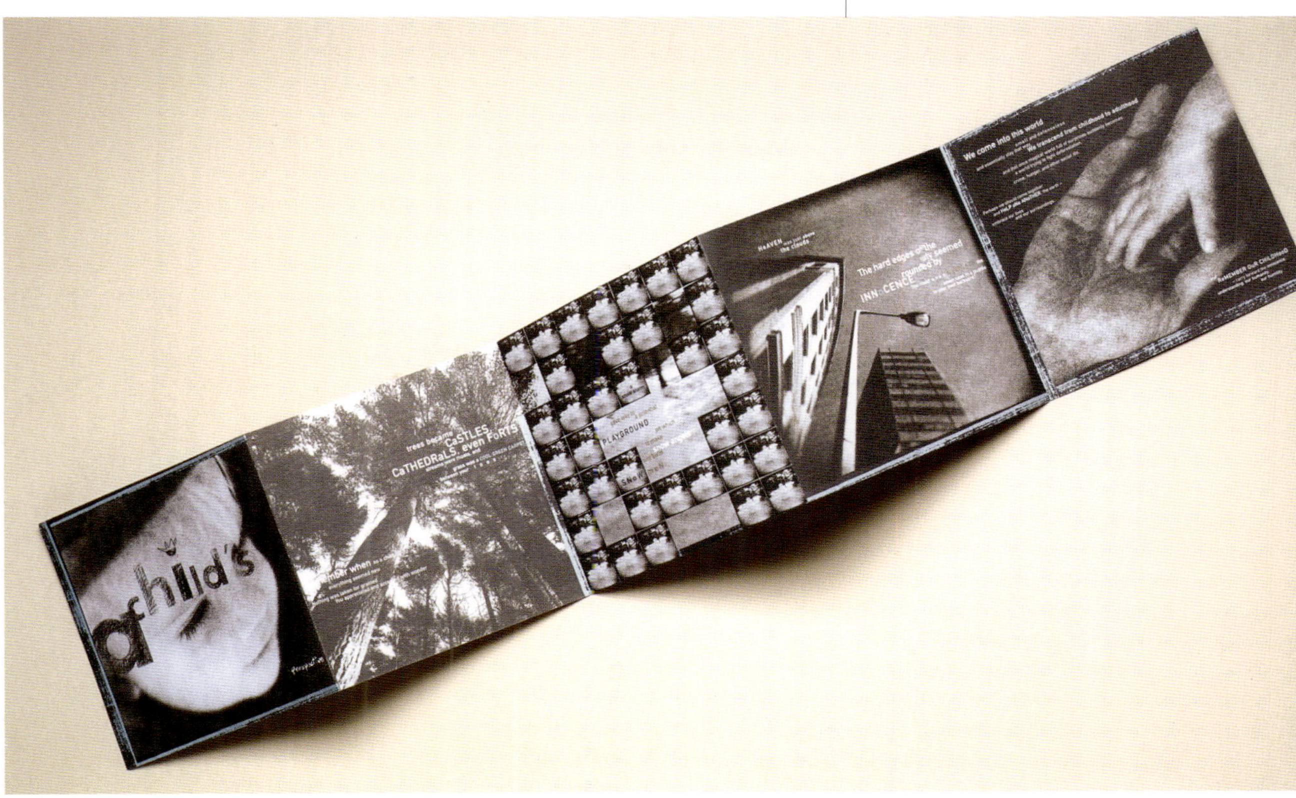

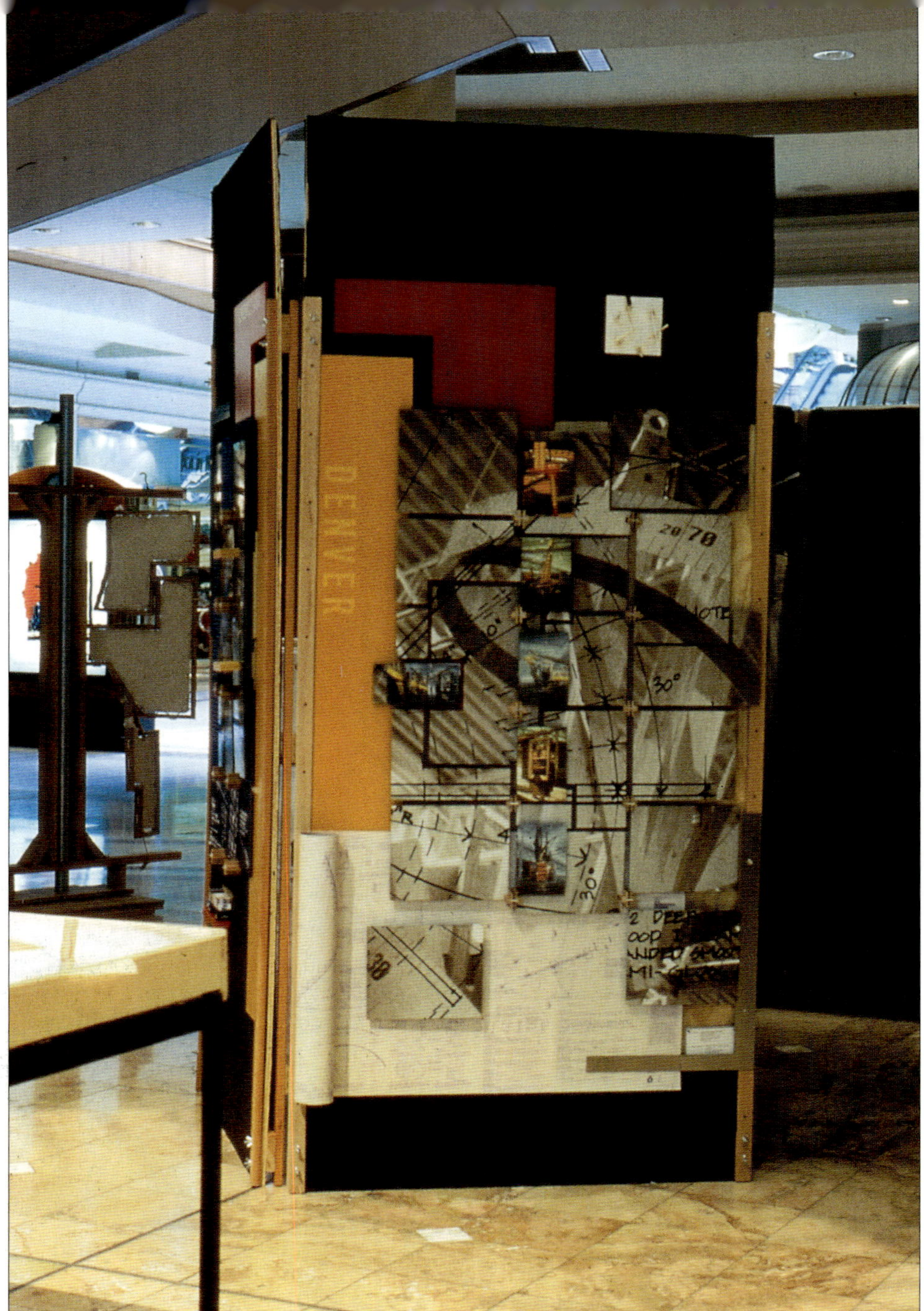


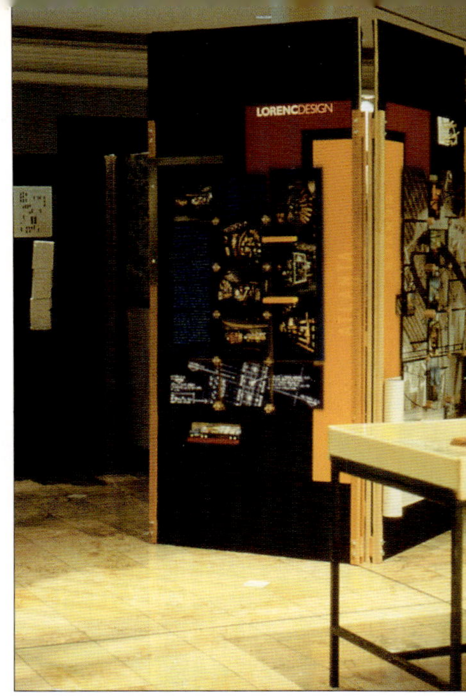


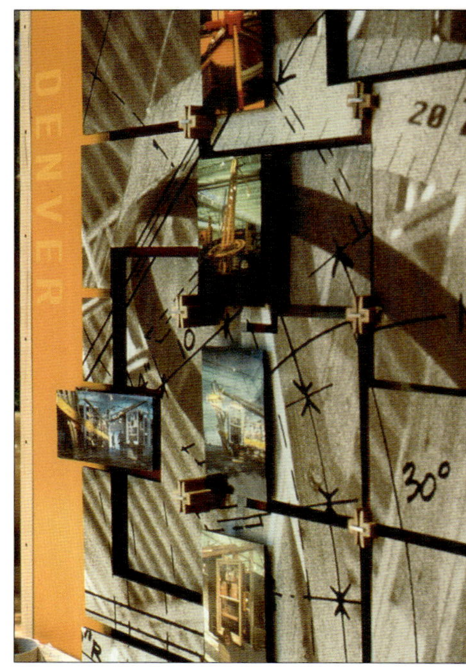


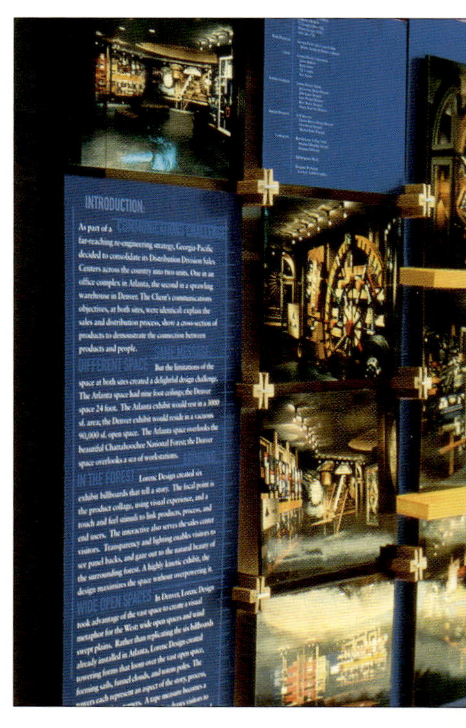


### AIA SHOW DISPLAY BOOTH

**Design Firm** *Lorenc Design*
**Art Director** *Jan Lorenc*
**Designer** *Rory Myers*
**Illustrators** *Rory Myers, Jan Lorenc*
**Photographer** *Jan Lorenc*

Impact with economy. That's the result of this high-impact photographic montage produced with color-output prints mounted on a plywood stand that is covered with foamcore board. The four-sided display tells a story in memorable images with a total price tag of $500 for labor and materials.

**THE ART DIRECTORS CLUB OF NEW YORK POSTCARD**

**Design Firm** *Mike Salisbury Communications*
**Art Director** *Mike Salisbury*
**Designer** *Mary Evelyn McGough*
**Illustrator** *Greg McClathy*

Who is this guy? I want to know more? These are the questions left with the recipient of this two-color postcard. The grainy, black-and-white close-up is an attention grabber, compelling you to read on.

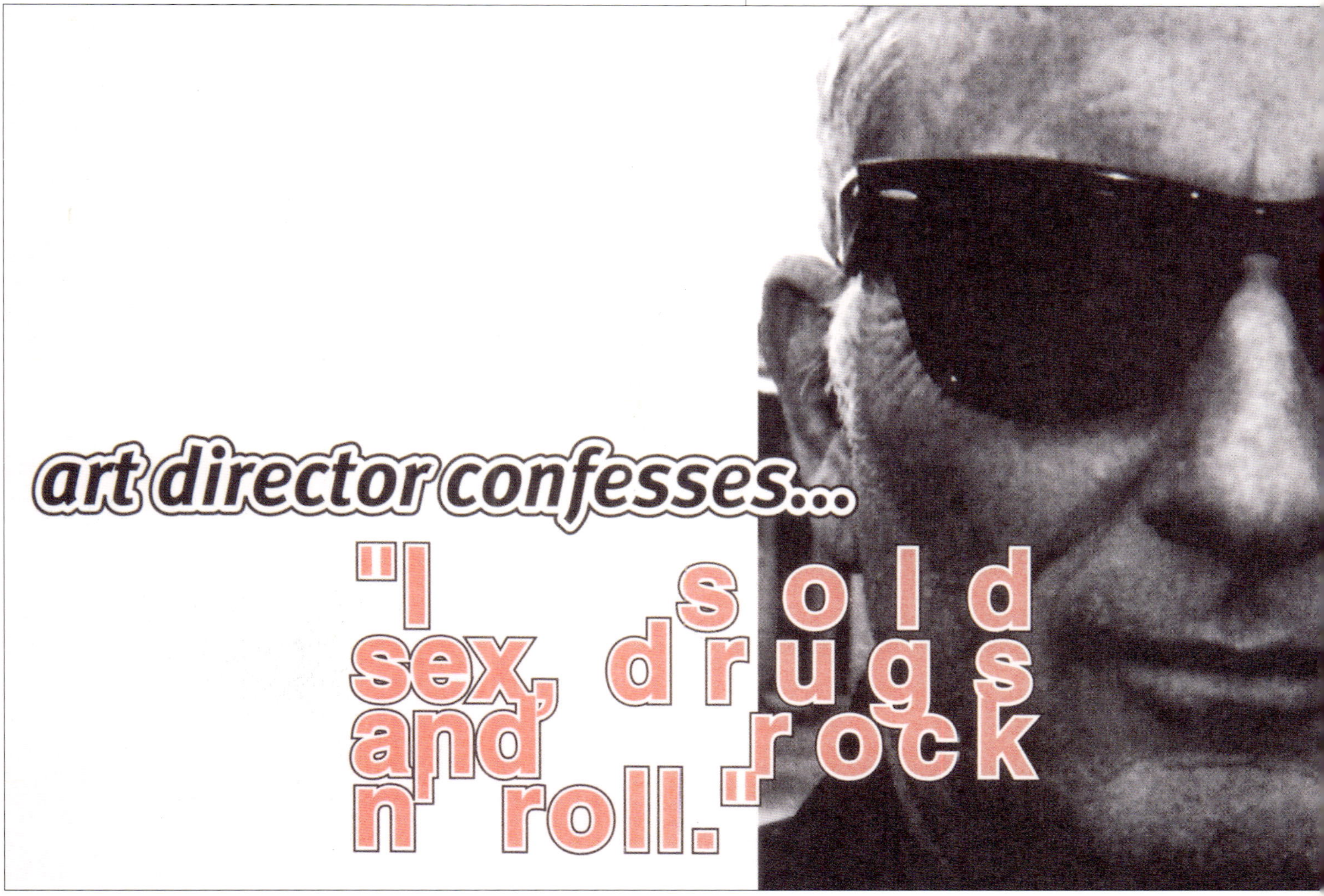

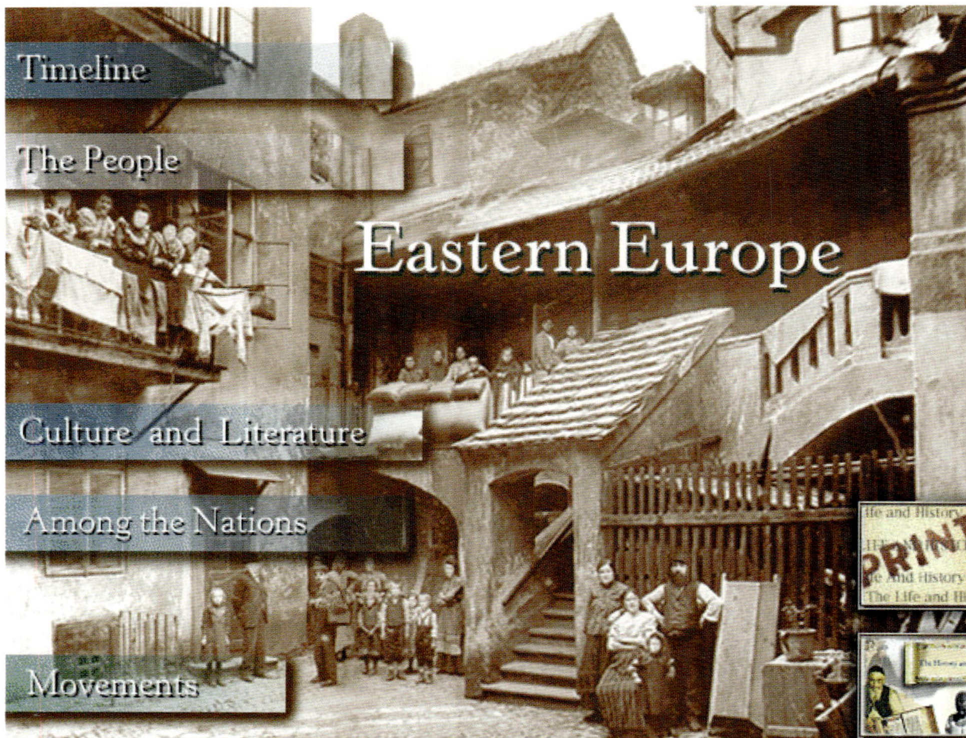


**MEMORIAL FOUNDATION FOR JEWISH CULTURE MULTIMEDIA SERIES**
**www.maxnm.com**

| | |
|---|---|
| **Design Firm** | *Maxima New Media* |
| **Art Director** | *Orit Kariv-Manor* |
| **Designer** | *Simcha Shtull* |
| **Programmer** | *Itamar Shutll-Trauring* |

This Web site comes to life with a series of black-and-white and sepia-tone photographs that work as both the backdrop and the navigational devices. The choice and style of the photos establish the site's reverence and its connection to both past and present.

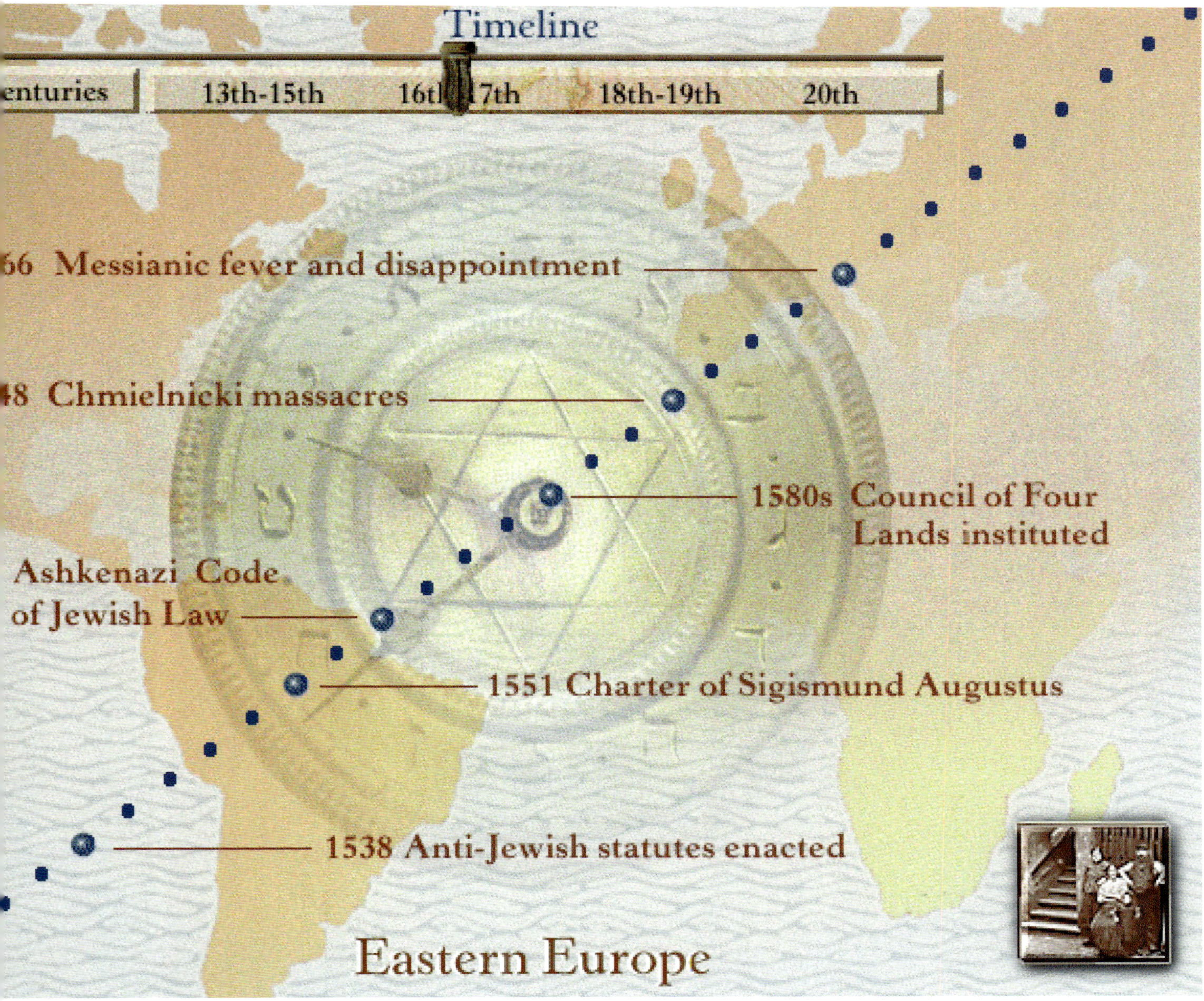
Timeline
enturies
13th-15th
16th-17th
18th-19th
20th
66 Messianic fever and disappointment
48 Chmielnicki massacres
1580s Council of Four Lands instituted
Ashkenazi Code of Jewish Law
1551 Charter of Sigismund Augustus
1538 Anti-Jewish statutes enacted
Eastern Europe

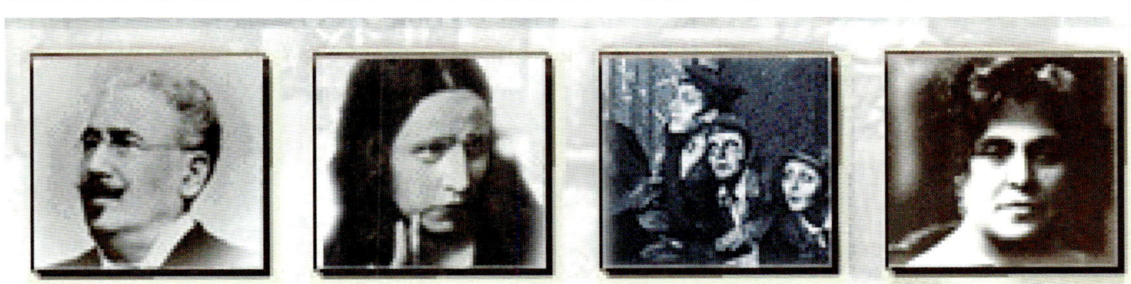

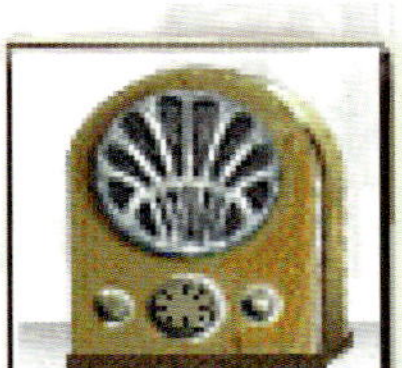

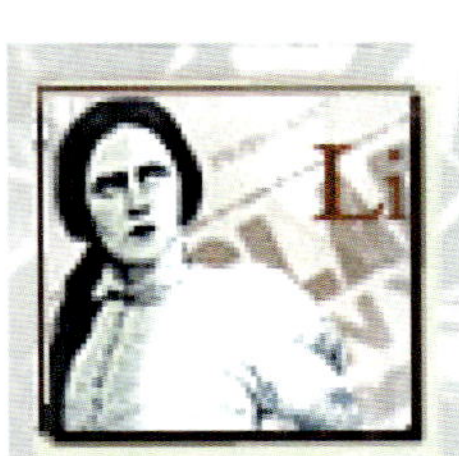
Li

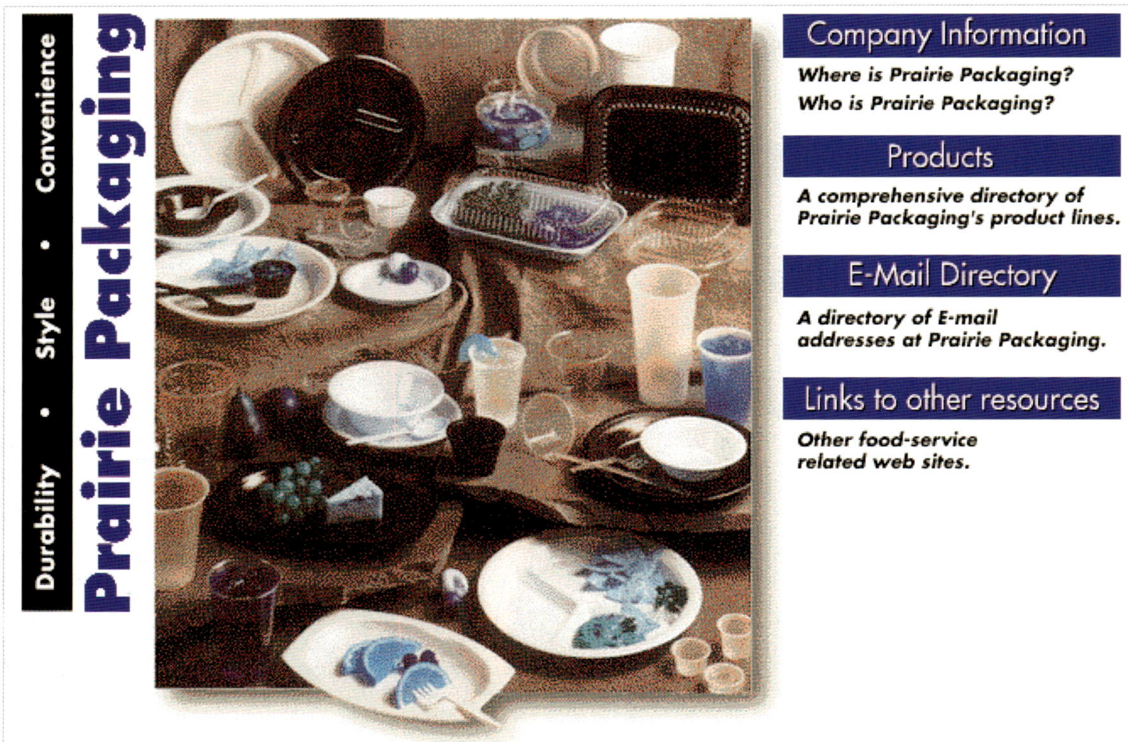


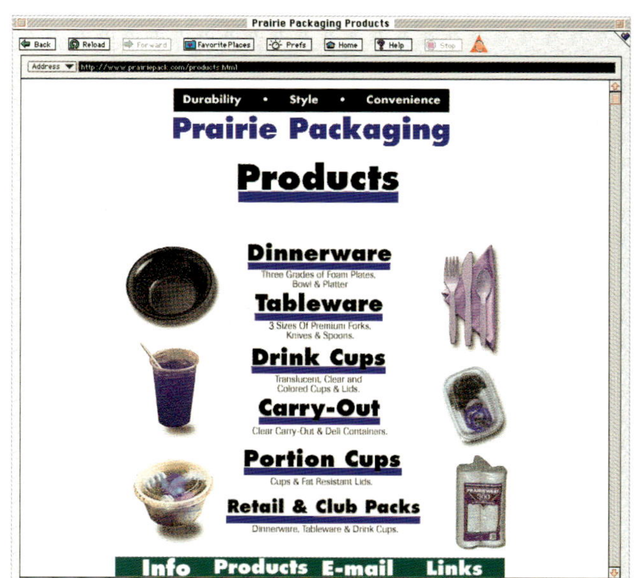


**PRAIRIE PACKAGING, INC. WEB SITE**
**www.prairiepack.com**

**Design Firm** *GE Neise Digital Communication*

Photographs of packaging that showcase its durability can look dull. However, in this example, exactly the opposite is true. All the images are organized and the result is energetic. Especially nice is the way the graphic elements complement the colors in the photography.

**LINCOLN PARK ZOO WEB SITE**
**www.lpzoo.com**

**Design Firm** *GE Neise Digital Communication*

Photographs and illustrations work in tandem throughout this site. Clever use of photos, such as the snake lurking behind the logo, along with the bright colors make visiting this site almost as much fun as the zoo itself.

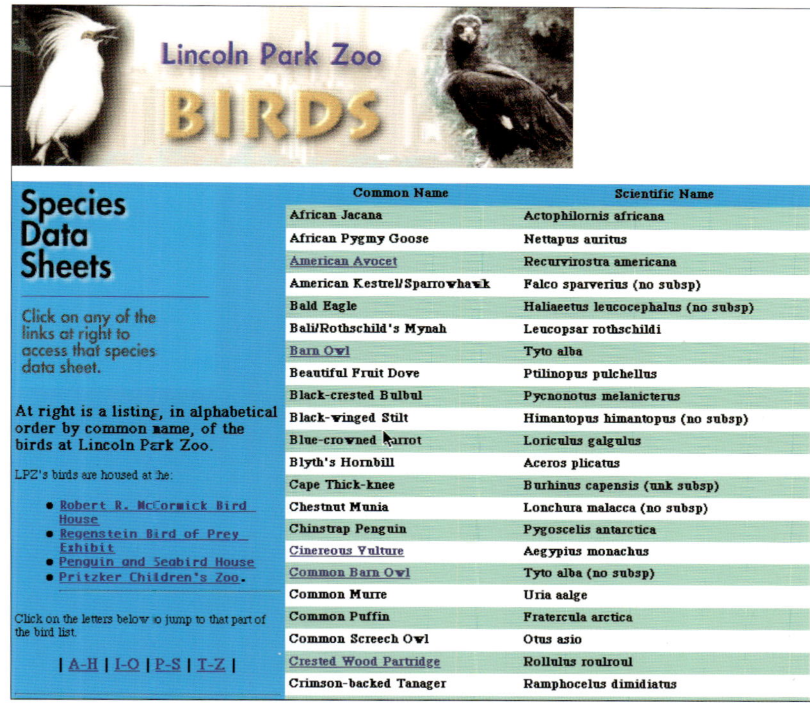


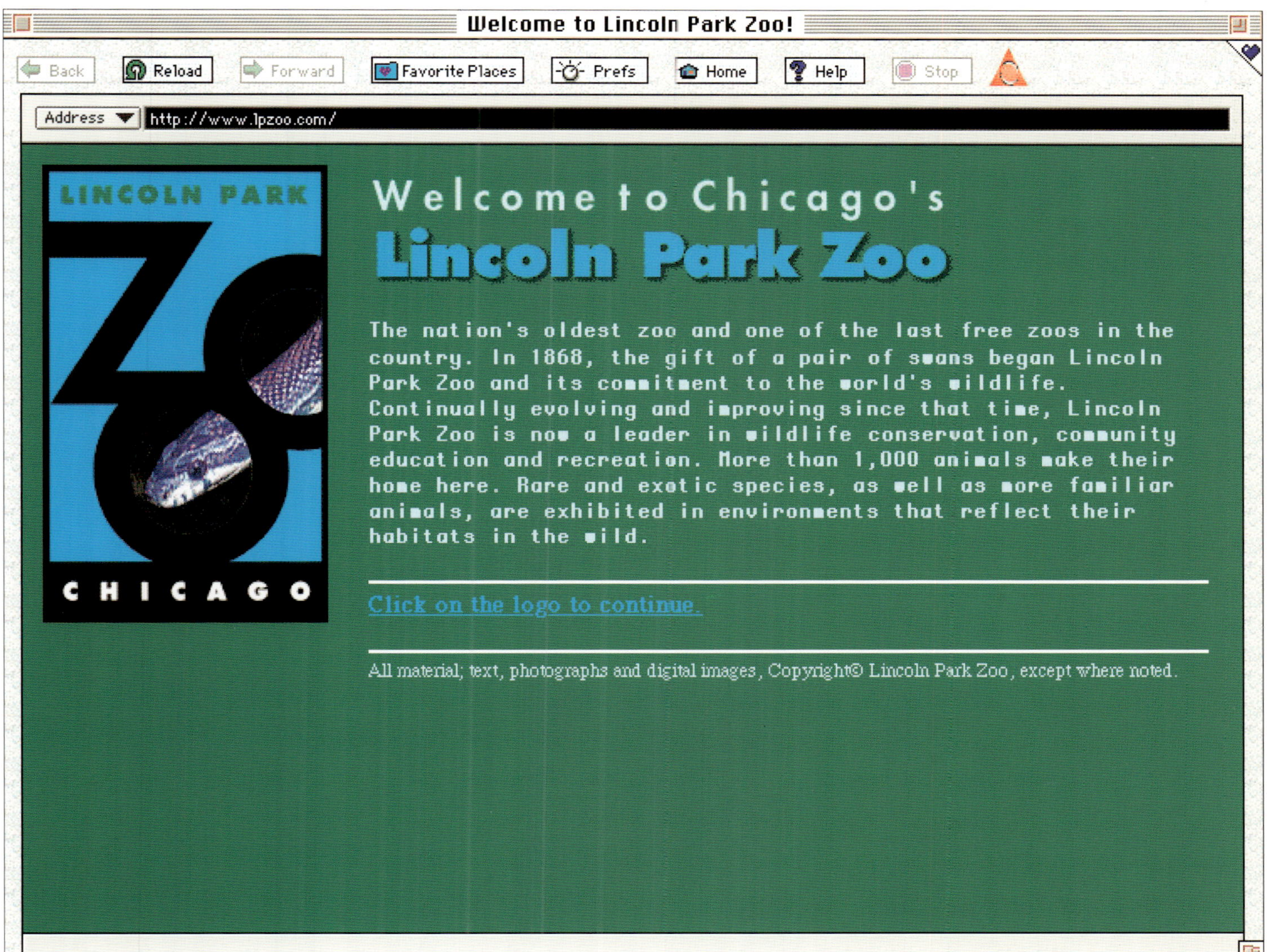

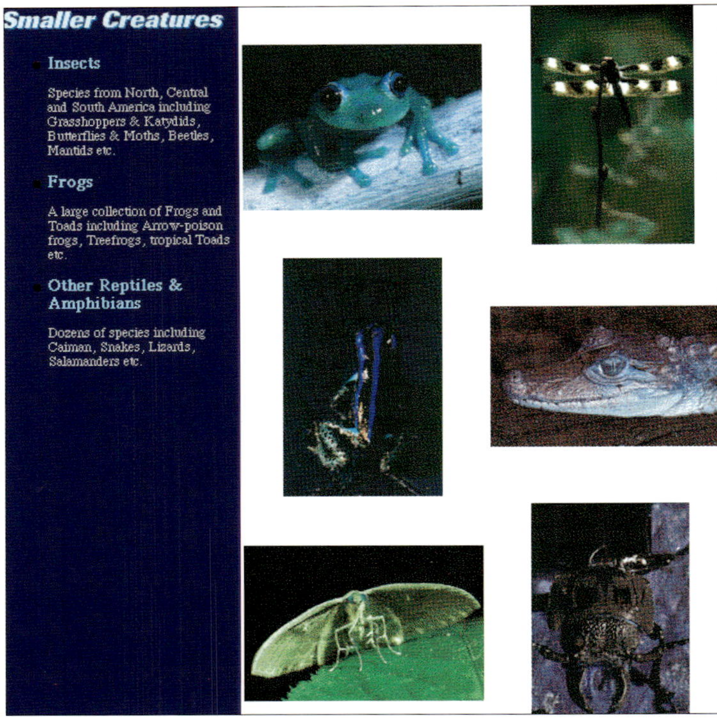


**GE NEISE DIGITAL COMMUNICATION WEB SITE**
**homepage.interaccess.com/~rcf/neise**

**Design Firm** *GE Neise Digital Communication*

A designer and a wildlife/nature photographer, Greg Neise displays both talents on this site that features his digital-design capabilities alongside his vast archive of stock photography, all of which is catalogued so that it is both easy to navigate and enjoyable.

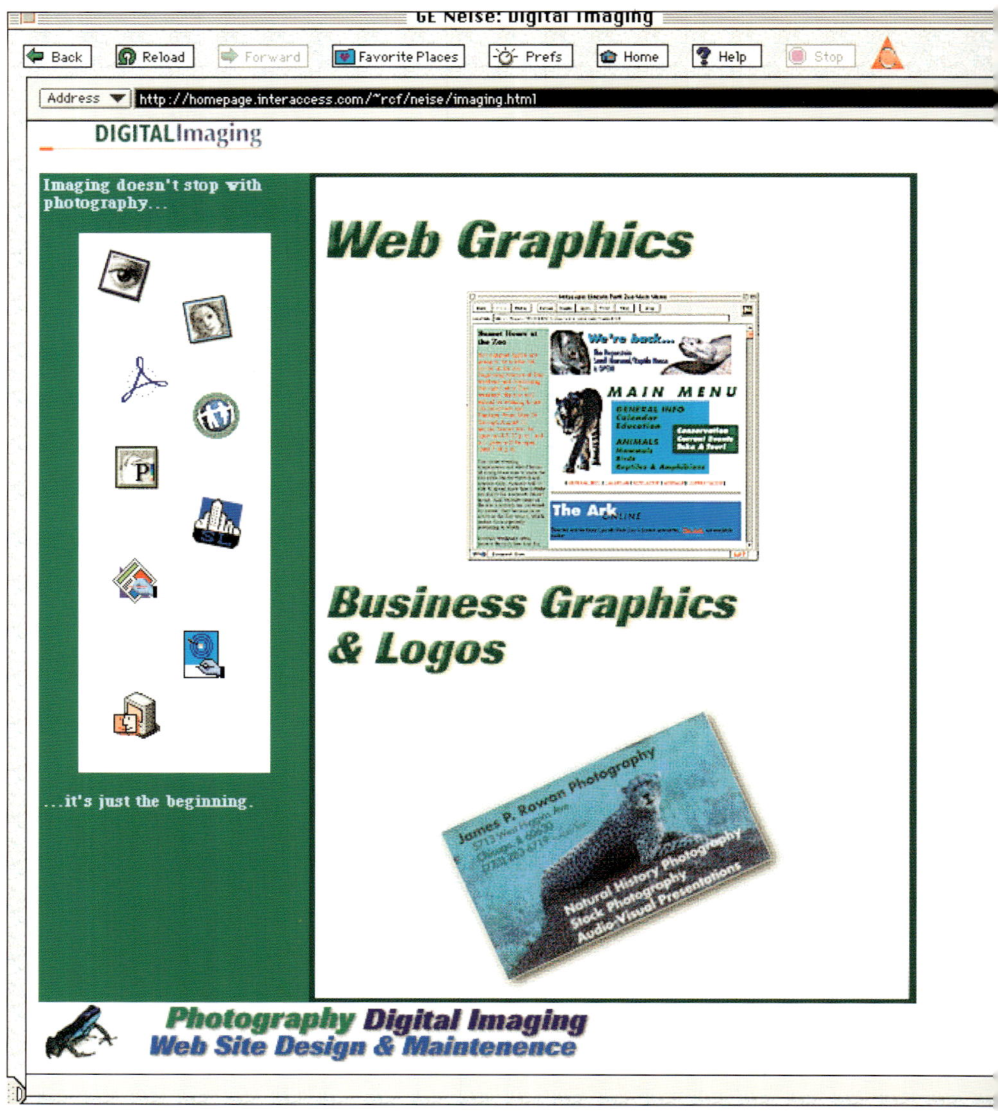

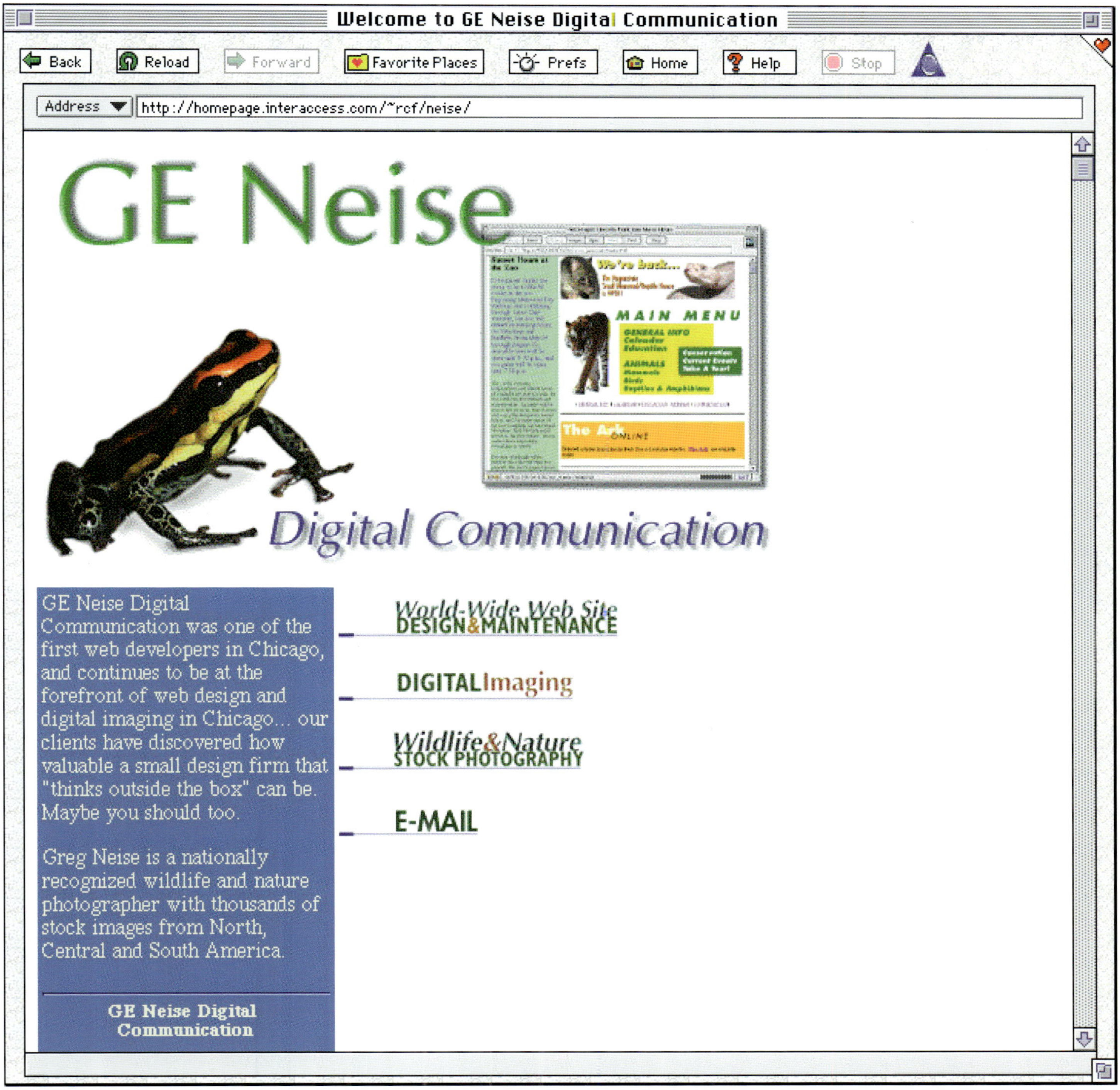

Welcome to GE Neise Digital Communication
Back
Reload
Forward
Favorite Places
Prefs
Home
Help
Stop
Address
http://homepage.interaccess.com/~rcf/neise/
GE Neise
MAIN MENU
Digital Communication
GE Neise Digital Communication was one of the first web developers in Chicago, and continues to be at the forefront of web design and digital imaging in Chicago... our clients have discovered how valuable a small design firm that "thinks outside the box" can be. Maybe you should too.
Greg Neise is a nationally recognized wildlife and nature photographer with thousands of stock images from North, Central and South America.
GE Neise Digital Communication
World-Wide Web Site DESIGN&MAINTENANCE
DIGITALImaging
Wildlife&Nature STOCK PHOTOGRAPHY
E-MAIL

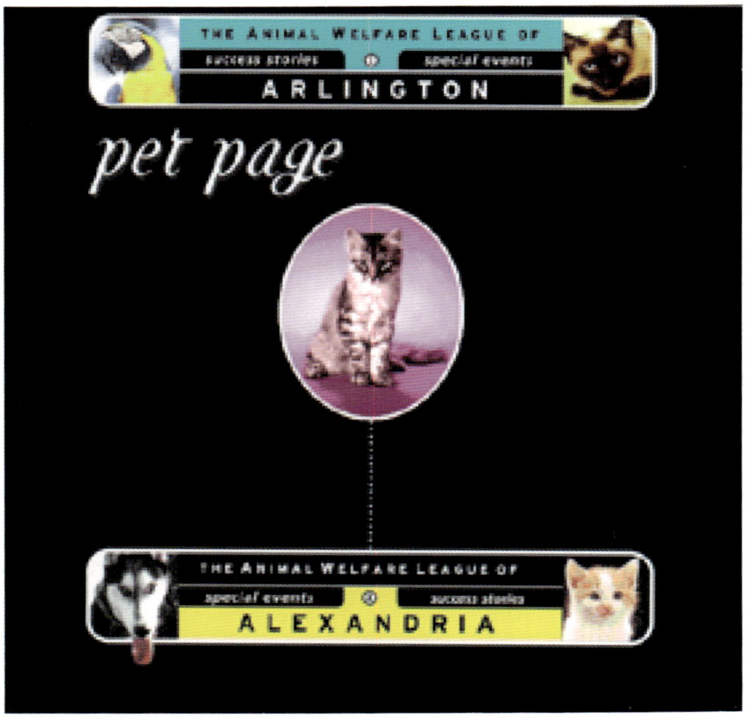


**ARLINGTON AND ALEXANDRIA ANIMAL HOSPITALS WEB SITE**
**www.petpage.org**

| | |
|---|---|
| **Design Firm** | *Grafik Communications, Ltd.* |
| **Creative Director** | *Judy Kirpich* |
| **Art Director** | *Johnny Vitorovich* |
| **Designer** | *Johnny Vitorovich* |
| **Photographers** | *Pam Soorenko, Pat Crowe, Oi Jakraat Veerasaran, Debbie Fox, Johnny Vitorovich, Susan Osborn, and various stock* |
| **Web Designers** | *Johnny Vitrovich, Judy Kirpich* |
| **Programmers** | *Johnny Vitrovich, Judy Kirpich* |

The design team contacted several photographers they had worked with previously to see if they would donate existing images or shoot original photography for this site. The response was positive and, more importantly, many had prior experience working with animals.

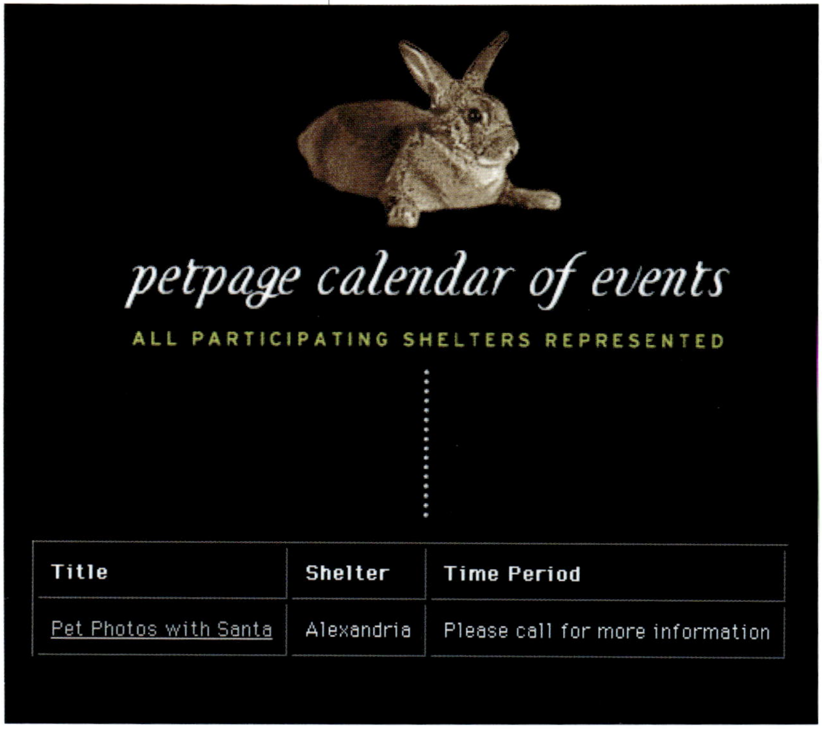

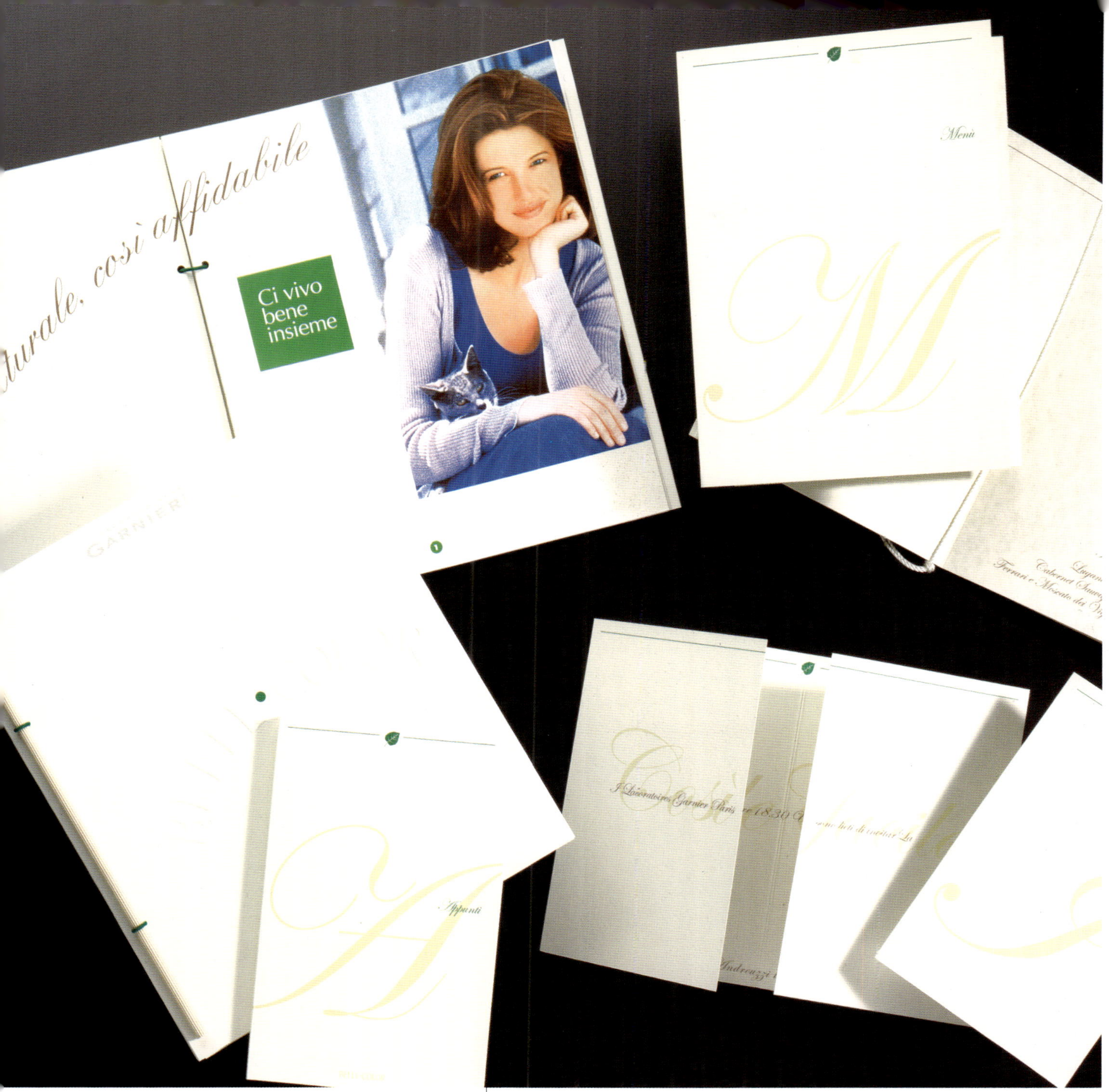


**LABORATOIRES GARNIER PARIS BROCHURE**

**Design Firm** *Giorgio Rocco Communications*
**Art Director** *Giorgio Rocco*
**Designer** *Giorgio Rocco*

Subtle colors on a blanket of white provide a smooth transition to the striking photograph that is the focus of this brochure, which is one element in a series of identity-program materials. The decision to concentrate attention on the color image proved highly effective in promoting Belle Color, a hair-coloring system.

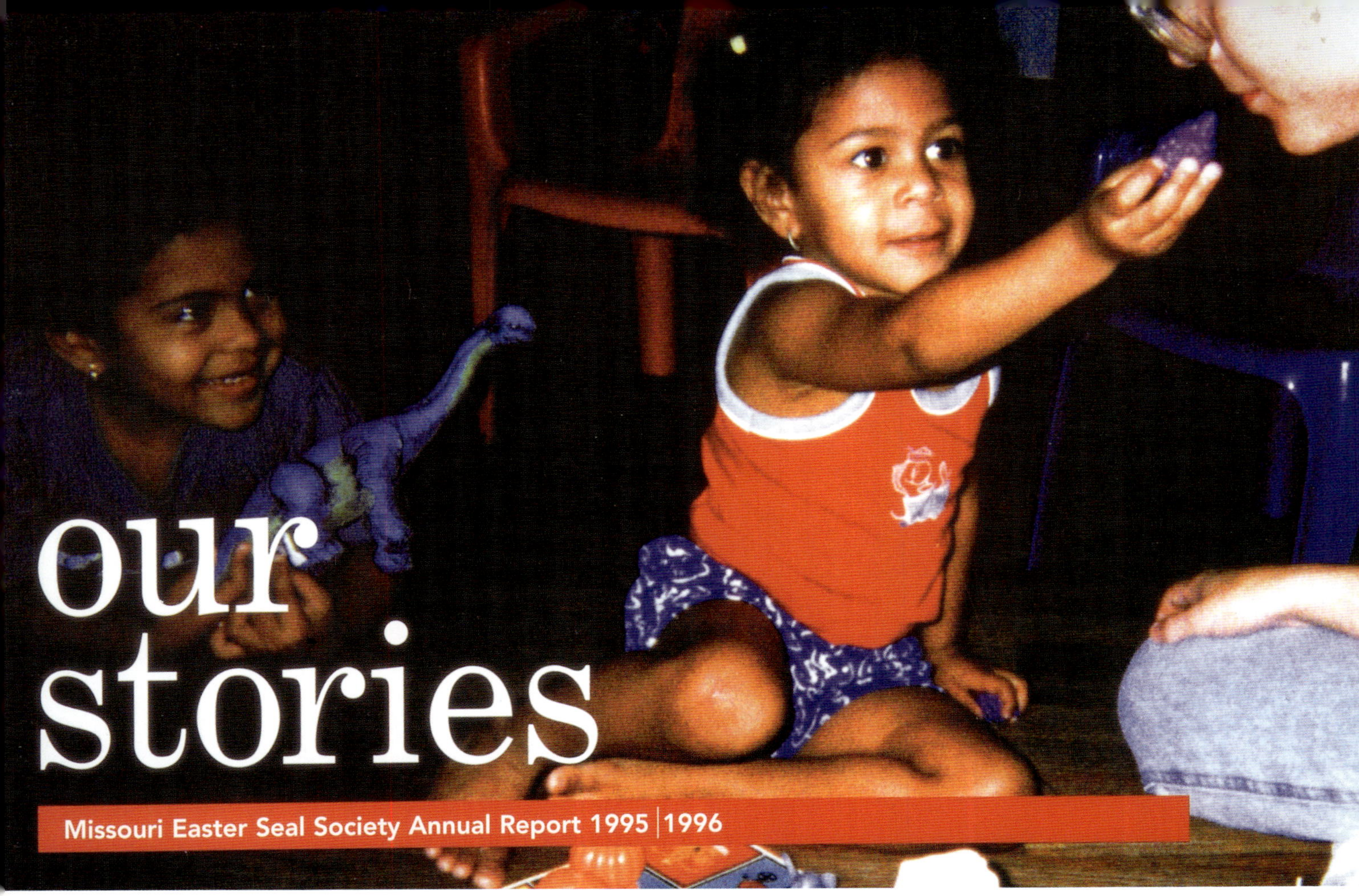


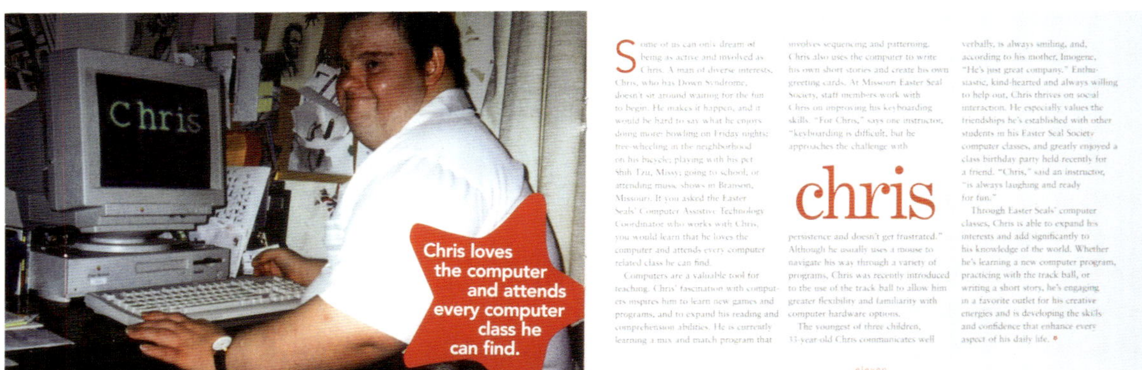


Some of us can only dream of being as active and involved as Chris. A man of diverse interests, Chris, who has Down Syndrome, doesn't sit around waiting for the fun to begin. He makes it happen, and it would be hard to say what he enjoys doing more: bowling on Friday nights; free-wheeling in the neighborhood on his bicycle; playing with his pet Shih Tzu, Missy; going to school, or attending music shows in Branson, Missouri. If you asked the Easter Seals' Computer Assistive Technology Coordinator who works with Chris, you would learn that he loves the computer and attends every computer related class he can find.

Computers are a valuable tool for teaching. Chris' fascination with computers inspires him to learn new games and programs, and to expand his reading and comprehension abilities. He is currently learning a mix and match program that involves sequencing and patterning. Chris also uses the computer to write his own short stories and create his own greeting cards. At Missouri Easter Seal Society, staff members work with Chris on improving his keyboarding skills. "For Chris," says one instructor, "keyboarding is difficult, but he approaches the challenge with

chris

persistence and doesn't get frustrated." Although he usually uses a mouse to navigate his way through a variety of programs, Chris was recently introduced to the use of the track ball to allow him greater flexibility and familiarity with computer hardware options.

The youngest of three children, 33-year-old Chris communicates well verbally, is always smiling, and, according to his mother, Imogene, "He's just great company." Enthusiastic, kind-hearted and always willing to help out, Chris thrives on social interaction. He especially values the friendships he's established with other students in his Easter Seal Society computer classes, and greatly enjoyed a class birthday party held recently for a friend. "Chris," said an instructor, "is always laughing and ready for fun."

Through Easter Seals' computer classes, Chris is able to expand his interests and add significantly to his knowledge of the world. Whether he's learning a new computer program, practicing with the track ball, or writing a short story, he's engaging in a favorite outlet for his creative energies and is developing the skills and confidence that enhance every aspect of his daily life.

eleven

**MISSOURI EASTER SEAL 1995–1996 ANNUAL REPORT**

**Design Firm** *Kiku Obata & Company*
**Art Director** *Liz Sullivan*
**Designer** *Liz Sullivan*
**Photographer** *Easter Seal Society clients*

Great photography doesn't always require a sizeable budget. To produce this annual report, a local photography shop donated disposable cameras and the organization's clients took all the candid shots. The photos convey what is at the heart of the organization by the people who are really involved.

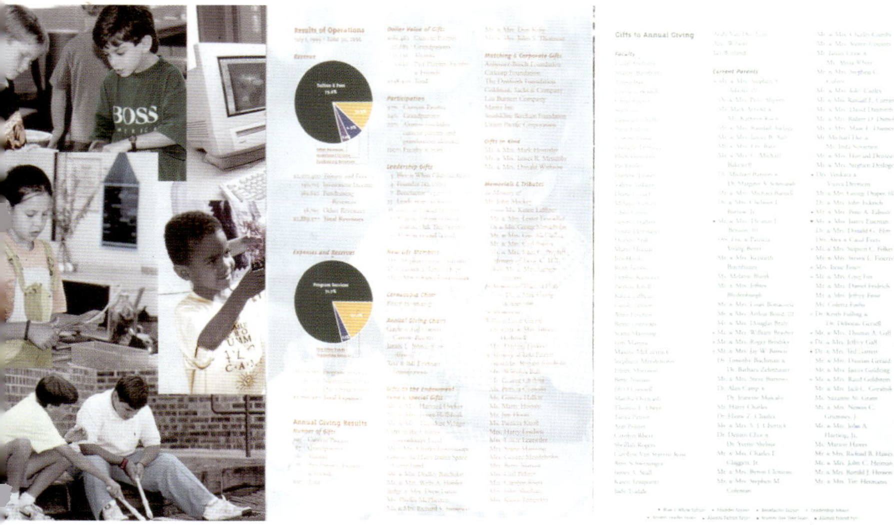

**THE COMMUNITY SCHOOL**
**1995–1996 ANNUAL REPORT**

**Design Firm** *Kiku Obata & Company*
**Art Director** *Amy Knopf*
**Designer** *Amy Knopf*

Black-and-white photos from the school's archive were chosen for a photomontage and hand tinted by the designer, giving character to this annual report's double gatefold four-color cover.

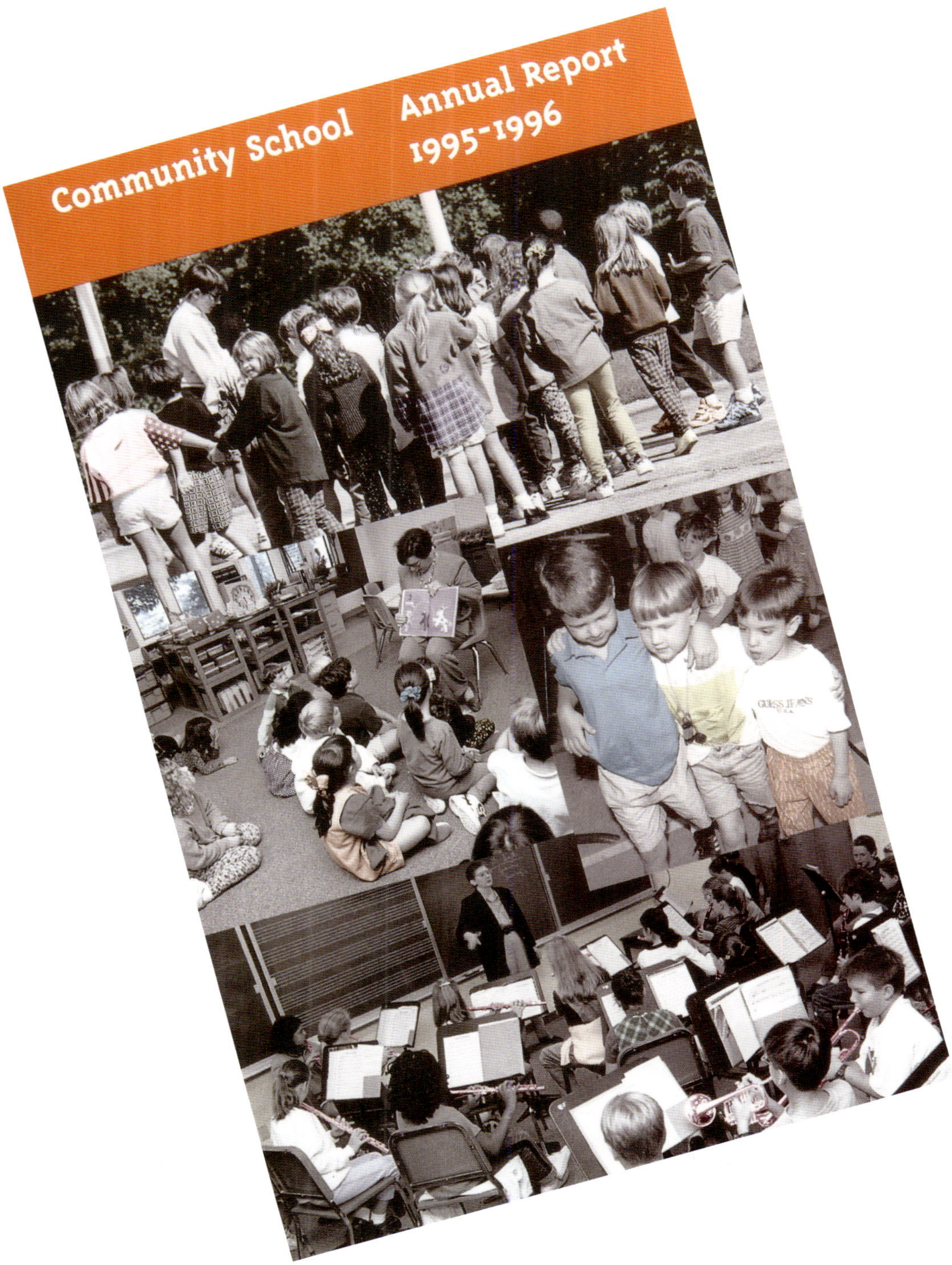

## KOEHLER McFADYEN & COMPANY BROCHURE

**Design Firm** *Hornall Anderson Design Works, Inc.*
**Art Director** *Jack Anderson*
**Designers** *Jack Anderson, Jana Wilson*
**Photographer** *Fred Houser*

To contain costs, photographs in this two-color brochure were printed as duotones, which emphasizes their dramatic imagery and high contrast. In all, the brochure looks deceptively expensive.

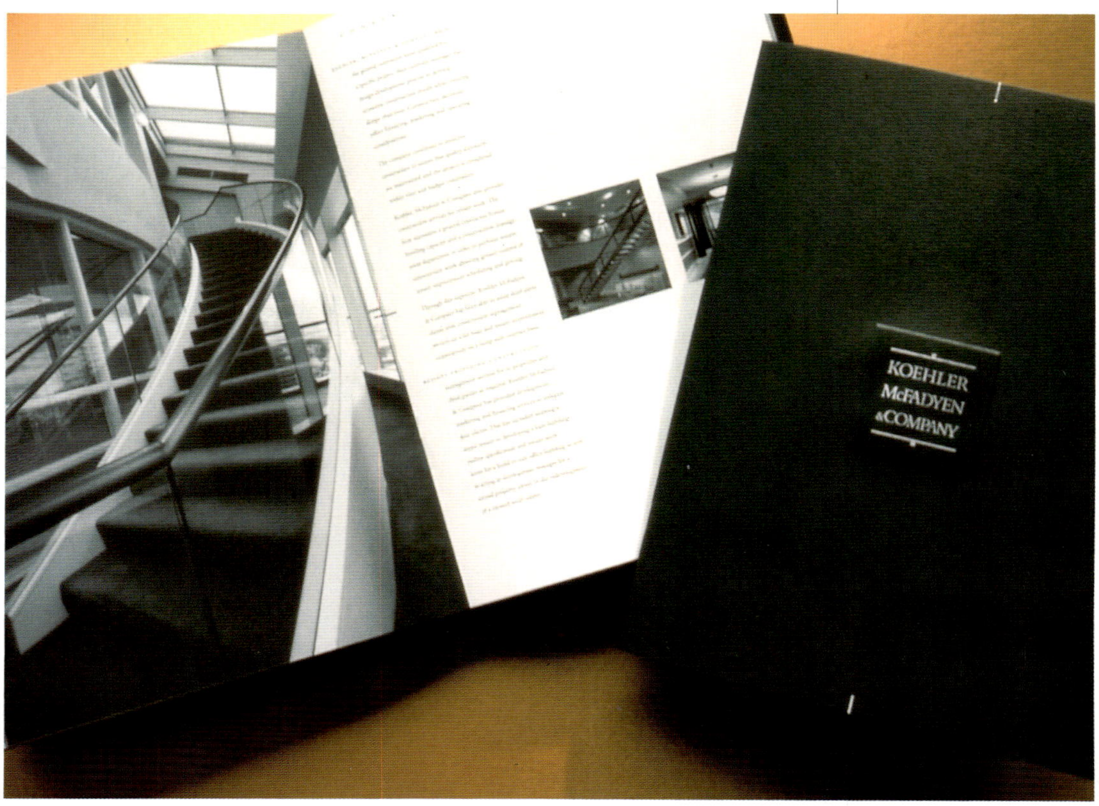

### WADSWORTH ATHENEUM SPRING SERENADE

**Design Firm** *Atlantic Design Works*
**Art Director** *Stacy W. Murray*
**Designer** *Stacy W. Murray*

Because the budget allowed only two-color printing, the designer converted existing color photographs to halftones and used metallic-gold ink as the second color. The result is elegant and sophisticated.

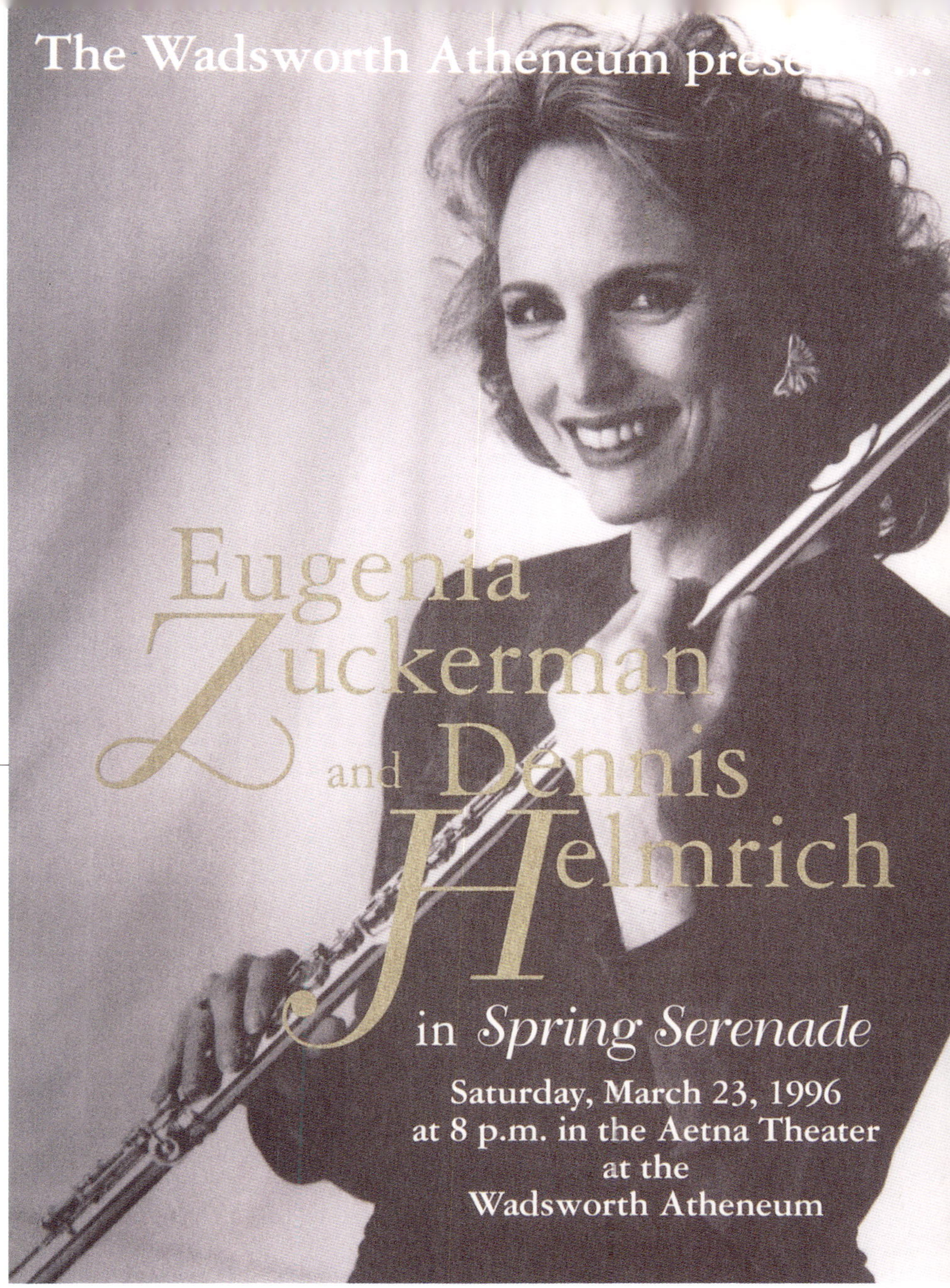


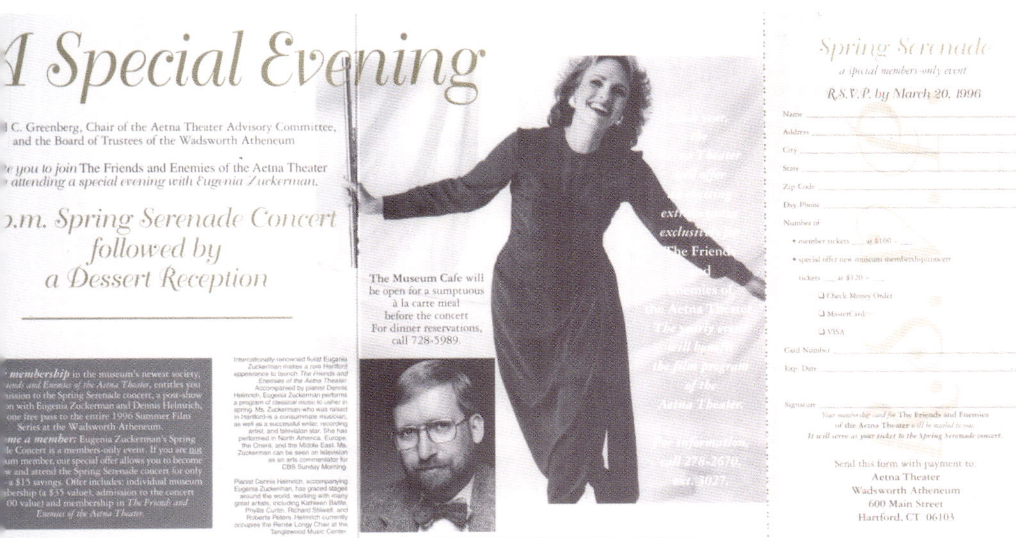

**SUBSTANCE ABUSE PROGRAM WEB SITE**
**darkwing.uoregon.edu/~kwiant**

**Design Firm** *G*
**Art Director** *Gary Leung*
**Designer** *Gary Leung*
**Photographers** *Miki Mace, Gary Leung, Nuri Kilani*

Instead of describing substance abuse, the photos at this site show it. Despite the seriousness of the subject, the photography and an animated GIF image that appears throughout make the site entertaining and informative.

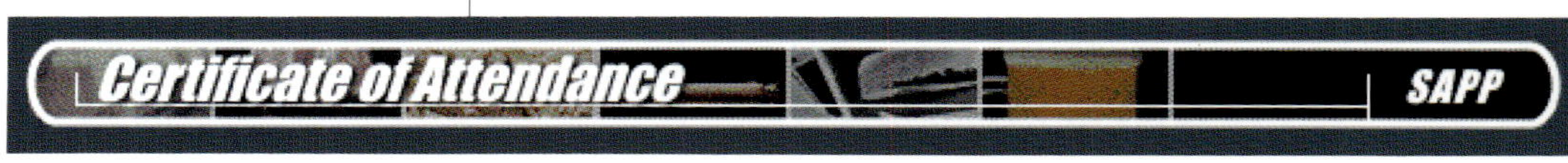


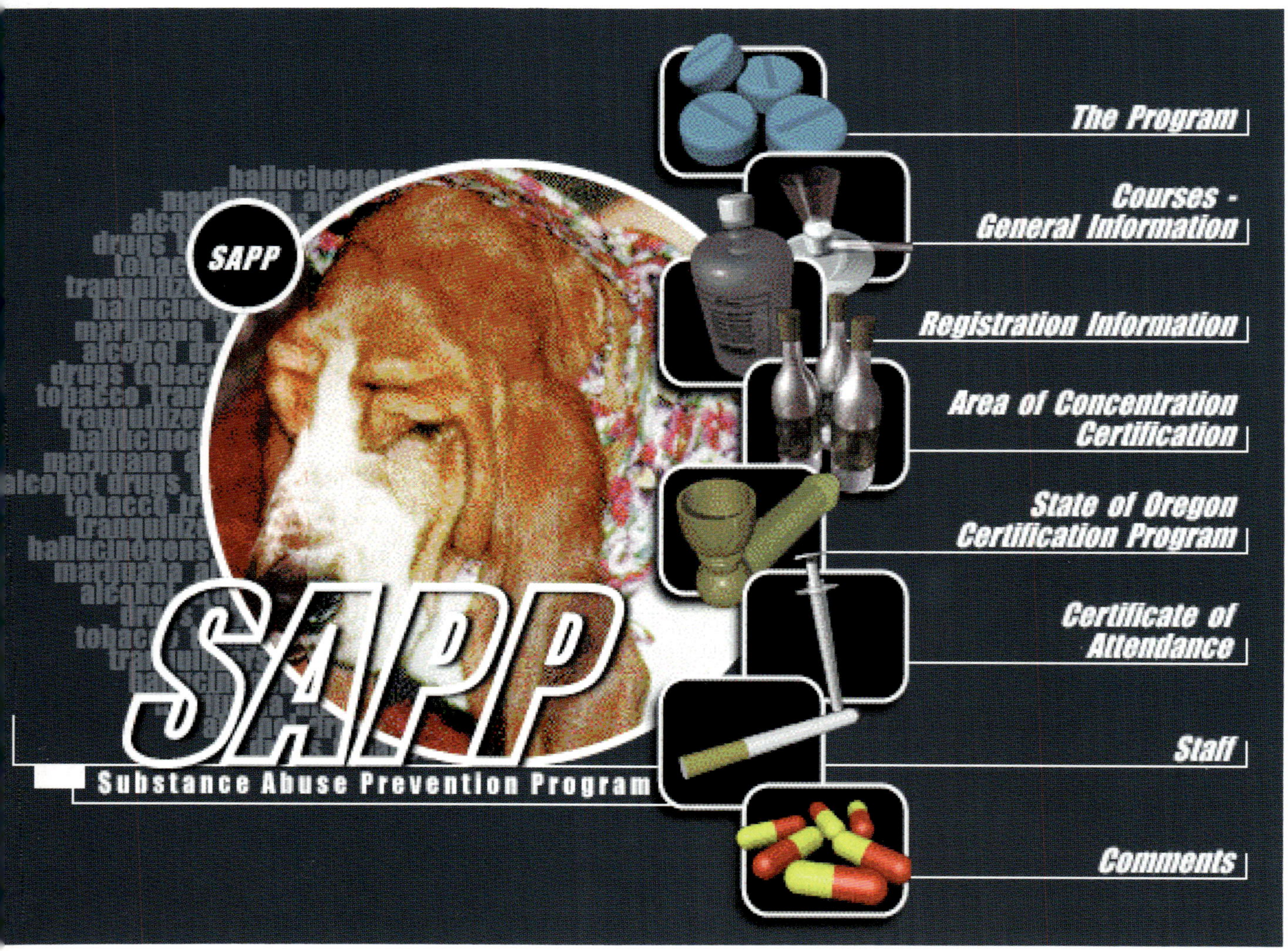

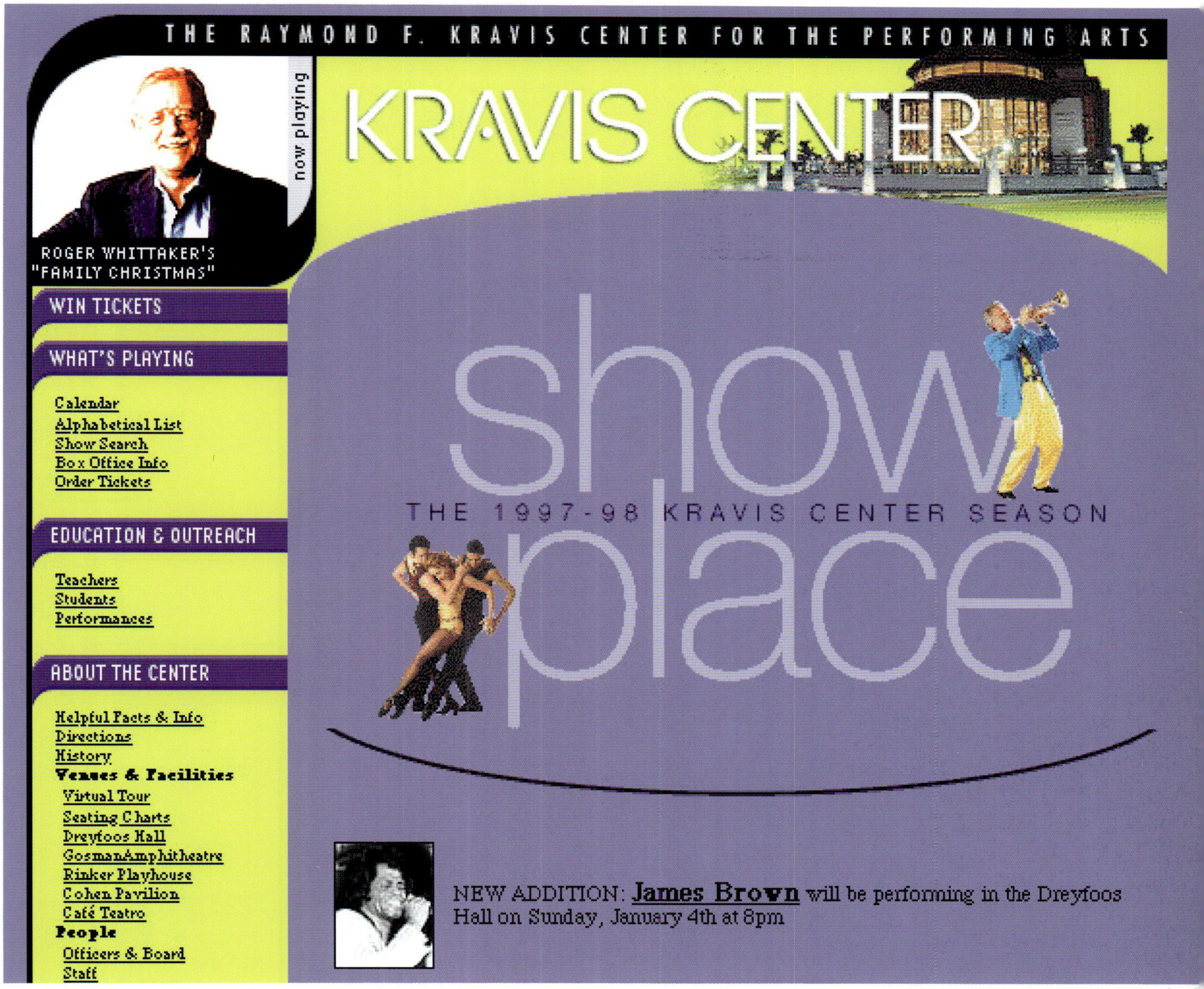


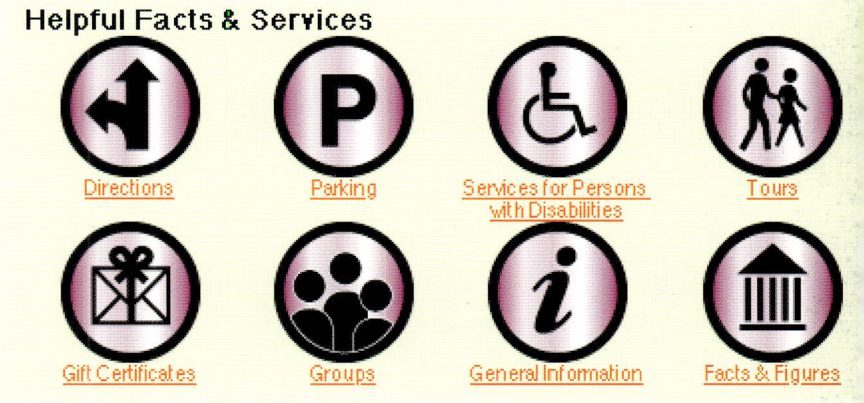


**THE RAYMOND F. KRAVIS CENTER FOR THE PERFORMING ARTS WEB SITE**
**www.kravis.org**

**Design Firm** *eman communications design, inc.*
**Art Director** *Tom Osborne*
**Designer** *Tom Osborne*
**Programmer** *Eric Norstrom*

The photography on this home page is so subtle yet so expertly integrated with the type that rather than being separate entities, they work together as one visual element.

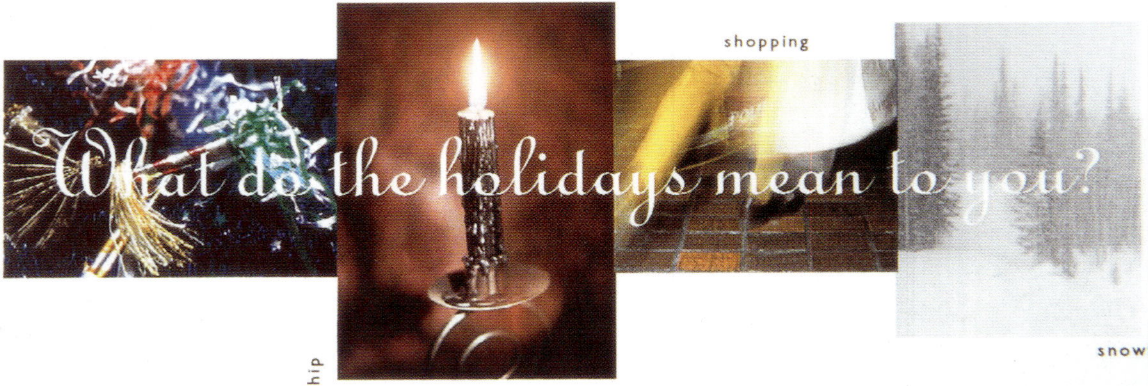
festivities
What do the holidays mean to you?
worship
shopping
snowfall

**HAL APPLE DESIGN & COMMUNICATIONS, INC.**
**HOLIDAY GREETING**

| | |
|---|---|
| **Design Firm** | *Hal Apple Design & Communications, Inc.* |
| **Art Director** | *Hal Apple* |
| **Designer** | *Andrea Del Guerico* |
| **Photographer** | *Jason Hashmi* |

Hal Apple Design's holiday greeting asks "What do the holidays mean to you?" The designer provides four possible responses, represented in photos as diverse in color and theme as the answers themselves.

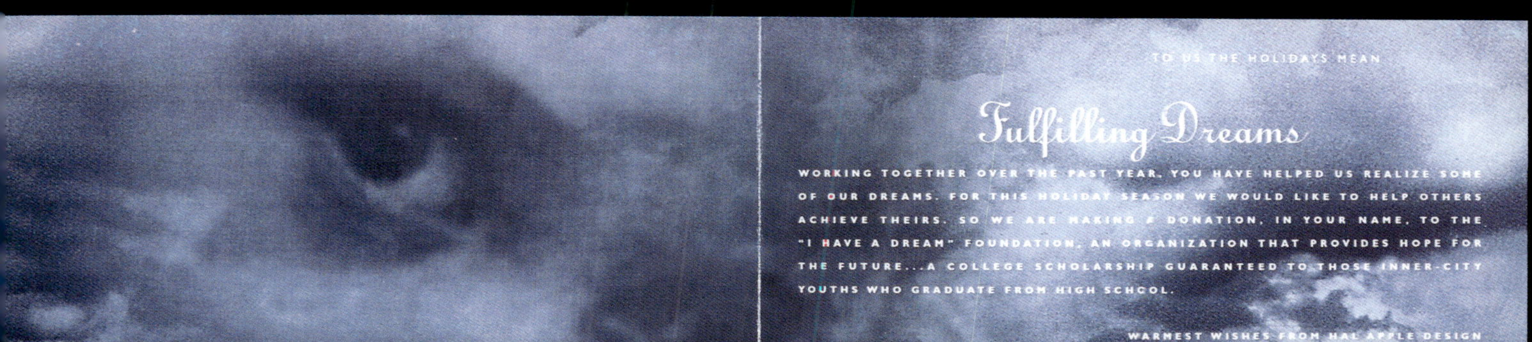

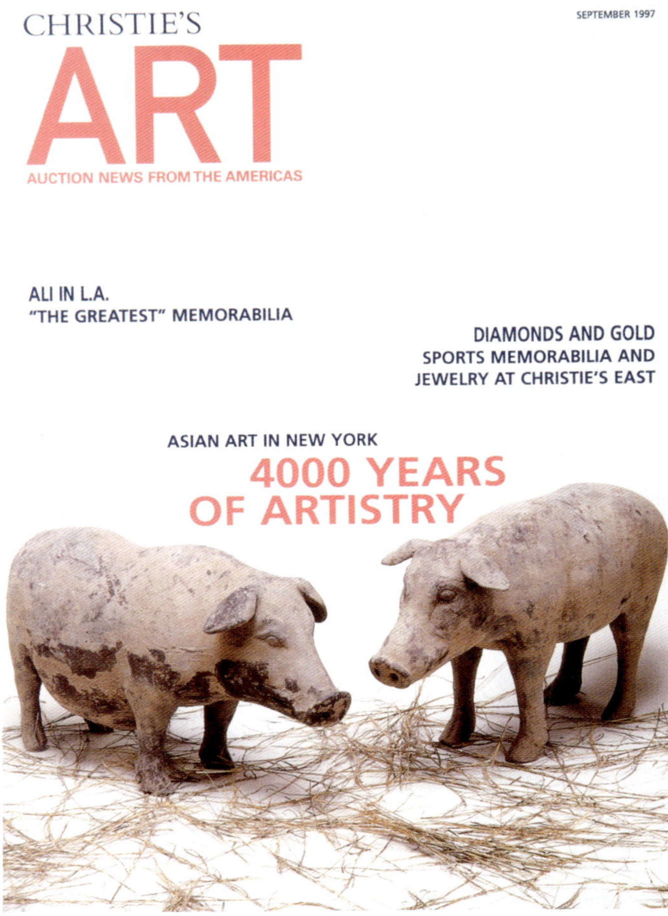


## CHRISTIE'S *ART AUCTION NEWS* CATALOG

**Design Firm** *Christie's Publications*
**Senior Editor** *Marissa Wilcox*
**Creative Director** *Skip Pollard*
**Designer** *Martin Schott*
**Senior Art Director** *Lynda Havell*

In a departure from traditional auction catalogs that stick to a rigid format, Christie's *Art Auction News* was redesigned for a more general audience. Photos float among copy blocks and the seventeenth-century terra-cotta pigs, which would have previously been posed on a pedestal, are photographed in hay.

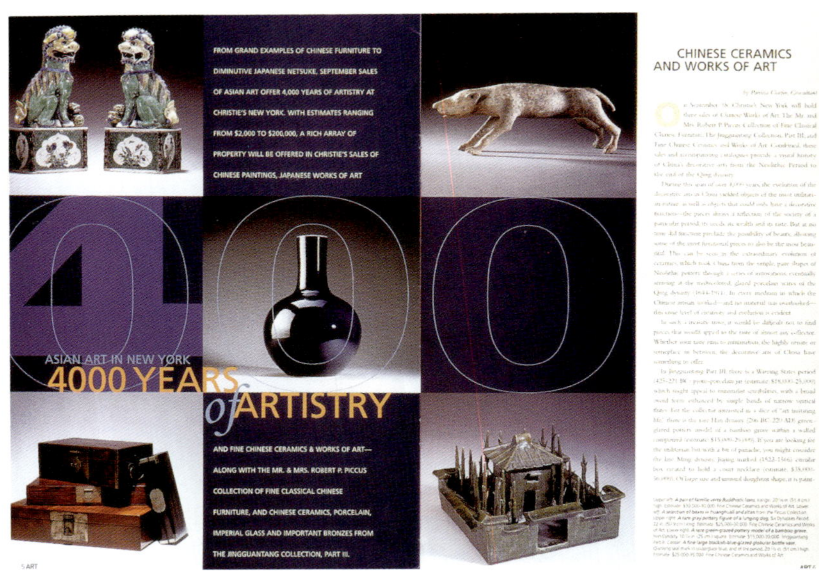

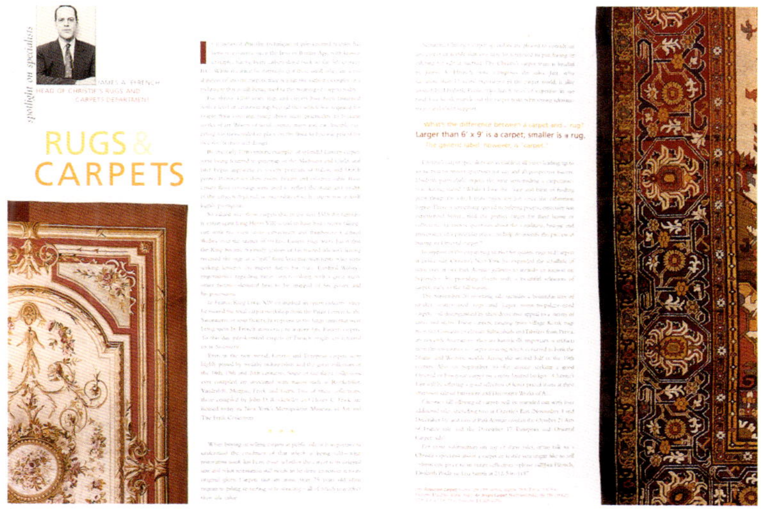


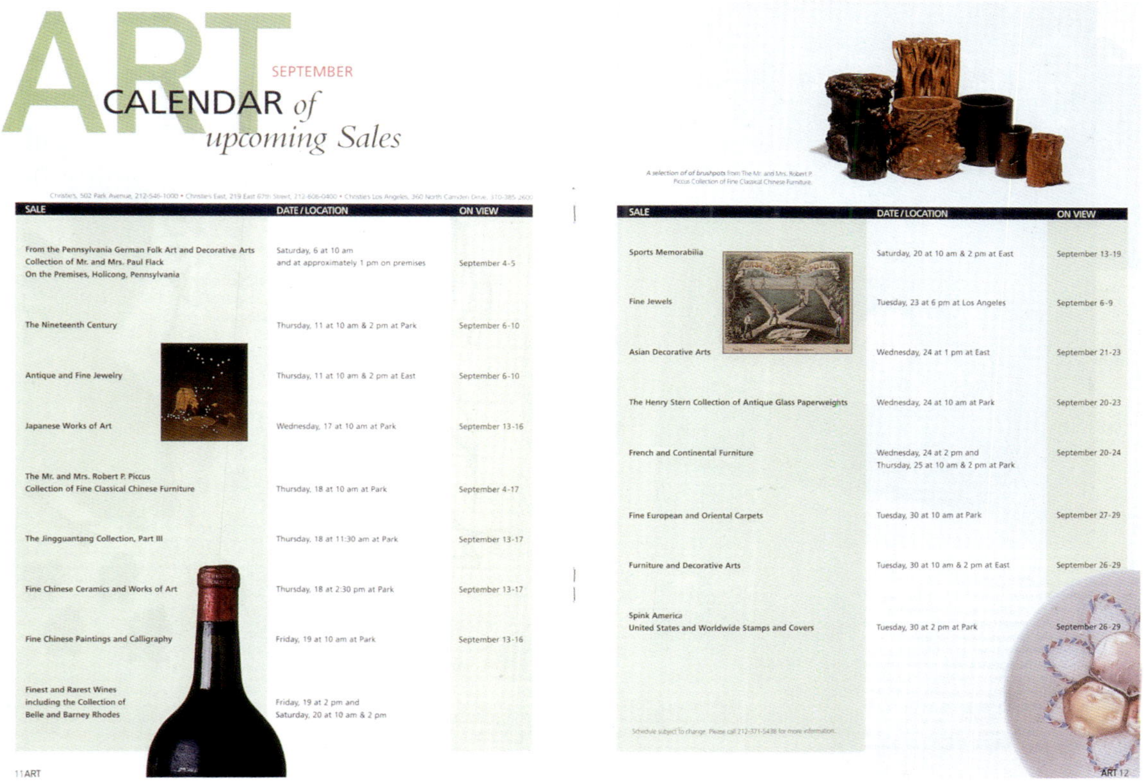

ART SEPTEMBER CALENDAR *of upcoming Sales*

Christie's, 502 Park Avenue, 212-546-1000 • Christie's East, 219 East 67th Street, 212-606-0400 • Christie's Los Angeles, 360 North Camden Drive, 310-385-2600

| SALE | DATE / LOCATION | ON VIEW |
|---|---|---|
| From the Pennsylvania German Folk Art and Decorative Arts Collection of Mr. and Mrs. Paul Flack On the Premises, Holicong, Pennsylvania | Saturday, 6 at 10 am and at approximately 1 pm on premises | September 4-5 |
| The Nineteenth Century | Thursday, 11 at 10 am & 2 pm at Park | September 6-10 |
| Antique and Fine Jewelry | Thursday, 11 at 10 am & 2 pm at East | September 6-10 |
| Japanese Works of Art | Wednesday, 17 at 10 am at Park | September 13-16 |
| The Mr. and Mrs. Robert P. Piccus Collection of Fine Classical Chinese Furniture | Thursday, 18 at 10 am at Park | September 4-17 |
| The Jingguantang Collection, Part III | Thursday, 18 at 11:30 am at Park | September 13-17 |
| Fine Chinese Ceramics and Works of Art | Thursday, 18 at 2:30 pm at Park | September 13-17 |
| Fine Chinese Paintings and Calligraphy | Friday, 19 at 10 am at Park | September 13-16 |
| Finest and Rarest Wines including the Collection of Belle and Barney Rhodes | Friday, 19 at 2 pm and Saturday, 20 at 10 am & 2 pm | |

11 ART

A selection of of brushpots from The Mr. and Mrs. Robert P. Piccus Collection of Fine Classical Chinese Furniture.

| SALE | DATE / LOCATION | ON VIEW |
|---|---|---|
| Sports Memorabilia | Saturday, 20 at 10 am & 2 pm at East | September 13-19 |
| Fine Jewels | Tuesday, 23 at 6 pm at Los Angeles | September 6-9 |
| Asian Decorative Arts | Wednesday, 24 at 1 pm at East | September 21-23 |
| The Henry Stern Collection of Antique Glass Paperweights | Wednesday, 24 at 10 am at Park | September 20-23 |
| French and Continental Furniture | Wednesday, 24 at 2 pm and Thursday, 25 at 10 am & 2 pm at Park | September 20-24 |
| Fine European and Oriental Carpets | Tuesday, 30 at 10 am at Park | September 27-29 |
| Furniture and Decorative Arts | Tuesday, 30 at 10 am & 2 pm at East | September 26-29 |
| Spink America United States and Worldwide Stamps and Covers | Tuesday, 30 at 2 pm at Park | September 26-29 |

Schedule subject to change. Please call 212-371-5438 for more information.

ART 12

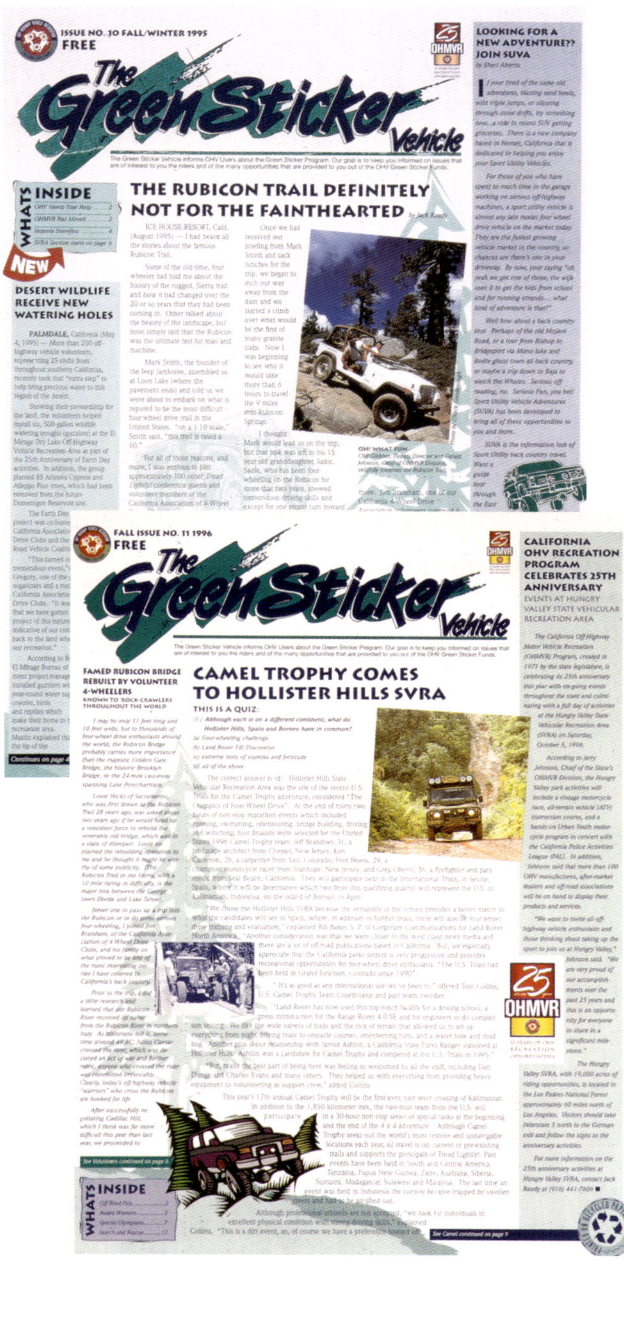

ISSUE NO. 10 FALL/WINTER 1995
FREE

# The Green Sticker Vehicle

LOOKING FOR A NEW ADVENTURE?? JOIN SUVA

WHAT'S INSIDE

NEW

DESERT WILDLIFE RECEIVE NEW WATERING HOLES

## THE RUBICON TRAIL DEFINITELY NOT FOR THE FAINTHEARTED

FALL ISSUE NO. 11 1996
FREE

# The Green Sticker Vehicle

CALIFORNIA OHV RECREATION PROGRAM CELEBRATES 25TH ANNIVERSARY

EVENTS AT HUNGRY VALLEY STATE VEHICULAR RECREATION AREA

FAMED RUBICON BRIDGE REBUILT BY VOLUNTEER 4-WHEELERS

## CAMEL TROPHY COMES TO HOLLISTER HILLS SVRA

THIS IS A QUIZ:

WHAT'S INSIDE

OHMVR

### CALIFORNIA STATE PARKS
### *THE GREEN STICKER VEHICLE* NEWSLETTER

**Design Firm** *University Media Services, California State University–Sacramento*
**Editors** *Priscilla Davis, Clifford R. Glidden, deputy director of Off-Highway Motor Vehicle Recreation Division*
**Designer** *Jim Molina, University Media Services, CSU–Sacramento*

Many of the photos in this newsletter are tilted slightly, creating a feeling for the rugged, hilly, off-highway terrain that the newsletter is all about and a lot of visual interest at the same time.

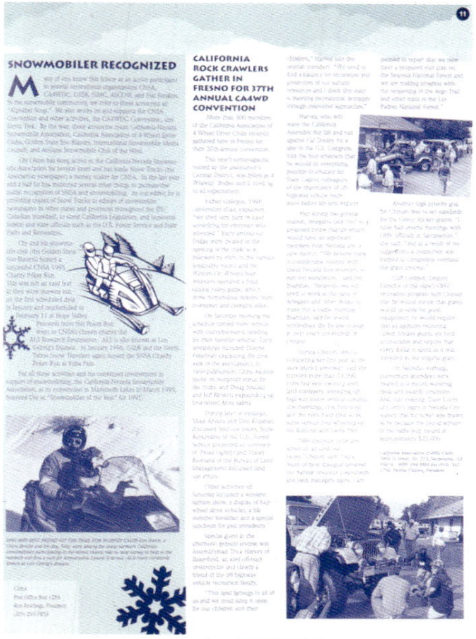
11
SNOWMOBILER RECOGNIZED
CALIFORNIA ROCK CRAWLERS GATHER IN FRESNO FOR 37TH ANNUAL CA4WD CONVENTION

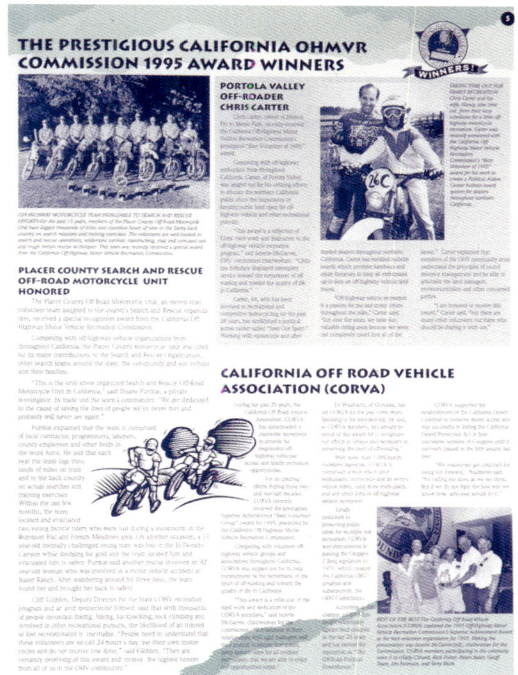
5
THE PRESTIGIOUS CALIFORNIA OHMVR COMMISSION 1995 AWARD WINNERS
WINNERS!
PORTOLA VALLEY OFF-ROADER CHRIS CARTER
PLACER COUNTY SEARCH AND RESCUE OFF-ROAD MOTORCYCLE UNIT HONORED
CALIFORNIA OFF ROAD VEHICLE ASSOCIATION (CORVA)

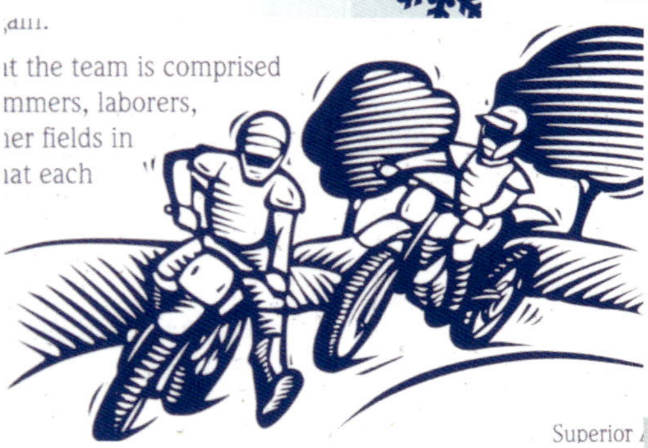
ain.
it the team is comprised
mmers, laborers,
ler fields in
lat each
Superior

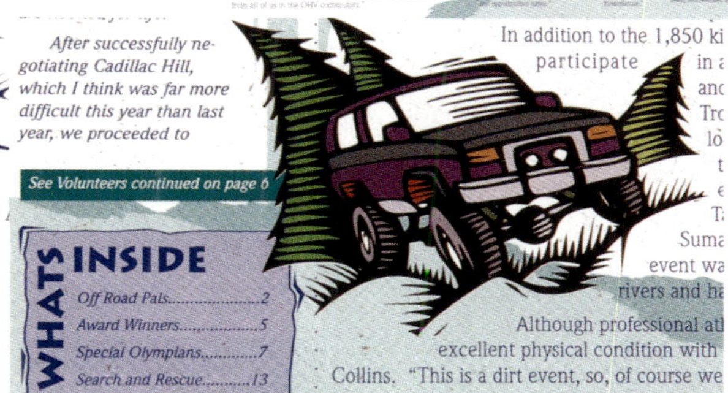
After successfully negotiating Cadillac Hill, which I think was far more difficult this year than last year, we proceeded to
See Volunteers continued on page 6
WHATS INSIDE
Off Road Pals....................2
Award Winners....................5
Special Olympians................7
Search and Rescue...............13
In addition to the 1,850 ki
participate in a
and
Tro
lo
t
e
T
Suma
event wa
rivers and ha
Although professional at
excellent physical condition with
Collins. "This is a dirt event, so, of course we

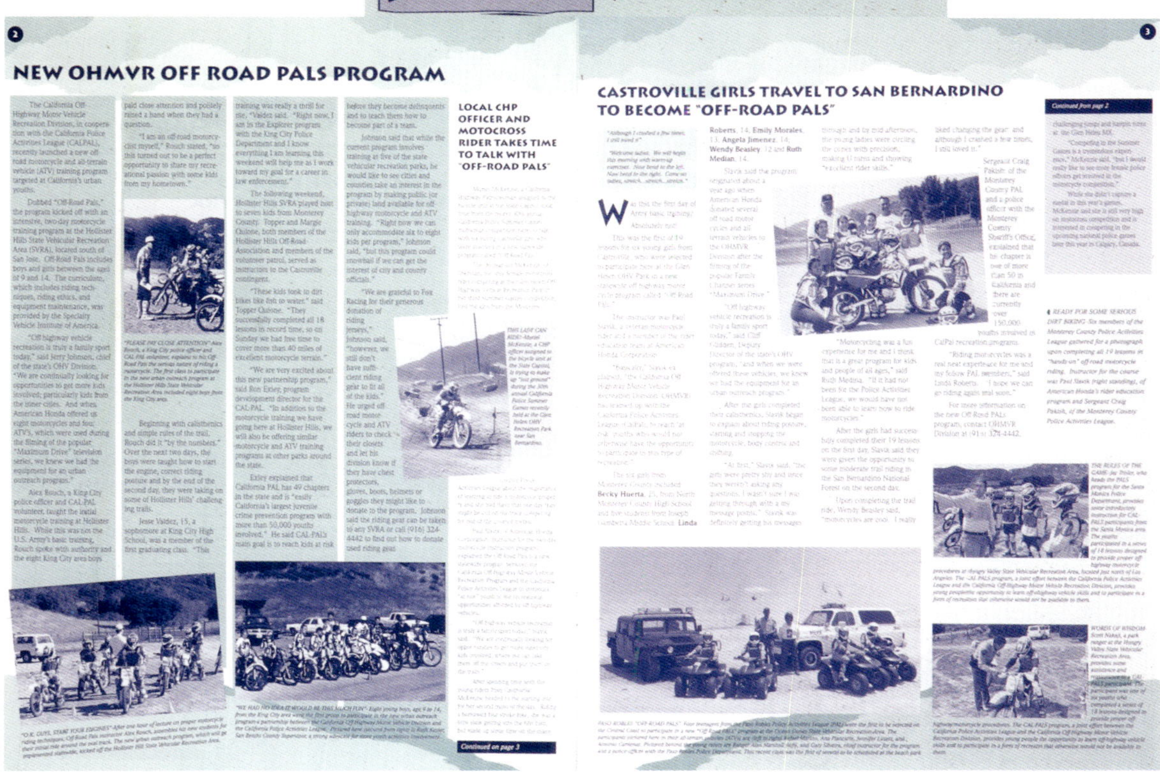
2
NEW OHMVR OFF ROAD PALS PROGRAM
LOCAL CHP OFFICER AND MOTOCROSS RIDER TAKES TIME TO TALK WITH "OFF-ROAD PALS"
Continued on page 3
3
CASTROVILLE GIRLS TRAVEL TO SAN BERNARDINO TO BECOME "OFF-ROAD PALS"
Continued from page 2

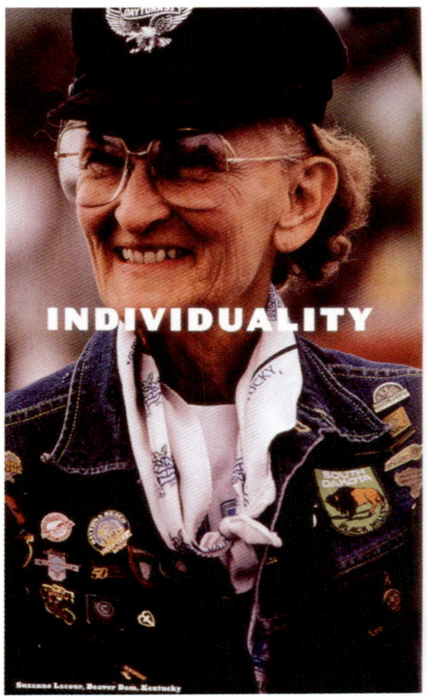


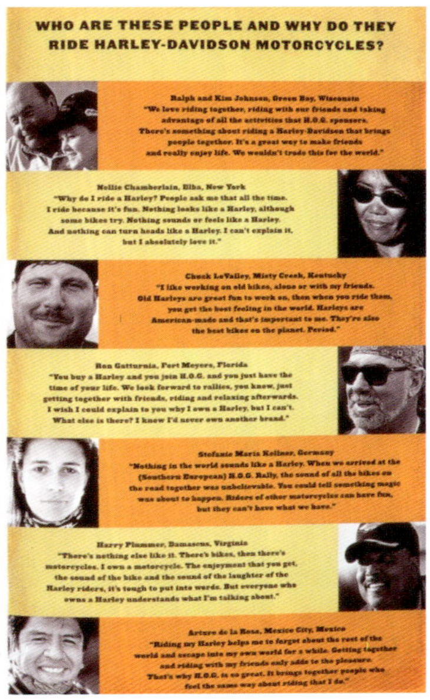


### HARLEY-DAVIDSON INC. 1996 ANNUAL REPORT

**Design Firm** *VSA Partners Inc.*
**Designers** *Curt Schreiber, Ken Fox, Fletcher Martin*
**Copywriter** *Ken Schmidt*

Harley-Davidson, a marketing success story for the ages, features actual accounts of Harley owners in this annual report. The extreme close-ups and intimate nature of many of the photos bring the stories home and show what makes the Harley rider so unique.

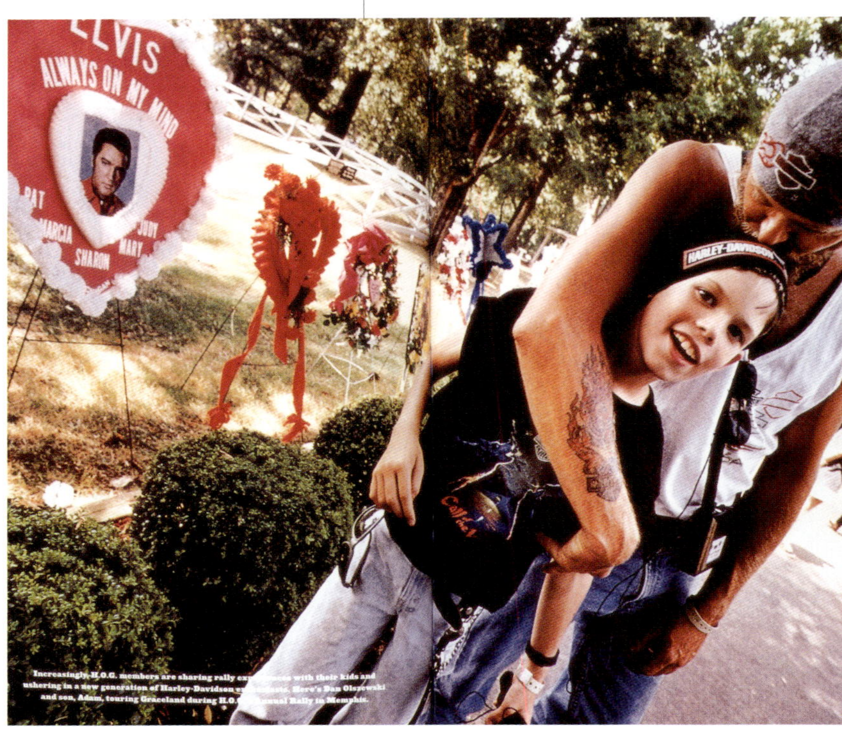

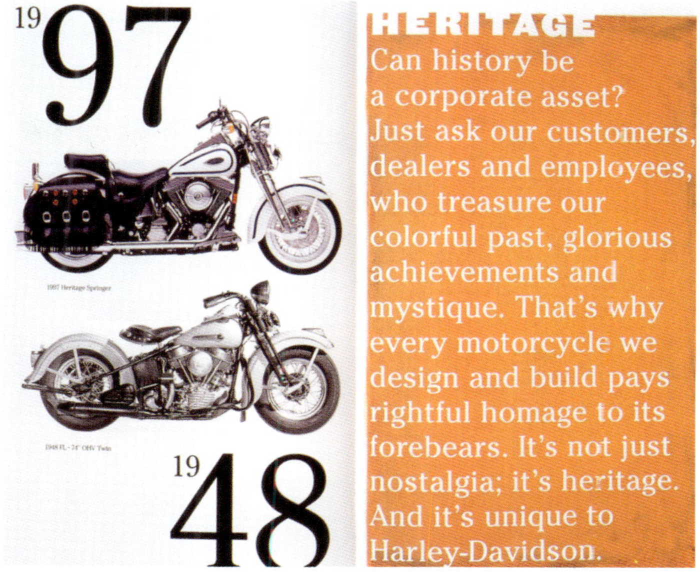

19 97

1997 Heritage Springer

1948 FL - 74" OHV Twin

19 48

**HERITAGE**

Can history be a corporate asset? Just ask our customers, dealers and employees, who treasure our colorful past, glorious achievements and mystique. That's why every motorcycle we design and build pays rightful homage to its forebears. It's not just nostalgia; it's heritage. And it's unique to Harley-Davidson.

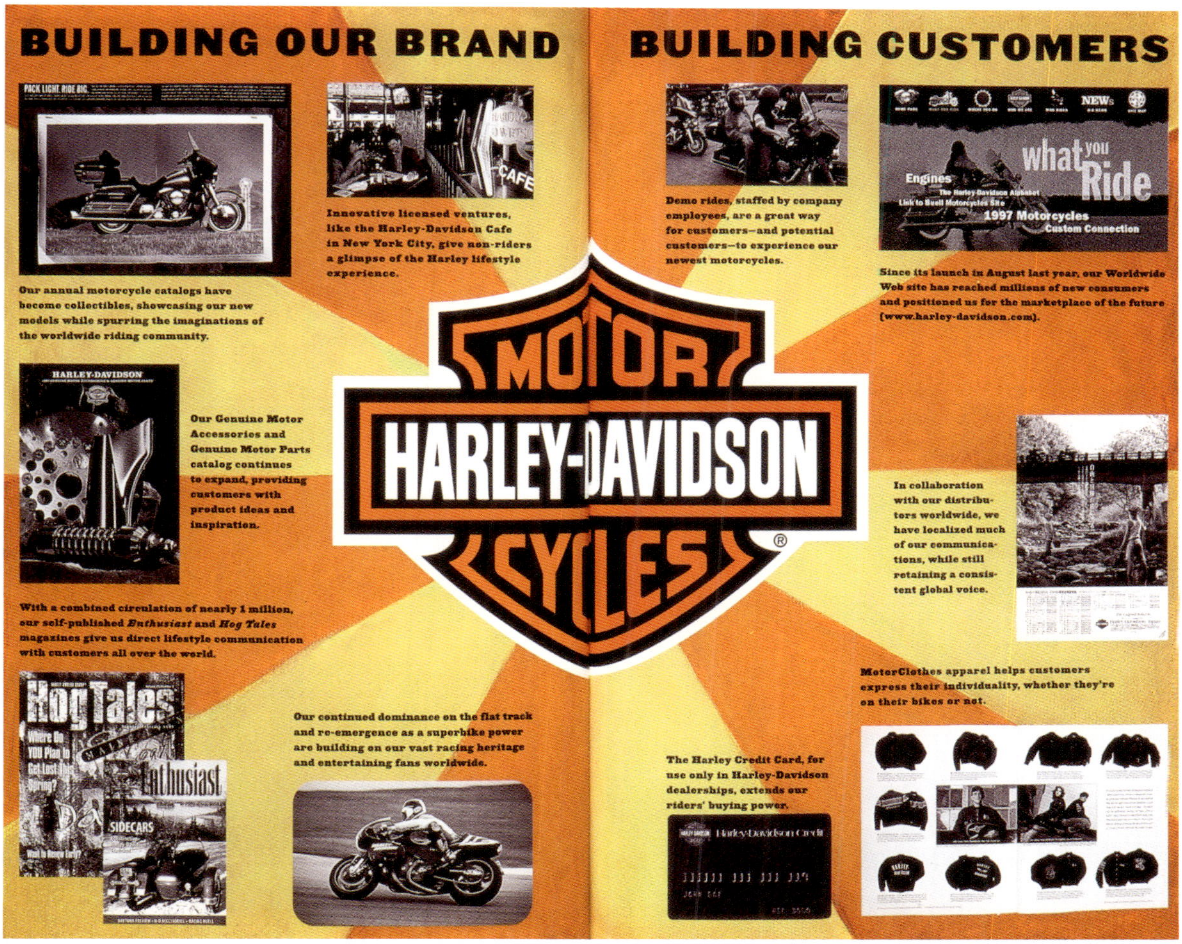

**BUILDING OUR BRAND**

Our annual motorcycle catalogs have become collectibles, showcasing our new models while spurring the imaginations of the worldwide riding community.

Innovative licensed ventures, like the Harley-Davidson Cafe in New York City, give non-riders a glimpse of the Harley lifestyle experience.

Our Genuine Motor Accessories and Genuine Motor Parts catalog continues to expand, providing customers with product ideas and inspiration.

With a combined circulation of nearly 1 million, our self-published *Enthusiast* and *Hog Tales* magazines give us direct lifestyle communication with customers all over the world.

Our continued dominance on the flat track and re-emergence as a superbike power are building on our vast racing heritage and entertaining fans worldwide.

**BUILDING CUSTOMERS**

Demo rides, staffed by company employees, are a great way for customers—and potential customers—to experience our newest motorcycles.

Since its launch in August last year, our Worldwide Web site has reached millions of new consumers and positioned us for the marketplace of the future (www.harley-davidson.com).

In collaboration with our distributors worldwide, we have localized much of our communications, while still retaining a consistent global voice.

MotorClothes apparel helps customers express their individuality, whether they're on their bikes or not.

The Harley Credit Card, for use only in Harley-Davidson dealerships, extends our riders' buying power.

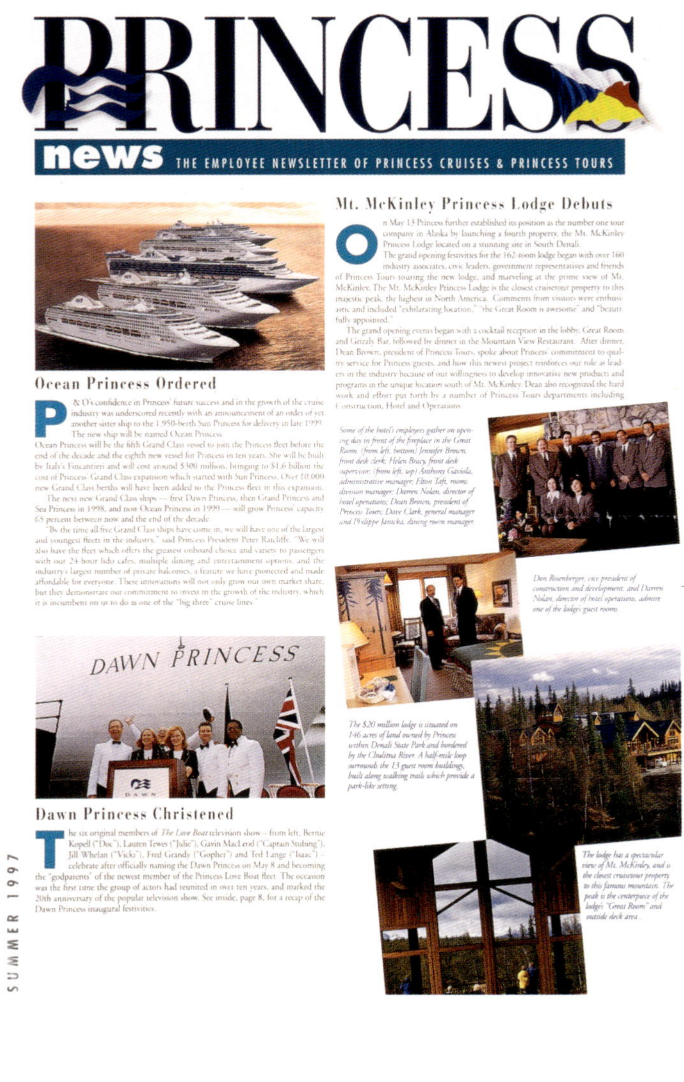
PRINCESS
**news** THE EMPLOYEE NEWSLETTER OF PRINCESS CRUISES & PRINCESS TOURS

## Ocean Princess Ordered

P&O's confidence in Princess' future success and in the growth of the cruise industry was underscored recently with an announcement of an order of yet another sister ship to the 1,950-berth Sun Princess for delivery in late 1999. The new ship will be named Ocean Princess.

Ocean Princess will be the fifth Grand Class vessel to join the Princess fleet before the end of the decade and the eighth new vessel for Princess in ten years. She will be built by Italy's Fincantieri and will cost around $300 million, bringing to $1.6 billion the cost of Princess' Grand Class expansion which started with Sun Princess. Over 10,000 new Grand Class berths will have been added to the Princess fleet in this expansion.

The next new Grand Class ships — first Dawn Princess, then Grand Princess and Sea Princess in 1998, and now Ocean Princess in 1999 — will grow Princess' capacity 65 percent between now and the end of the decade.

"By the time all five Grand Class ships have come in, we will have one of the largest and youngest fleets in the industry," said Princess President Peter Ratcliffe. "We will also have the fleet which offers the greatest onboard choice and variety to passengers with our 24-hour lido cafes, multiple dining and entertainment options, and the industry's largest number of private balconies, a feature we have pioneered and made affordable for everyone. These innovations will not only grow our own market share, but they demonstrate our commitment to invest in the growth of the industry, which it is incumbent on us to do as one of the "big three" cruise lines."

DAWN PRINCESS

## Dawn Princess Christened

The six original members of *The Love Boat* television show – from left, Bernie Kopell ("Doc"), Lauren Tewes ("Julie"), Gavin MacLeod ("Captain Stubing"), Jill Whelan ("Vicki"), Fred Grandy ("Gopher") and Ted Lange ("Isaac") – celebrate after officially naming the Dawn Princess on May 8 and becoming the "godparents" of the newest member of the Princess Love Boat fleet. The occasion was the first time the group of actors had reunited in over ten years, and marked the 20th anniversary of the popular television show. See inside, page 8, for a recap of the Dawn Princess inaugural festivities.

## Mt. McKinley Princess Lodge Debuts

On May 13 Princess further established its position as the number one tour company in Alaska by launching a fourth property, the Mt. McKinley Princess Lodge located on a stunning site in South Denali.

The grand opening festivities for the 162-room lodge began with over 160 industry associates, civic leaders, government representatives and friends of Princess Tours touring the new lodge, and marveling at the prime view of Mt. McKinley. The Mt. McKinley Princess Lodge is the closest cruisetour property to this majestic peak, the highest in North America. Comments from visitors were enthusiastic and included "exhilarating location," "the Great Room is awesome" and "beautifully appointed."

The grand opening events began with a cocktail reception in the lobby, Great Room and Grizzly Bar, followed by dinner in the Mountain View Restaurant. After dinner, Dean Brown, president of Princess Tours, spoke about Princess' commitment to quality service for Princess guests, and how this newest project reinforces our role as leaders in the industry because of our willingness to develop innovative new products and programs in the unique location south of Mt. McKinley. Dean also recognized the hard work and effort put forth by a number of Princess Tours departments including Construction, Hotel and Operations.

*Some of the hotel's employees gather on opening day in front of the fireplace in the Great Room. (from left, bottom) Jennifer Brown, front desk clerk; Helen Bruce, front desk supervisor; (from left, top) Anthony Gaviola, administrative manager; Elton Taft, rooms division manager; Darren Nolan, director of hotel operations; Dean Brown, president of Princess Tours; Dave Clark, general manager and Philippe Janicka, dining room manager.*

*Don Rosenberger, vice president of construction and development, and Darren Nolan, director of hotel operations, admire one of the lodge's guest rooms.*

*The $20 million lodge is situated on 146 acres of land owned by Princess within Denali State Park and bordered by the Chulitna River. A half-mile loop surrounds the 13 guest room buildings, built along walking trails which provide a park-like setting.*

*The lodge has a spectacular view of Mt. McKinley, and is the closest cruisetour property to this famous mountain. The peak is the centerpiece of the lodge's "Great Room" and outside deck area.*

SUMMER 1997

### PRINCESS CRUISES *PRINCESS NEWS* NEWSLETTER

**Design Firm** *Princess Cruises*
**Designer** *Lisa Juarez*
**Editor** *Julie Benson*

Such a photo-intense newsletter can become busy, but the streamlined format is maintained by sticking with a four-column grid layout; anchoring small photos to a single, large image placed slightly off center; and calling attention to more active photos by feathering their edges.

PRINCESS
**news** THE EMPLOYEE NEWSLETTER OF PRINCESS CRUISES & PRINCESS TOURS

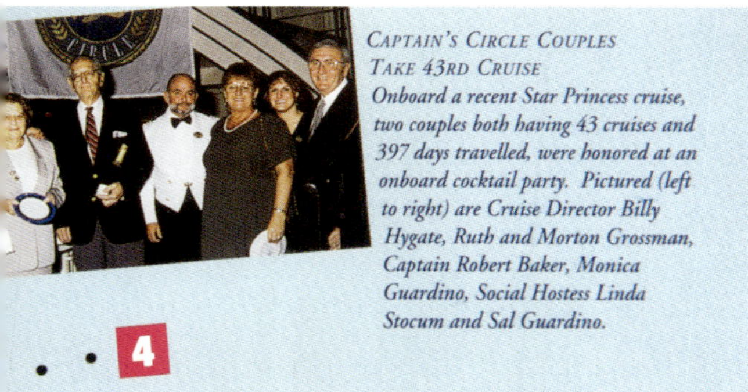


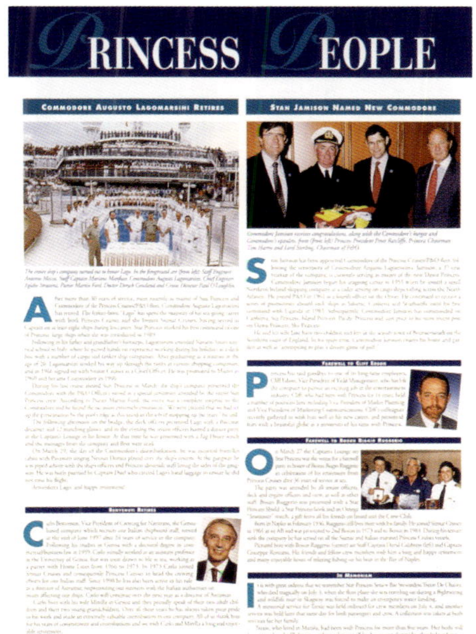


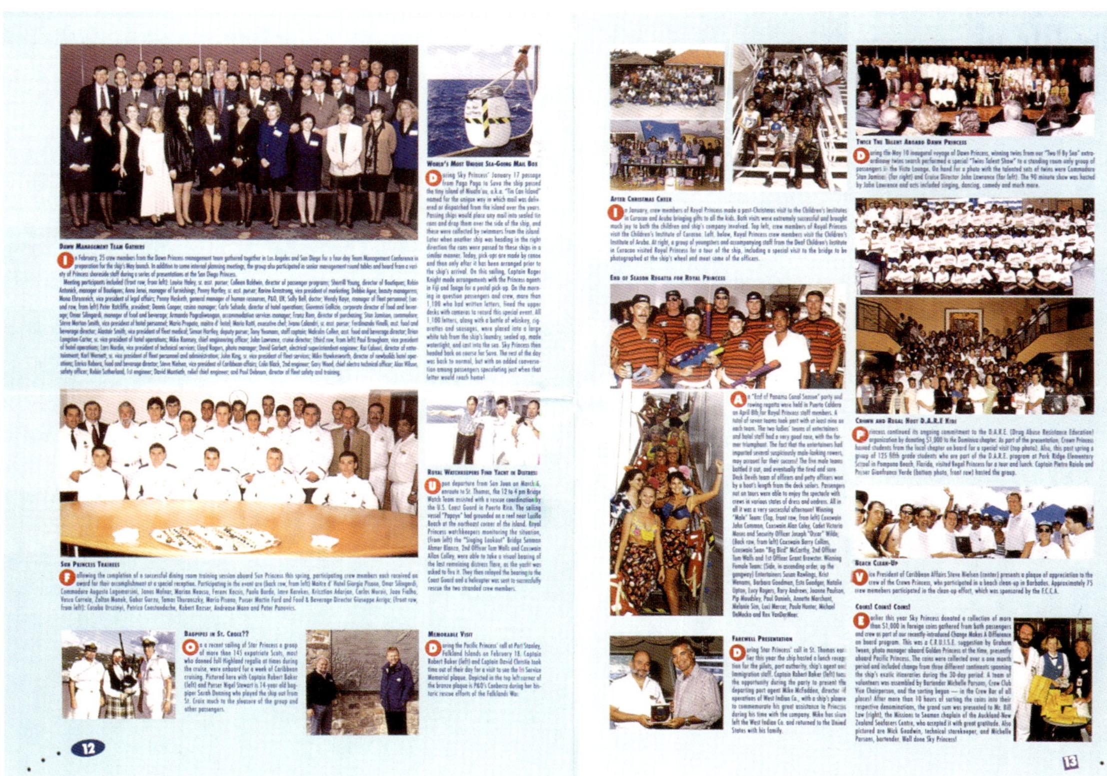

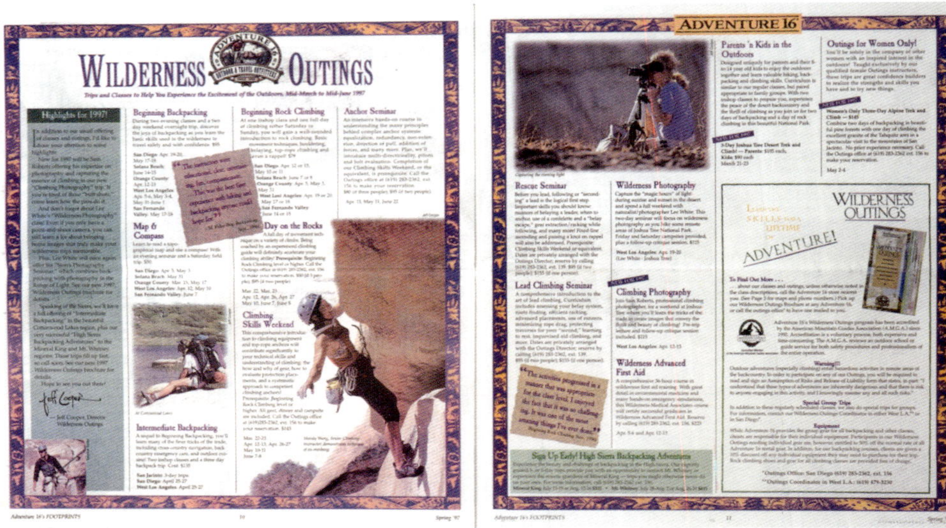
WILDERNESS OUTINGS

ADVENTURE 16

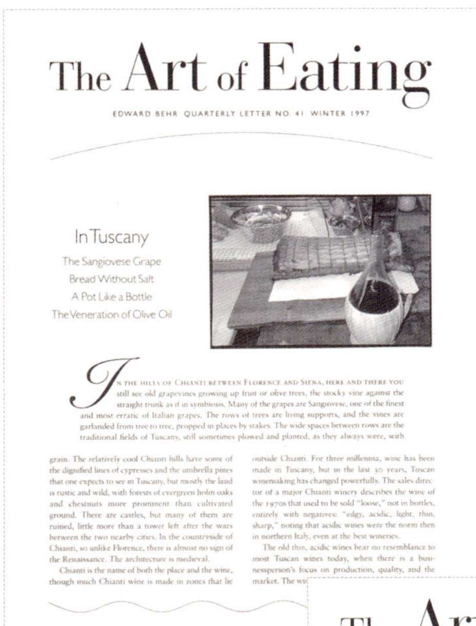
The Art of Eating

EDWARD BEHR QUARTERLY LETTER NO. 41 WINTER 1997

In Tuscany

The Sangiovese Grape

Bread Without Salt

A Pot Like a Bottle

The Veneration of Olive Oil

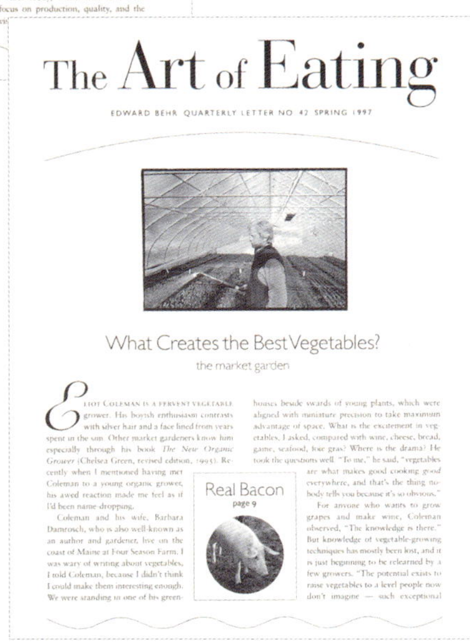
The Art of Eating

EDWARD BEHR QUARTERLY LETTER NO. 42 SPRING 1997

What Creates the Best Vegetables?

the market garden

Real Bacon

page 9

**EDWARD BEHR'S *THE ART OF EATING***

**Designers** *Keith Chamberlin, Edward Behr*

**Editor** *Edward Behr*

**Writer** *Edward Behr*

The art of simplicity is exemplified in *The Art of Eating,* where articulate copy is complemented by unobtrusive black-and-white photography.

### ADVENTURE 16 *FOOTPRINTS* NEWSLETTER

**Design Firm** *Taylor Graphics*
**Designer** *Marjorie Taylor*
**Editor** *Peter Jensen*

Outdoor photography is a must for a wilderness outfitter and despite the fact that this newsletter is printed on newsprint, the photos reproduce extremely well. The secret: use color sparingly.

### H. J. HEINZ CO. 1996 ANNUAL REPORT

**Design Firm** *RKC! (Robinson Kurtin Communications! Inc.)*
**Copywriters** *Eleanor Foa Dienstag, Eleanor Foa Associates; Jack Kennedy, Ketchum PR*

There is no staid photography in this Heinz annual report. An extra-large photo of toddlers on its cover piques reader curiosity. Inside, the tots appear in a spread that transitions nicely with the procuct photography.

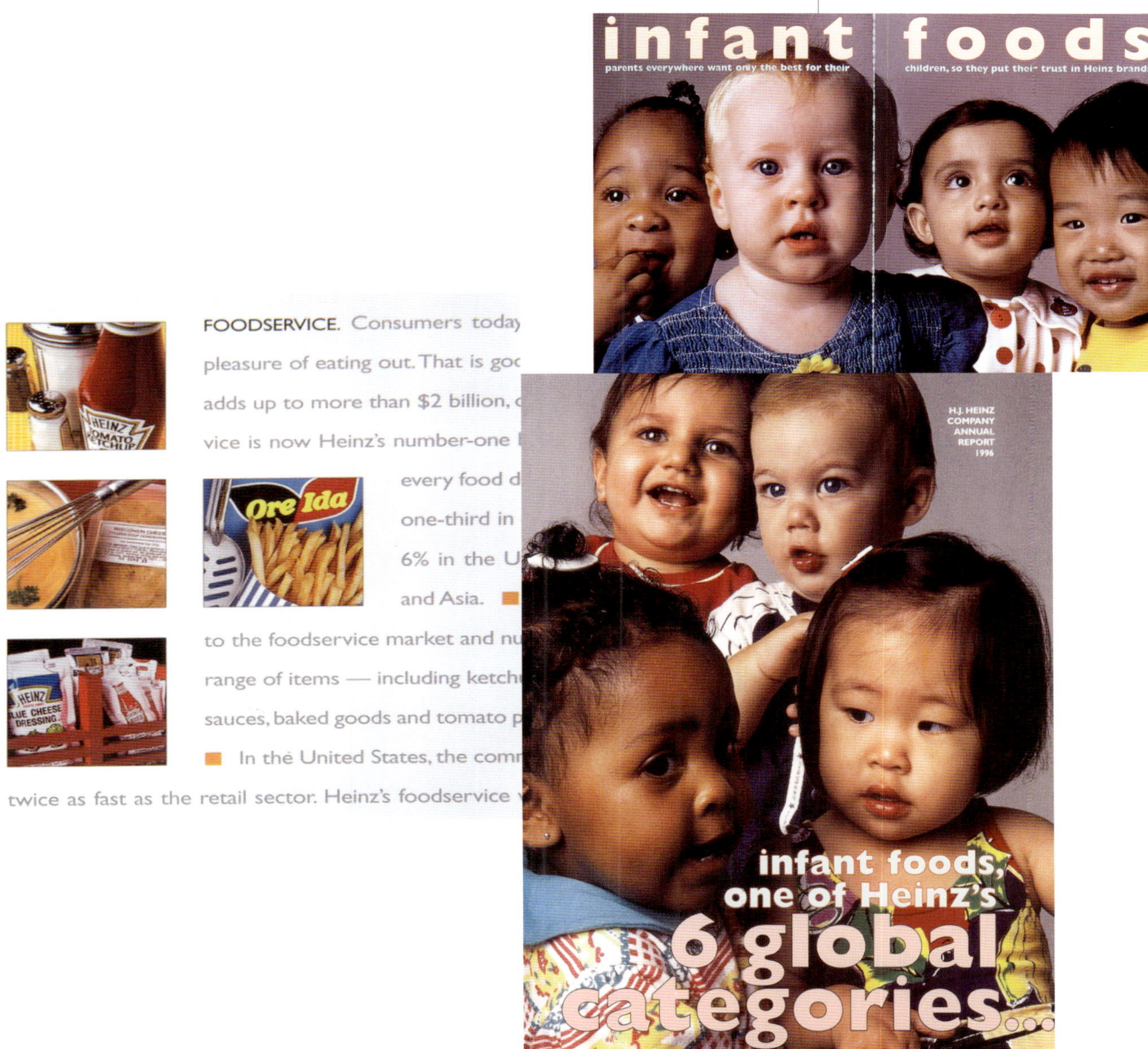

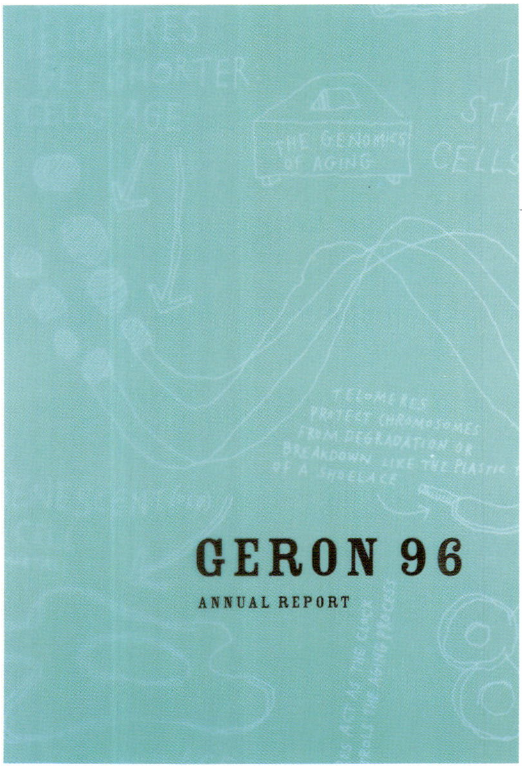


### GERON 1996 ANNUAL REPORT

**Design Firm** *Cahan & Associates*
**Art Director** *Bill Cahan*
**Designer** *Bob Dinetz*
**Illustrator** *Carole Melis*

This annual report about a scientific-research lab avoids sterile images. Instead, scientists provided photos of themselves, which were used as full-page images. Other shots, as well as copy, were laid out in a grid reminiscent of the pattern found throughout Geron's labs.

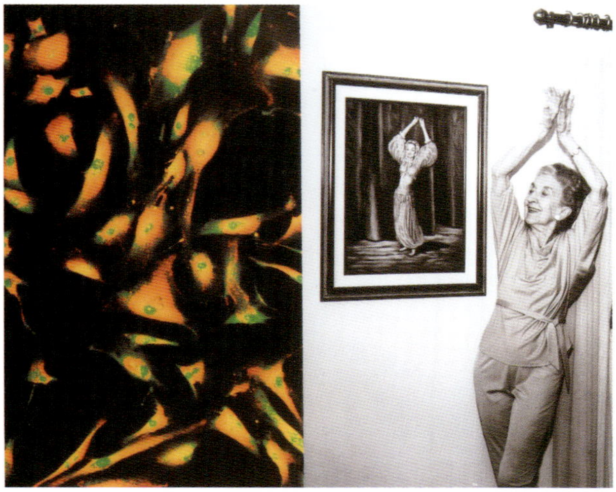

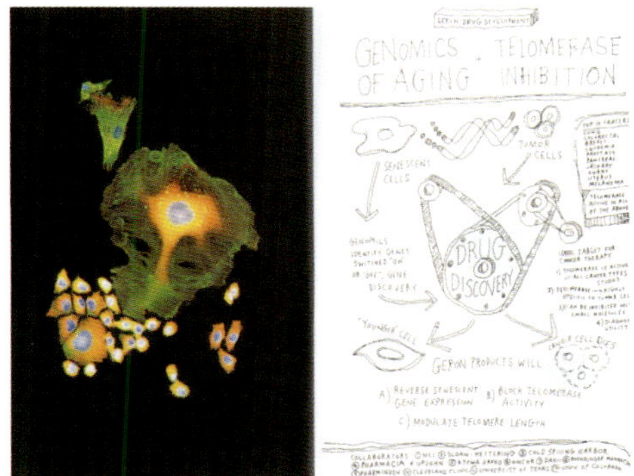
GENOMICS OF AGING
TELOMERASE INHIBITION
DRUG DISCOVERY

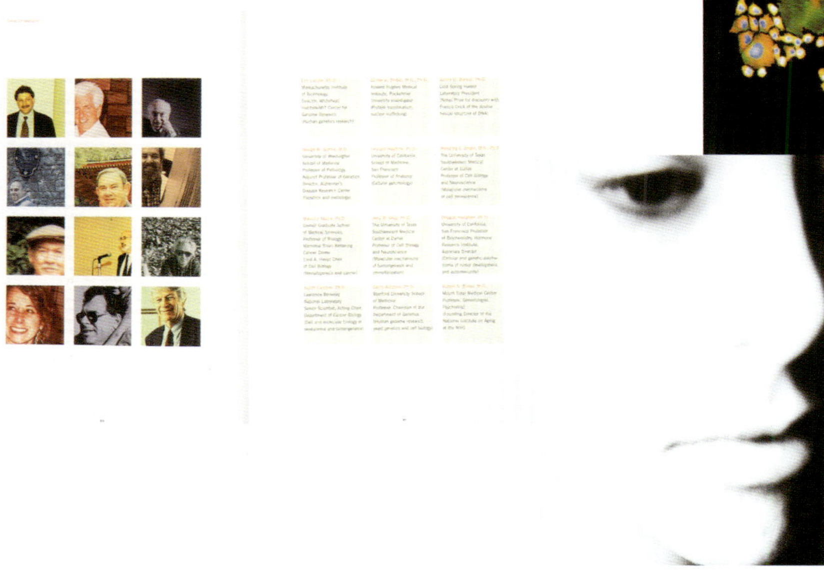

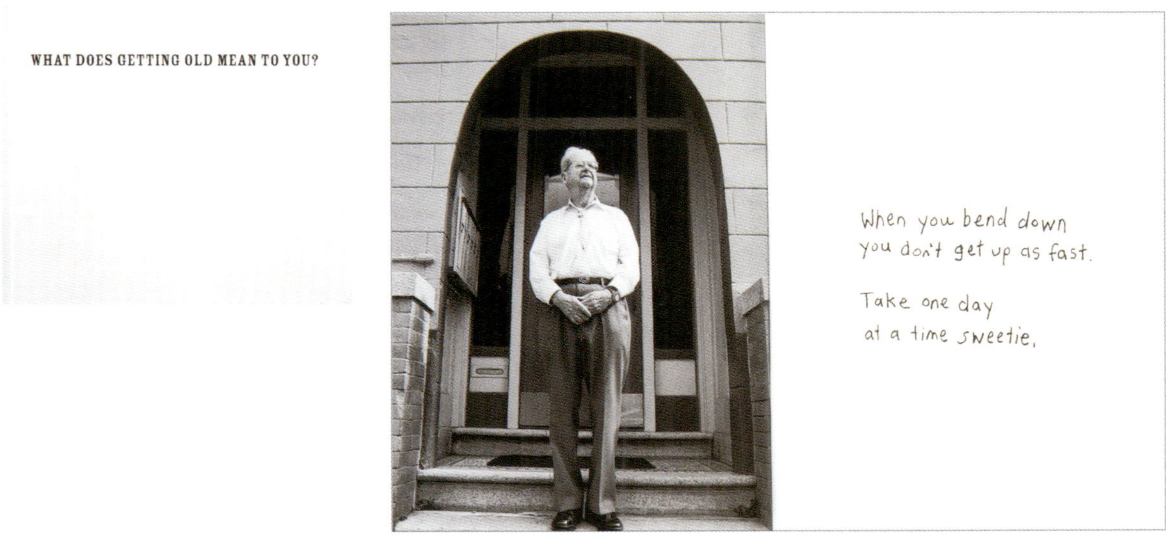
WHAT DOES GETTING OLD MEAN TO YOU?
When you bend down
you don't get up as fast.
Take one day
at a time sweetie.

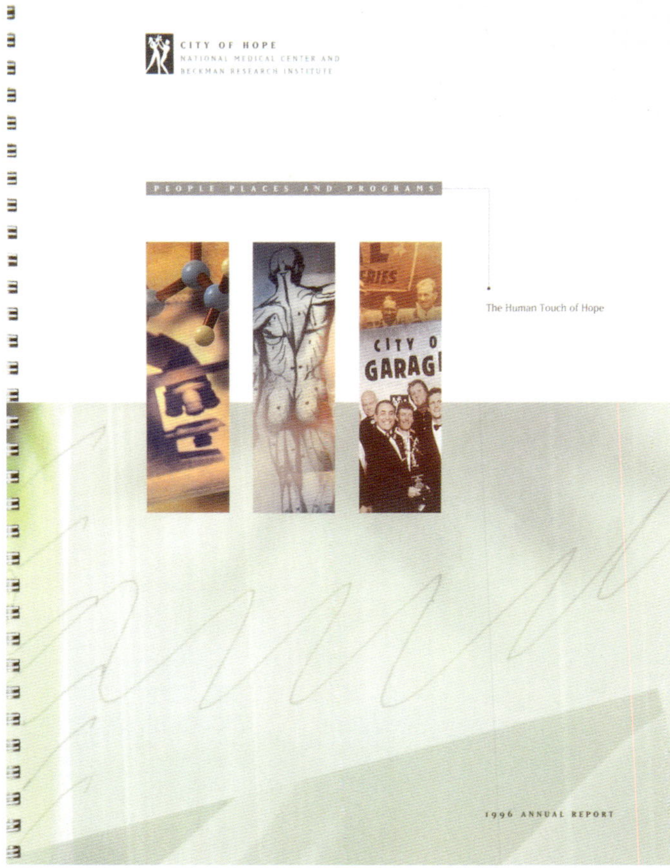
CITY OF HOPE
NATIONAL MEDICAL CENTER AND
BECKMAN RESEARCH INSTITUTE
PEOPLE PLACES AND PROGRAMS
The Human Touch of Hope
1996 ANNUAL REPORT

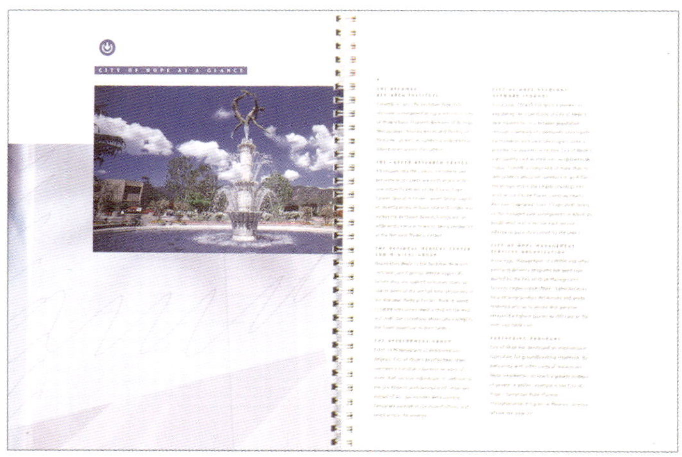
CITY OF HOPE AT A GLANCE

## CITY OF HOPE 1996 ANNUAL REPORT

**Design Firm** *Kimberly Baer Design*
**Designer** *Maggie van Oppen*
**Illustrator** *Richard Tuschman*
**Photographer** *Mark Robert Halper*

The photo collages created for City of Hope's annual report are composed of objects and images that, together, communicate the organization's message. Finding individual photographs that communicate as much would have been difficult, if not impossible.

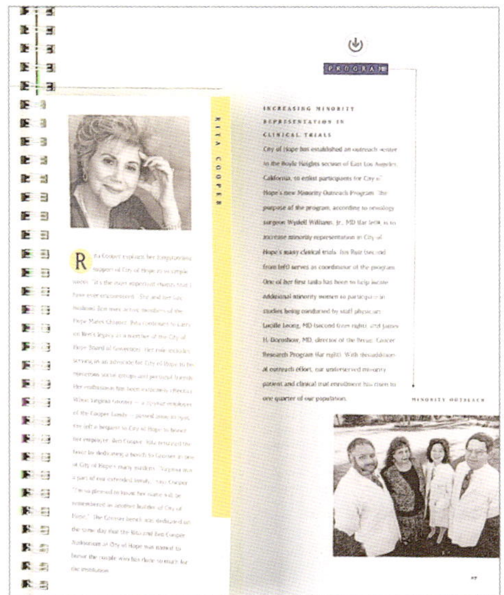


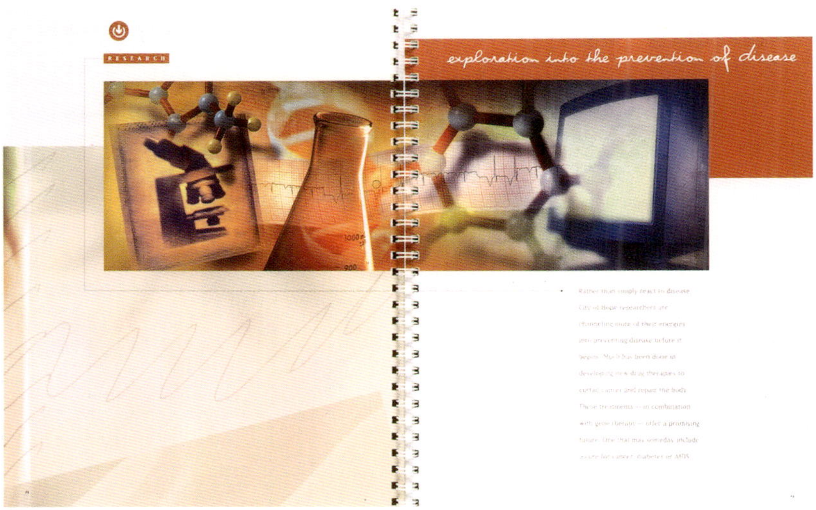


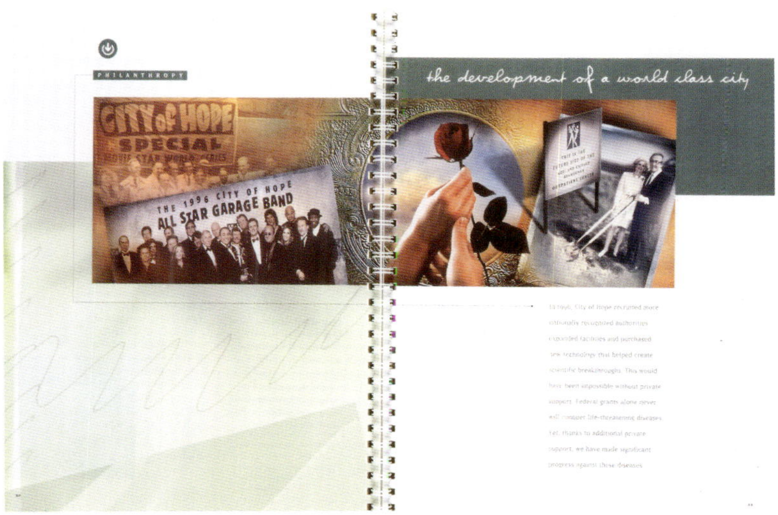

## ST. JUDE MEDICAL INC. 1996 ANNUAL REPORT

**Design Firm** *Larsen Design + Interactive*
**Designer** *Tim Larsen*

Showing a virtual timeline of happy, healthy former patients, all with their own unique story to tell, St. Jude Medical's annual report gets personal. The photos include people who appear to have just stepped out of their daily life expressly for these shots. Aside from the personality of the poses, this represents a great technique for enlivening static group photos.

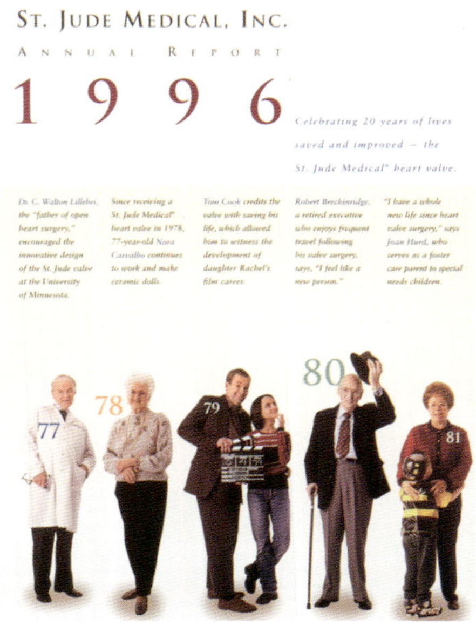


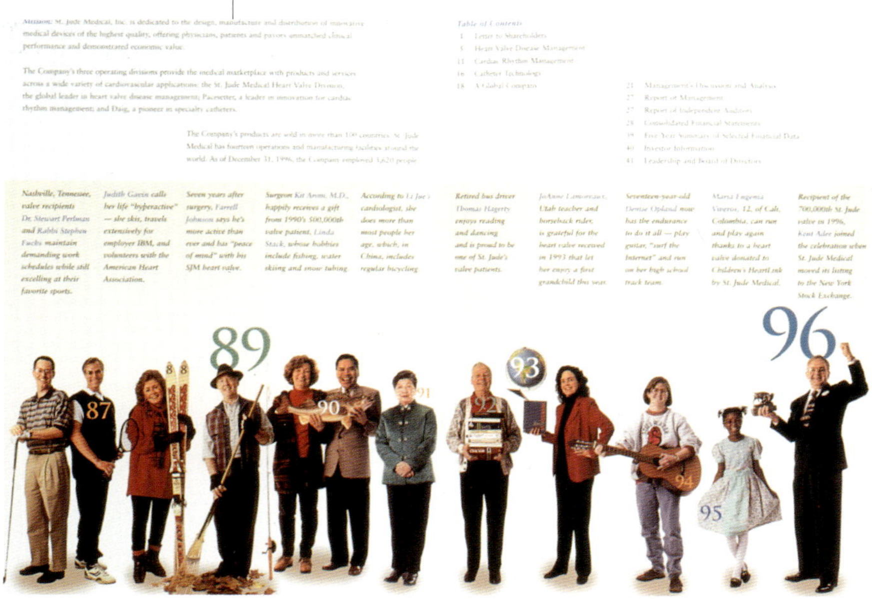

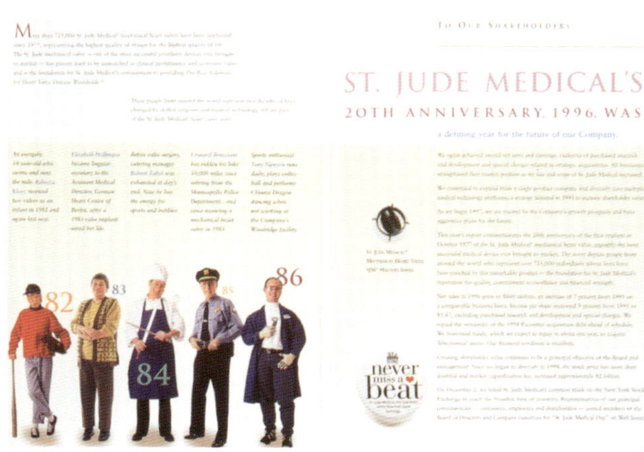

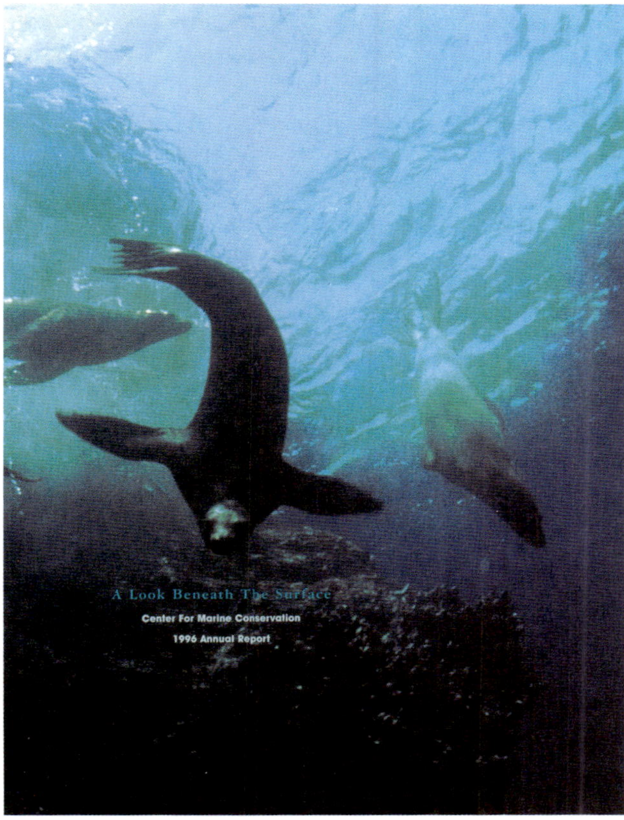


## CENTER FOR MARINE CONSERVATION 1996 ANNUAL REPORT

**Design Firm** *Sibley Peteet Design, in association with GSD&M Advertising*
**Art Directors** *Rex Peteet, Mark Brinkman*
**Designers** *Rex Peteet, Mark Brinkman*

There are plenty of photographs of the ocean and marine life within the Center for Marine Conservation annual report. What makes them different is the designers' desire to look beneath the surface, resulting in an exquisite opening spread where a vellum sheet obscures a coral reef until the reader peers underneath.

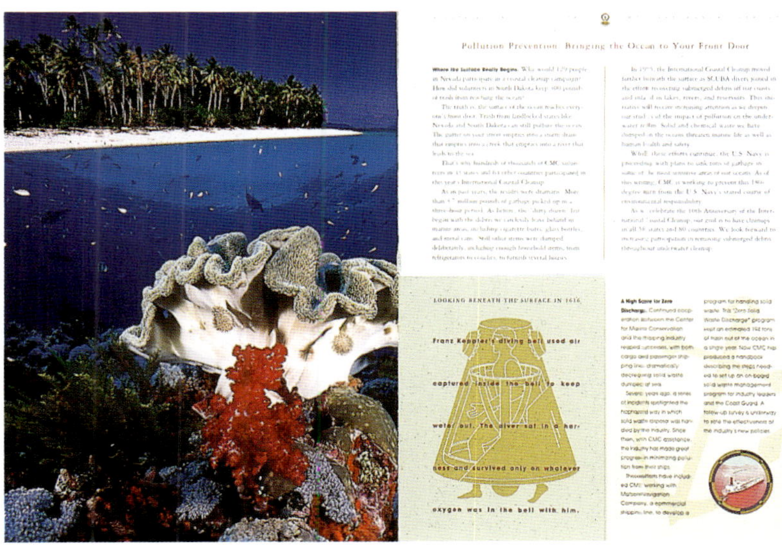

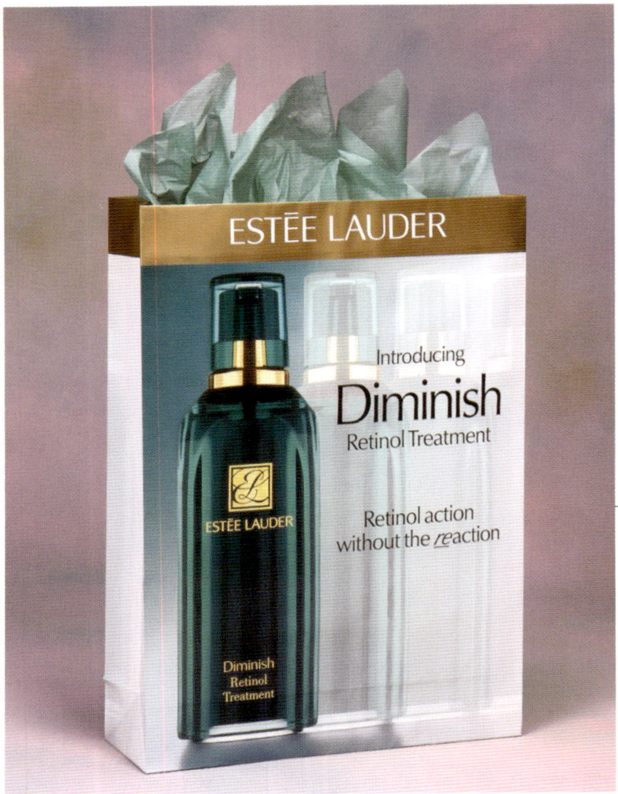


**LA PRAIRIE BAG**

**Art Director** *Ched Vakorich*
**Bag Manufacturer** *S. Posner Sons Inc*

The refreshingly clean and clear images of the organic ingredients in the products that are shown on the packaging reinforce the brand image.

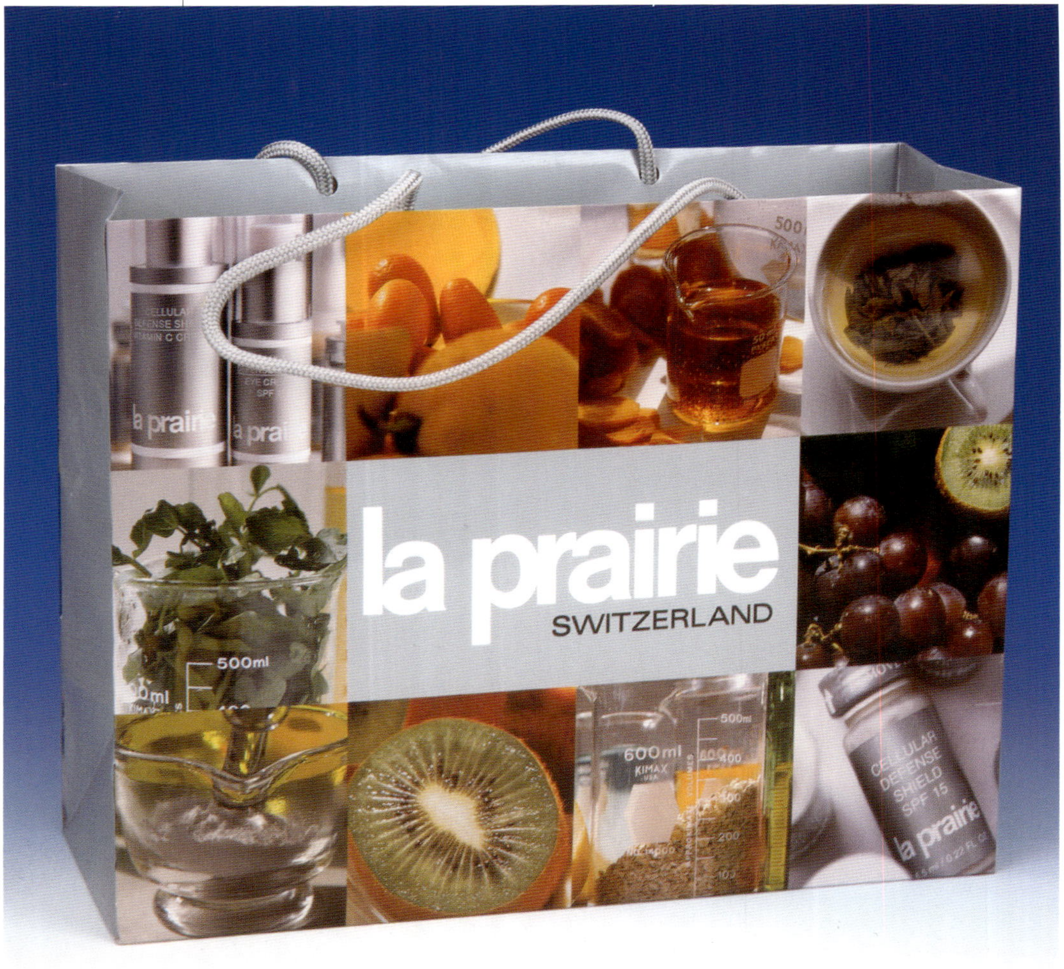

**ESTÉE LAUDER DIMINISH PACKAGING**

**Design Firm** *Estée Lauder in-house*
**Bag Manufacturer** *Modern Arts Packaging*

By screening back the photograph of Estée Lauder's Diminish, the photo does exactly what the product promises.

**CARNET DE VOL BAG**

**Design Firm** *Carré Noir*
**Art Director** *Jean-Christophe Cribelier*
**Designer** *Jean-Christophe Cribelier*
**Bag Manufacturer** *Lambacel*

This stylized photograph of a smart dresser in motion graphically illustrates ready-to-wear for the man on the move.

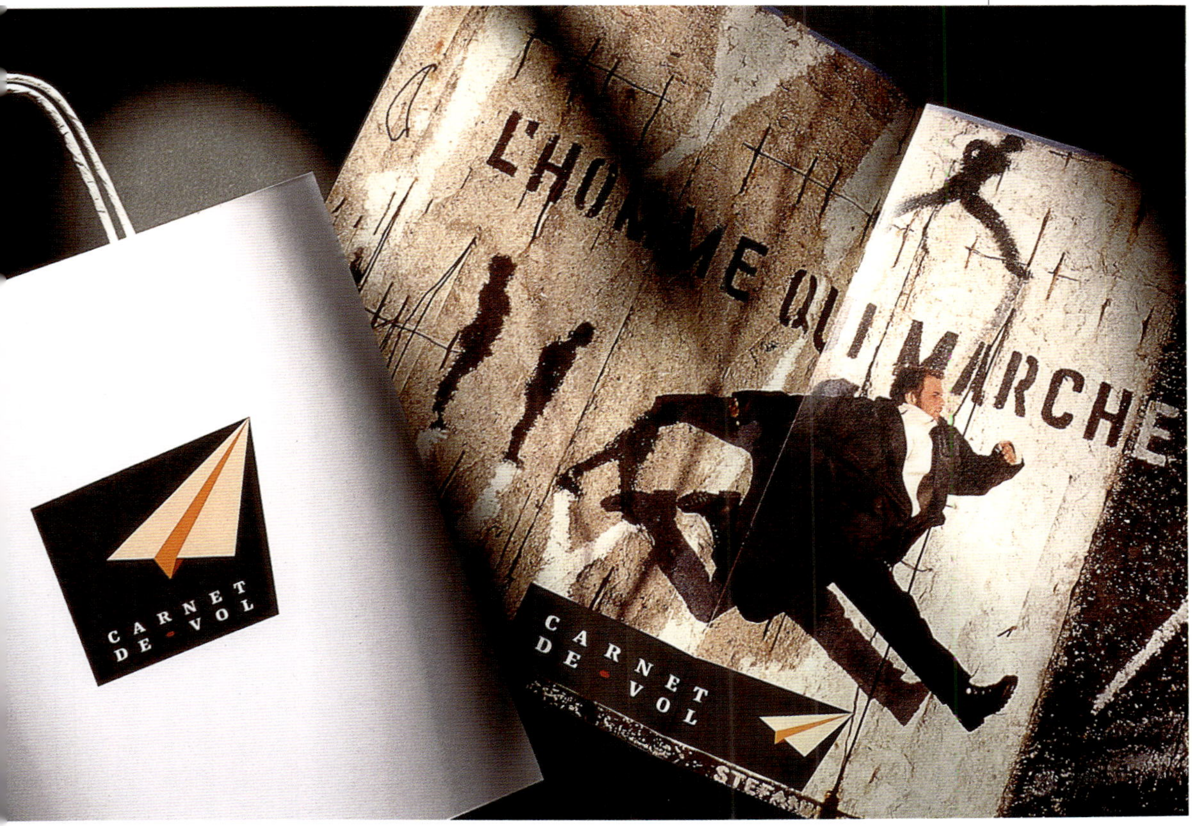

**DAYTON HUDSON CORPORATION**
**50 YEARS OF GIVING COMMEMORATIVE BAG**

**Design Firm** *design guys*
**Art Director** *Steven Sikora*
**Designers** *Richard Boynton, Steven Sikora, Amy Kirkpatrick*

Black-and-white close-ups of children's smiles and long shots of children at play were chosen to commemorate Dayton Hudson's involvement in the community. The bag was used at all of Dayton Hudson's stores from discount merchandisers to their upscale department stores.

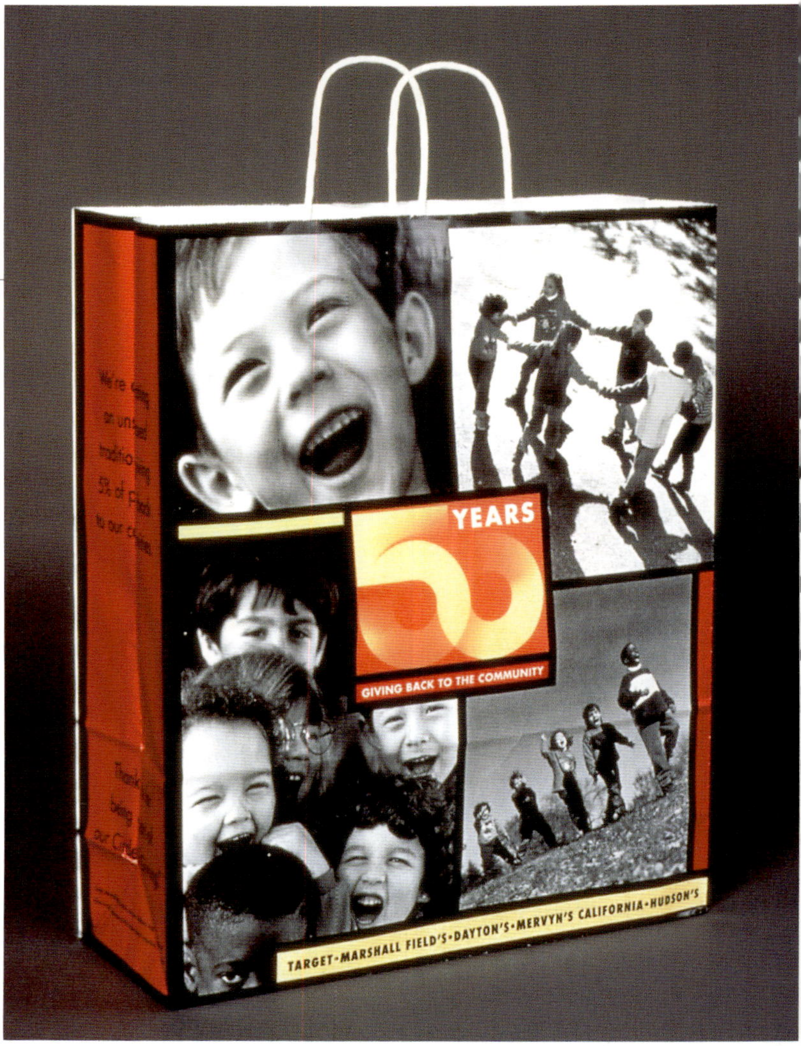


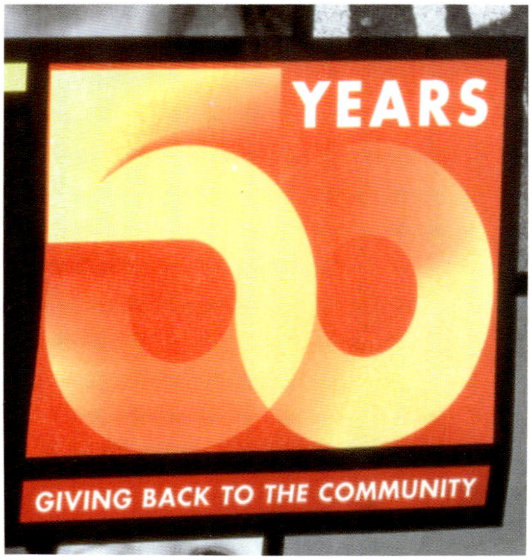

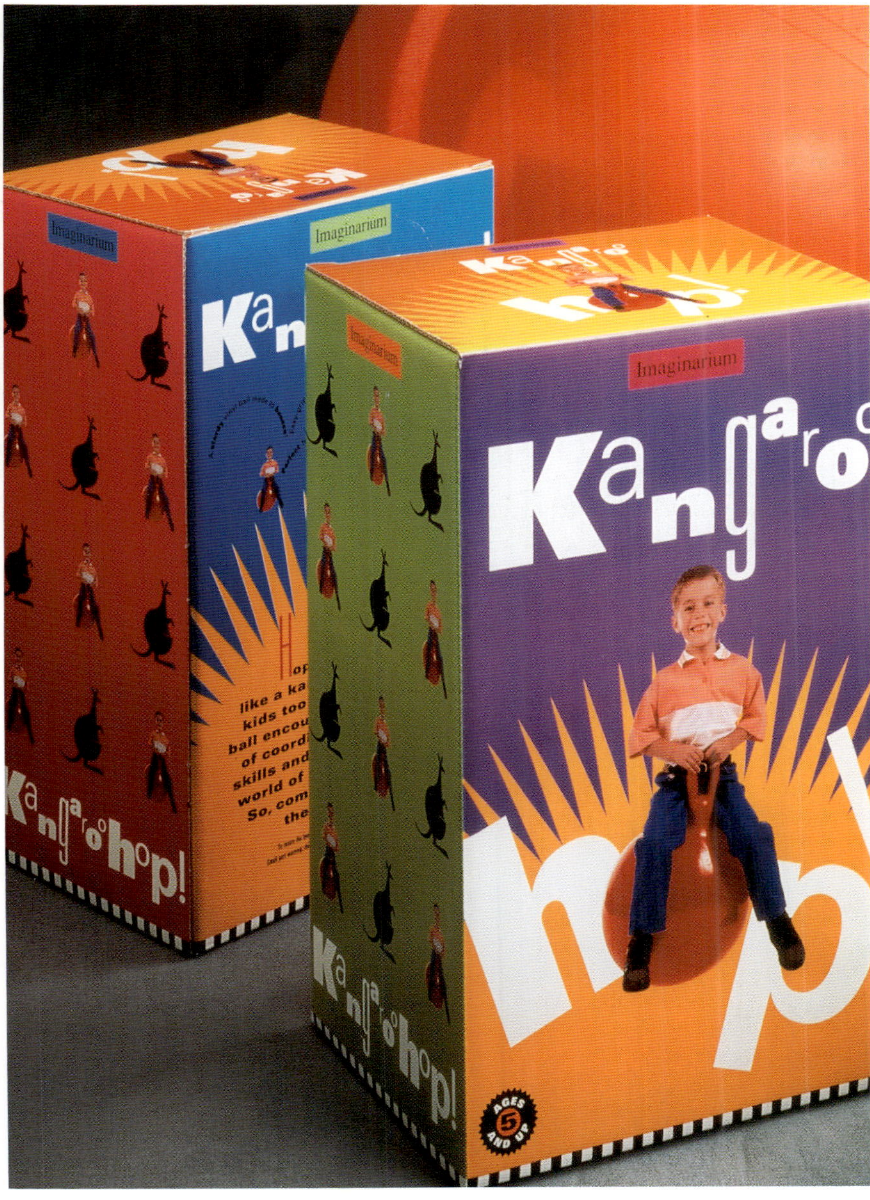


**IMAGINARIUM KANGAROO HOP! PACKAGING**

**Design Firm** *Gee & Chung Design*
**Art Director** *Earl Gee*
**Designer** *Earl Gee*
**Photographer** *Sandra Frank*

By integrating an actual photograph of a child using the toy against a stylized, colorful, graphic background, the design couples what is real with what is imagined.

**DRAKE'S PACKAGING**

**Design Firm** *Berni Design*
**Art Director** *Mark Eckstein*

Drake's recognizable product photography looks fresh and realistic. Moreover, shoppers' familiarity with the photographs and overall design makes this snack-food box comfort-food packaging.

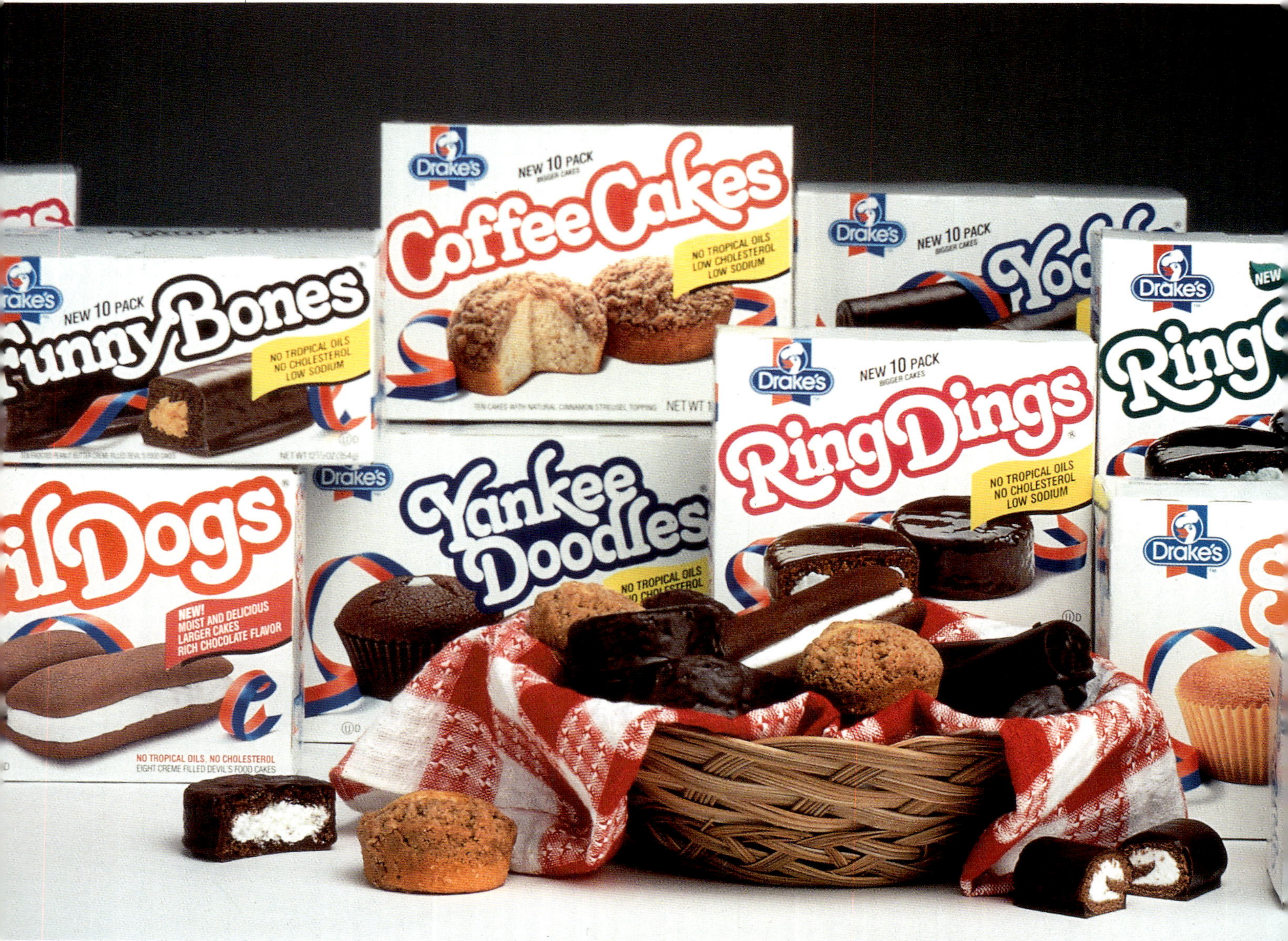

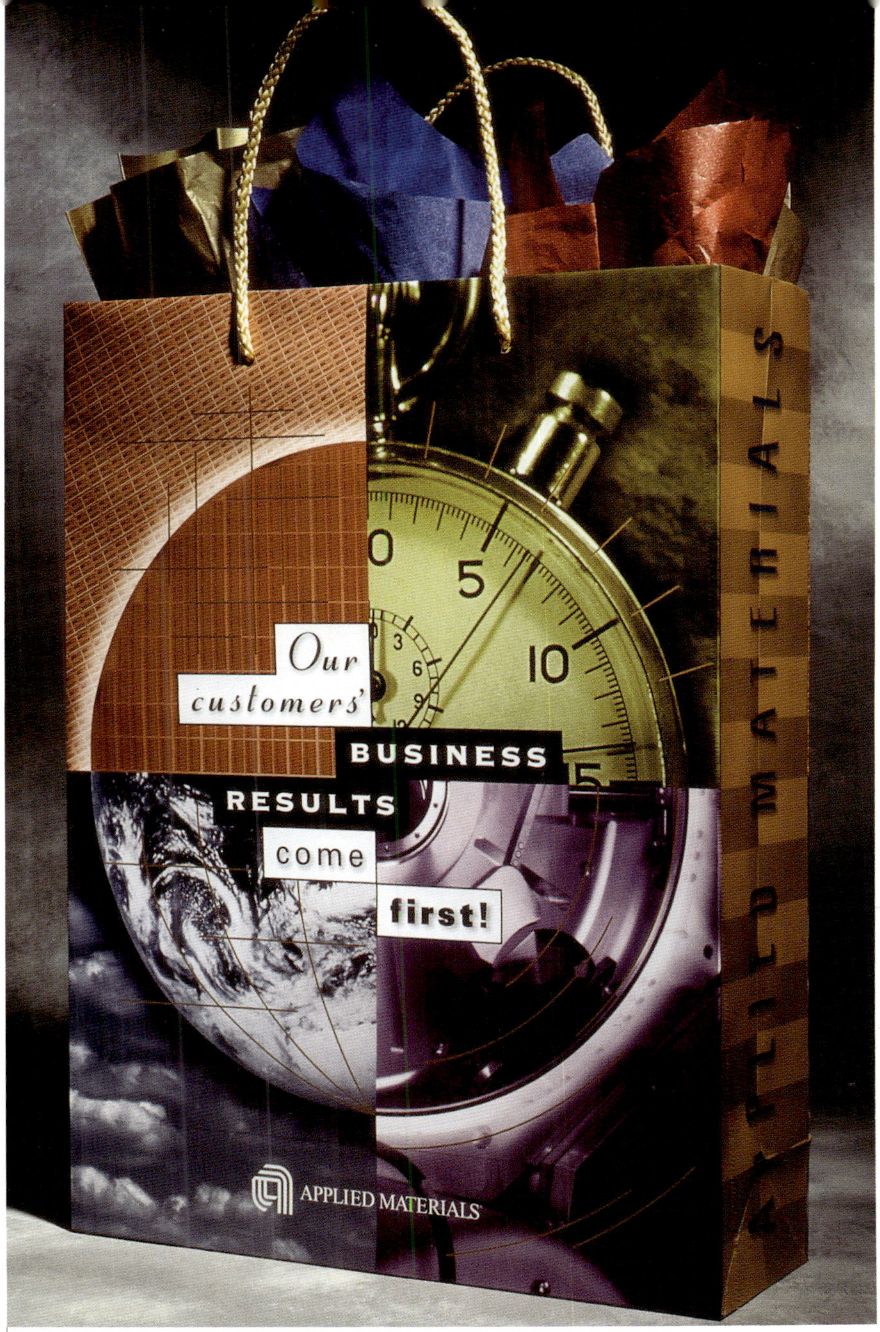


**APPLIED MATERIALS BAG**

| | |
|---|---|
| **Design Firm** | *Gee & Chung Design* |
| **Art Director** | *Earl Gee* |
| **Designers** | *Earl Gee, Fani Chung* |
| **Bag Manufacturer** | *Commonwealth Packaging Company* |

The four distinctly different photographs used on this bag have one thing in common: their circular shape. Together, the individual capabilities they represent combine to showcase the company as a whole—in all, a unique approach to presenting such value-added intangibles.

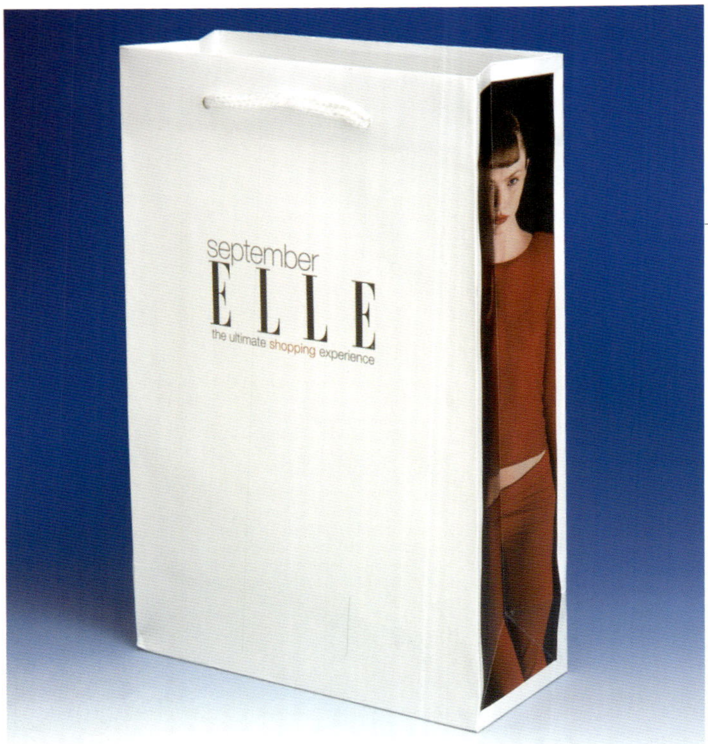


**SEPTEMBER *ELLE*/HACHETTE FILIPACCHI BAG**

**Design Firm** *Elle in-house*
**Art Director** *Rob Nolan*
**Bag Manufacturer** *Modern Arts Packaging*

The element of surprise is demonstrated on a bag for an upscale fashion magazine that sneaks in a shot of a long, lean model where you would least expect it—on the bag's gusset.

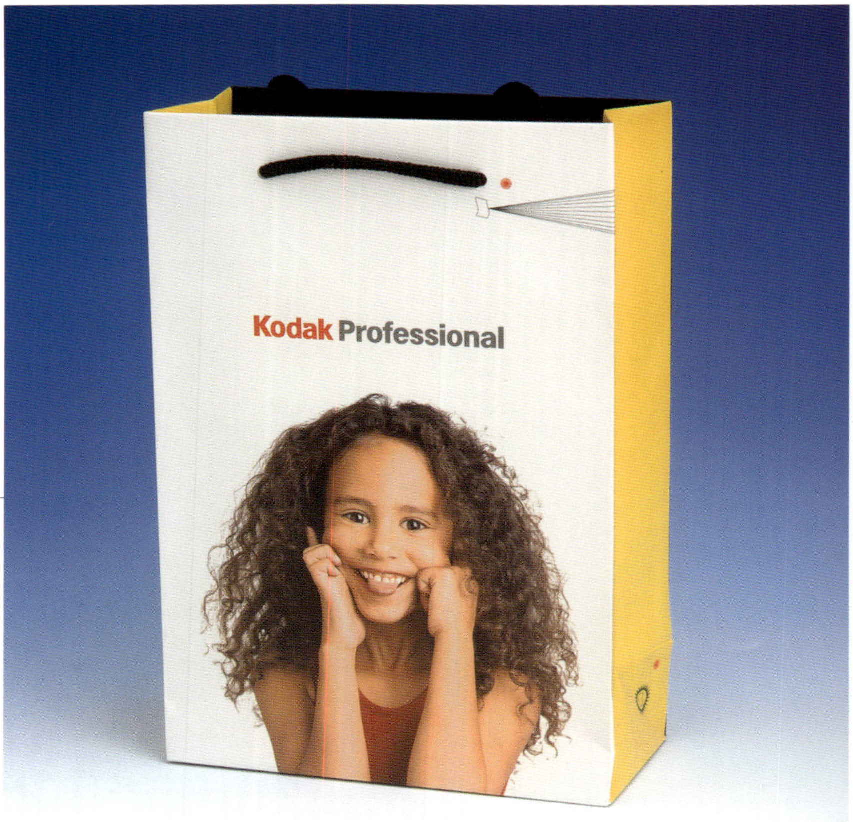


**KODAK BAG**

**Design Firm** *Saatchi & Saatchi Business Communications*
**Bag Manufacturer** *Modern Arts Mexico*

The photography is fun, the reproduction is high quality, and the look is eye catching. One wouldn't expect anything less from Kodak, especially since the bag is used to promote the high-level performance of Kodak film.

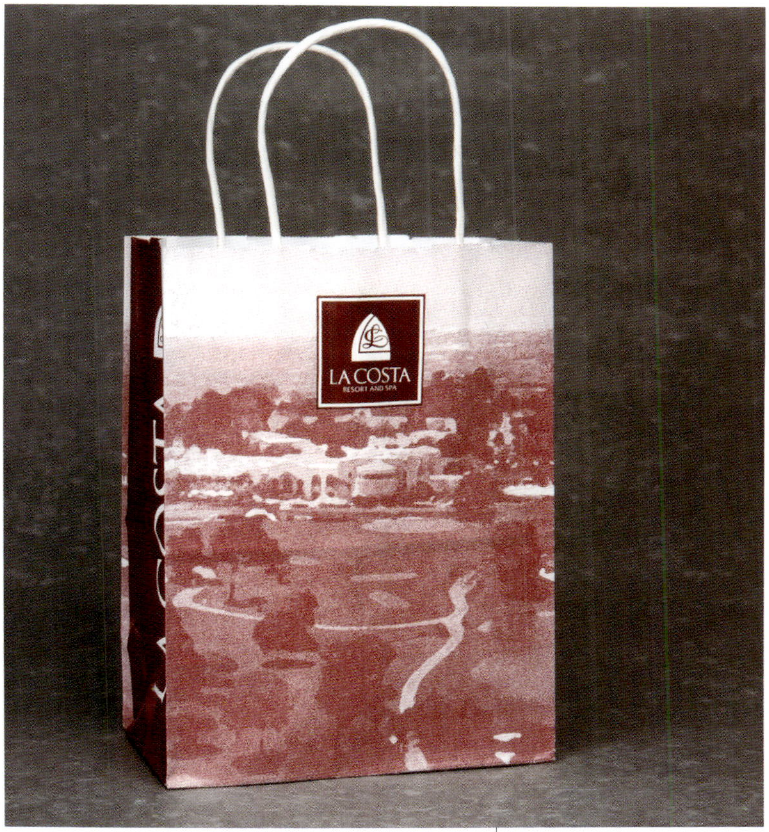


**LA COSTA BAG**

**Design Firm** *Jim Parker*
**Bag Manufacturer** *Bonita Pioneer Packaging*

A one-color sepia-tone shot of the resort gives La Costa an understated elegance that differentiates the design from other resorts' promotional pieces that feature sun-bleached beaches and lapis-colored waters.

**KOBE FASHION MUSEUM SYNAPSE AUDIO-VISUAL INSTALLATION**

**Design Firm** *Why Not Associates*
**Designers** *Andy Altman, Dave Ellis, Patrick Morrissey, Iain Cadby*
**Photographers** *Rocco Redondo, Richard Woolf, Hulton Deutsch, PhotoDisc, Inc.*

This Japanese museum took photography to a new level when it projected more than 5,000 photos onto four walls and the floor as part of a multimedia presentation.

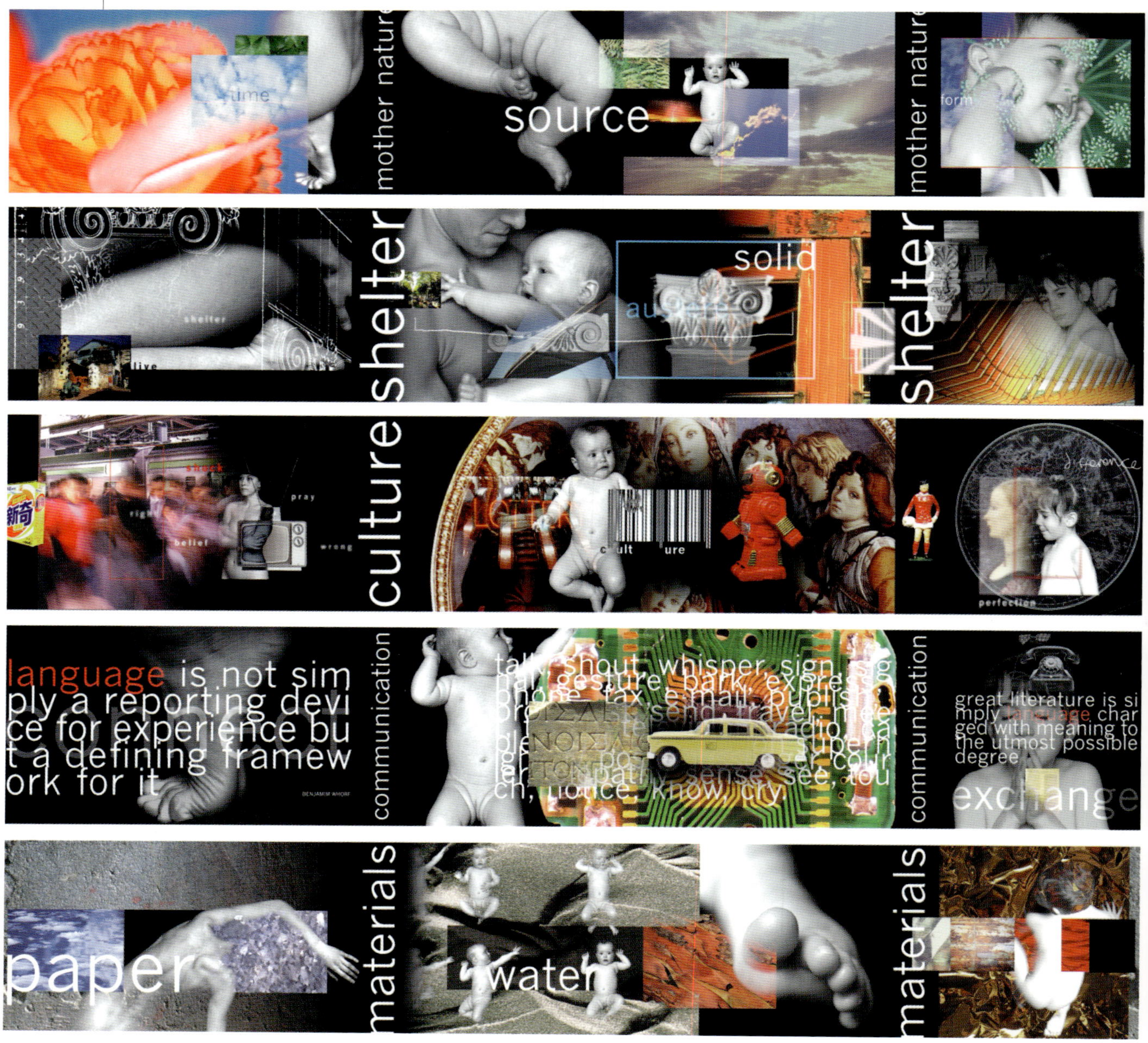

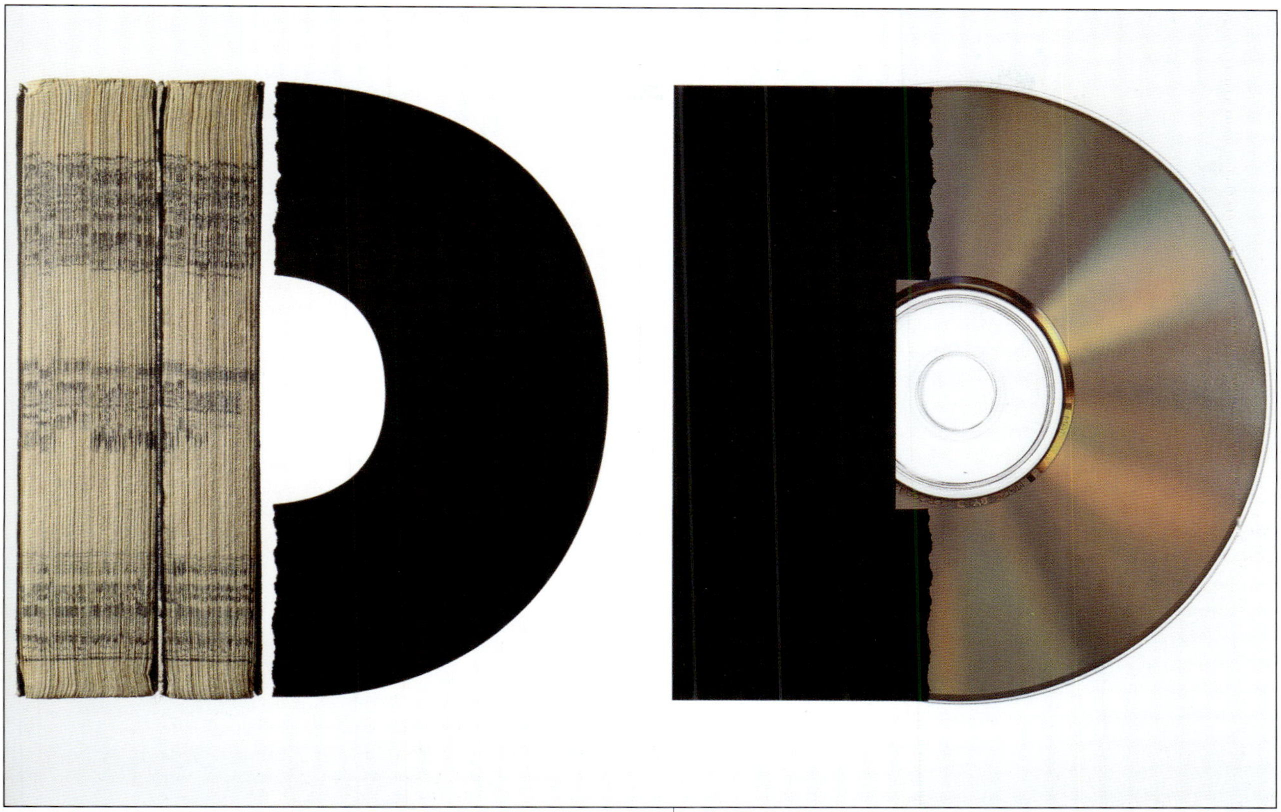

**DDD GALLERY YESTERDATA/DATATODAY POSTER**

**Design Firm** *Kan & Lau Design Consultants*
**Art Director** *Kan Tai-Keung*
**Designer** *Kan Tai-Keung*
**Illustrator** *Benson Kwun*
**Photographer** *C. K. Wong*

Integrating photography and type produced an interesting effect as demonstrated on this poster for a Japanese art gallery. A photo of an antique book and a compact disc visually compose the double *D* in the gallery's initials while contrasting the time-honored versus the timely methods of storing and retrieving information.

## AMAZONIA EXPEDITIONS BROCHURE

**Design Firm** *Asylum*
**Art Director** *Cheryl Dasher*
**Designer** *Cheryl Dasher*

An expeditionary map is the backdrop for a series of wildlife shots, close-up images of plant foliage, and object photography, all of which appear three-dimensional, inviting the reader to step into the adventure.

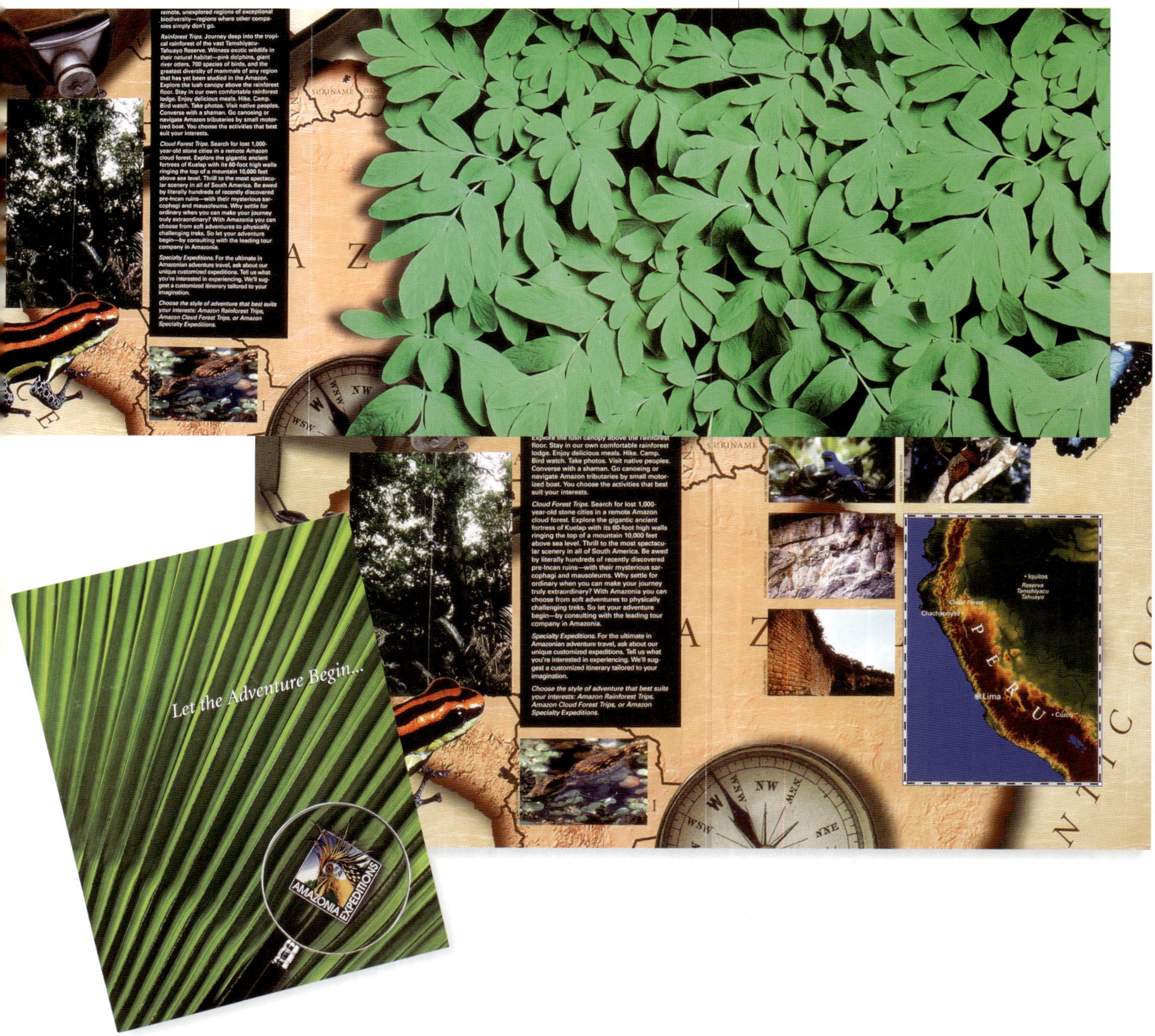

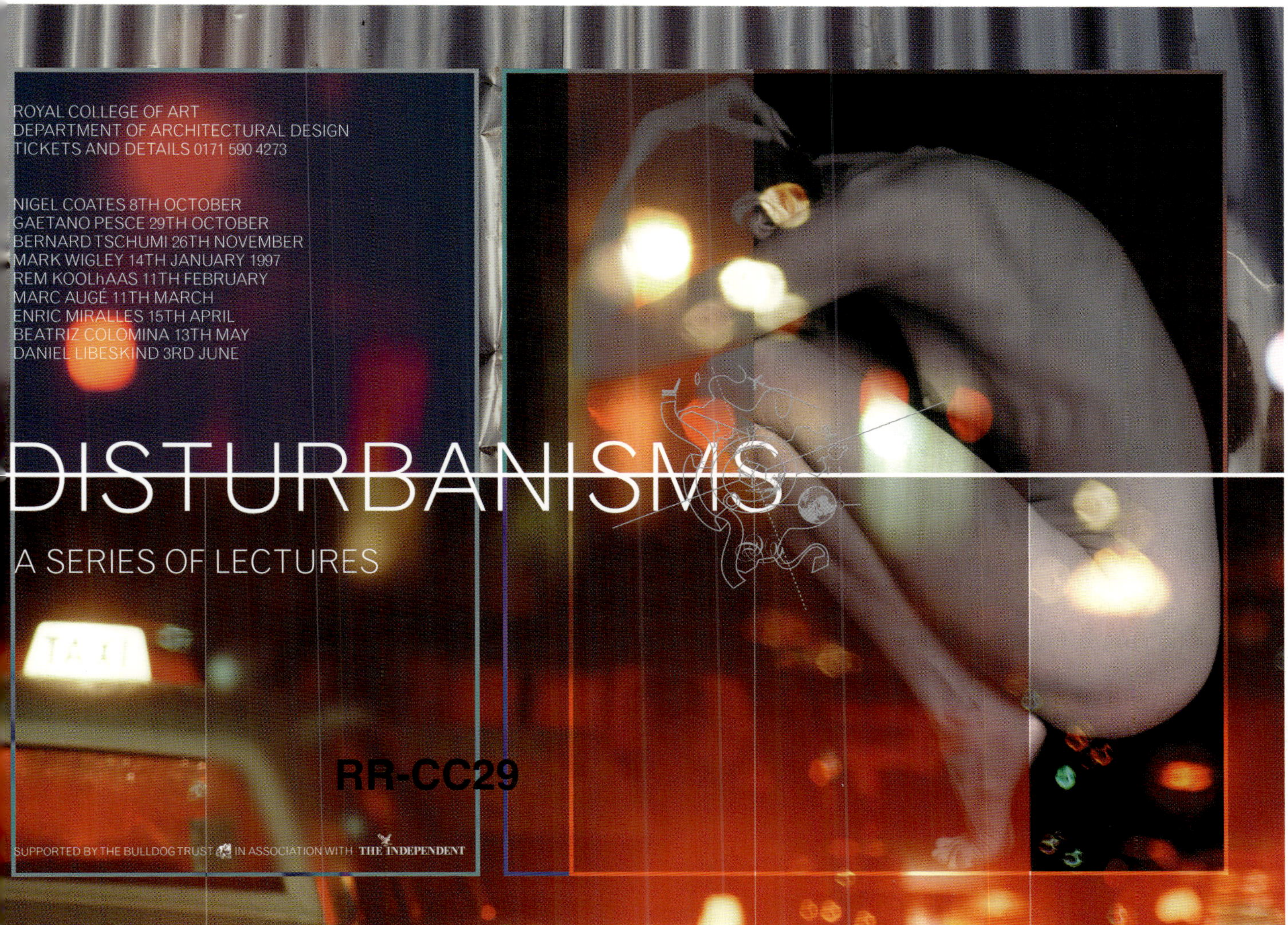


**THE ROYAL COLLEGE OF ART DISTURBANISMS POSTER**

**Design Firm** *Why Not Associates*
**Designers** *Andy Altmann, David Ellis, Patrick Morrissey, Iain Cadby*
**Photographer** *Rocco Redondo, PhotoDisc, Inc.*

Photos of everyday images—the taxi and traffic lights—are in stark contrast to the lone woman, curled in the fetal position. So real becomes the scene when the images are combined, that one can almost hear the blare of car horns and understand why she wants to escape.

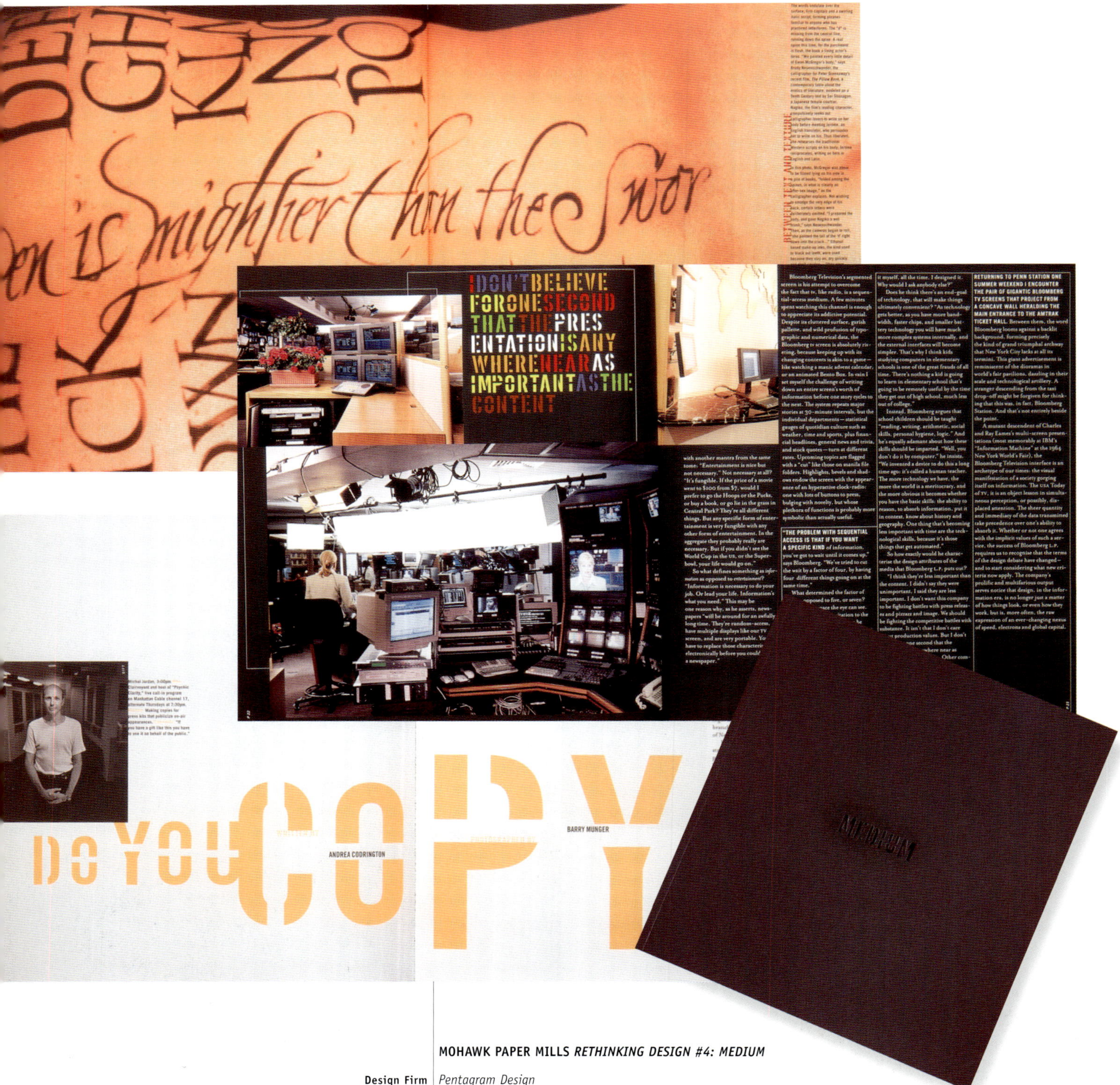


**MOHAWK PAPER MILLS *RETHINKING DESIGN #4: MEDIUM***

**Design Firm** *Pentagram Design*
**Partner** *Michael Bierut*
**Designers** *Michael Bierut, Jacqueline Thaw*

Writers talk about shifting between different mediums in this paper promotion. Many of the photographic images are busy and chaotic, giving a sense of urgency that any copywriter could appreciate.

**THE ROYAL ACADEMY OF ARTS LIVING BRIDGES POSTER**

**Design Firm** *Why Not Associates*
**Designers** *Andy Altmann, Davis Ellis, Patrick Morrissey, Iain Cadby*
**Photographer** *Rocco Redondo*

The image of the man in this poster has an almost translucent quality. Where his form meets the peaceful, calm water there is a certain indefinable spirituality that gives the design its impact.

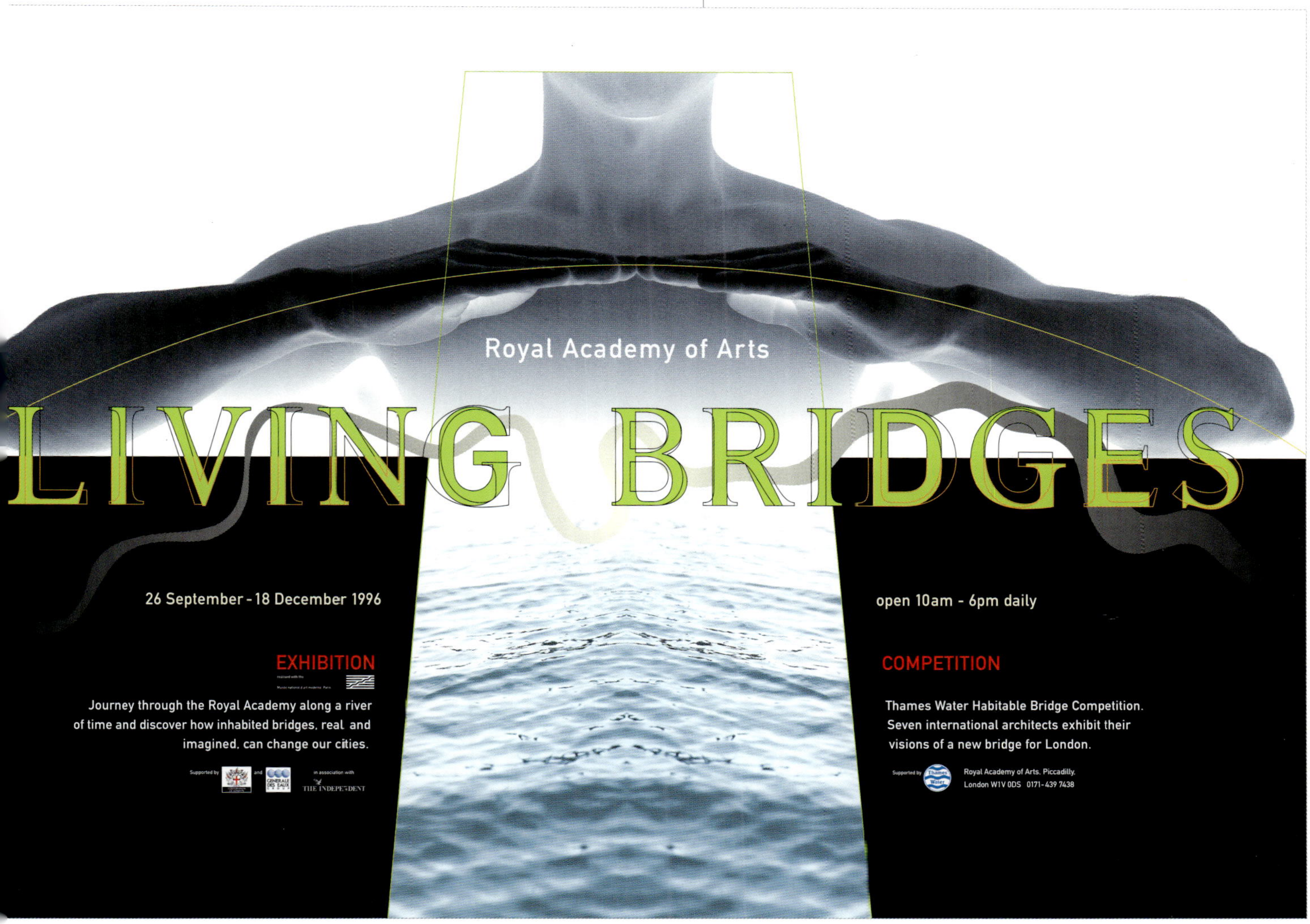

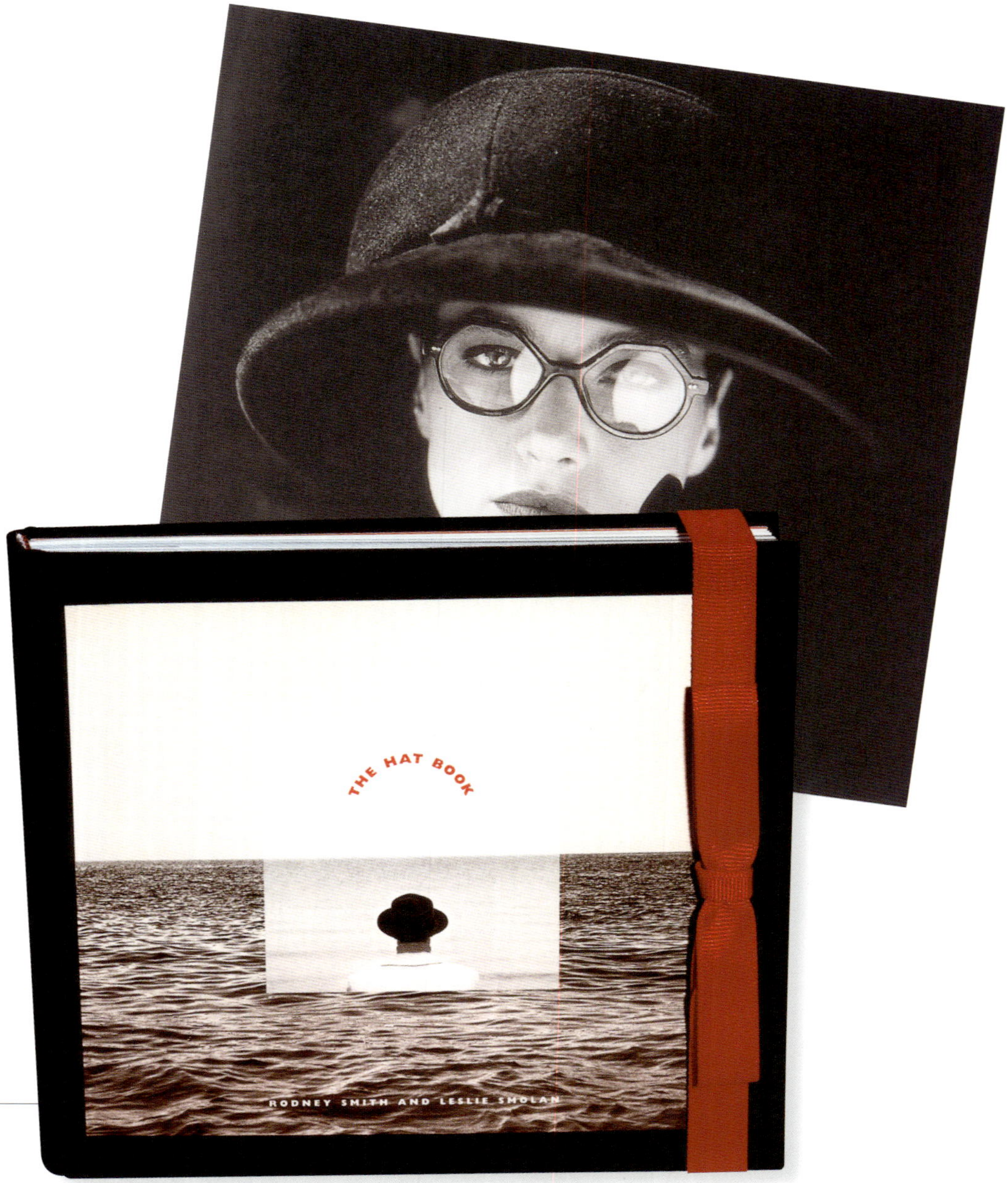


## THE HAT BOOK

**Design Firm** *Carbone Smolan Associates*
**Creative Director** *Mires Design*
**Art Director** *Scott Mires*
**Designers** *Leslie Smolan, Jennifer Domer*
**Illustrators** *Miguel Perez, Scott Mires*
**Photographer** *Rodney Smith*

*The Hat Book* features a collection of tri-tone black-and-white photographs reproduced on 100-lb. Mohawk Superfine paper. This is a prime example of how rich and multidimensional black-and-white photography can be.

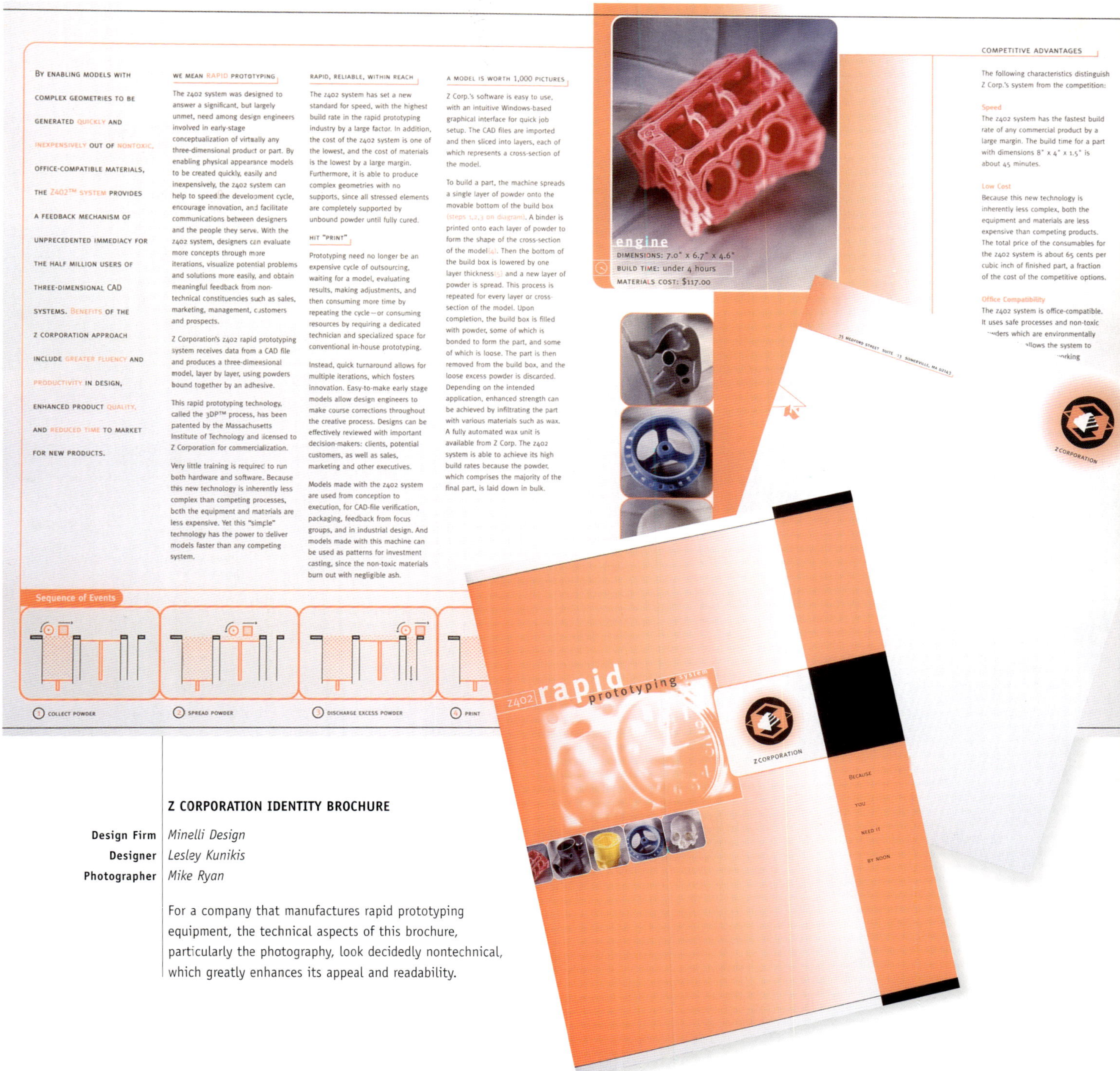


## Z CORPORATION IDENTITY BROCHURE

**Design Firm** *Minelli Design*
**Designer** *Lesley Kunikis*
**Photographer** *Mike Ryan*

For a company that manufactures rapid prototyping equipment, the technical aspects of this brochure, particularly the photography, look decidedly nontechnical, which greatly enhances its appeal and readability.

## CERROSOLO IMAGE BROCHURE

**Design Firm** *Media Artists Inc.*
**Art Director** *Michael Connell*
**Designer** *Michael Connell*
**Illustrator** *Mario Sacchi*
**Photographer** *Xandi Kreuzeder*
**Copywriter** *J. C. Maribona*

It is surprising that this treasure trove of sepia-tone photographs of outdoor and religious images is for a snowboard manufacturer. Nevertheless, executed as four-color process in rich browns and sepias, the images transport the imagination to another realm in a way that standard action photography could not.

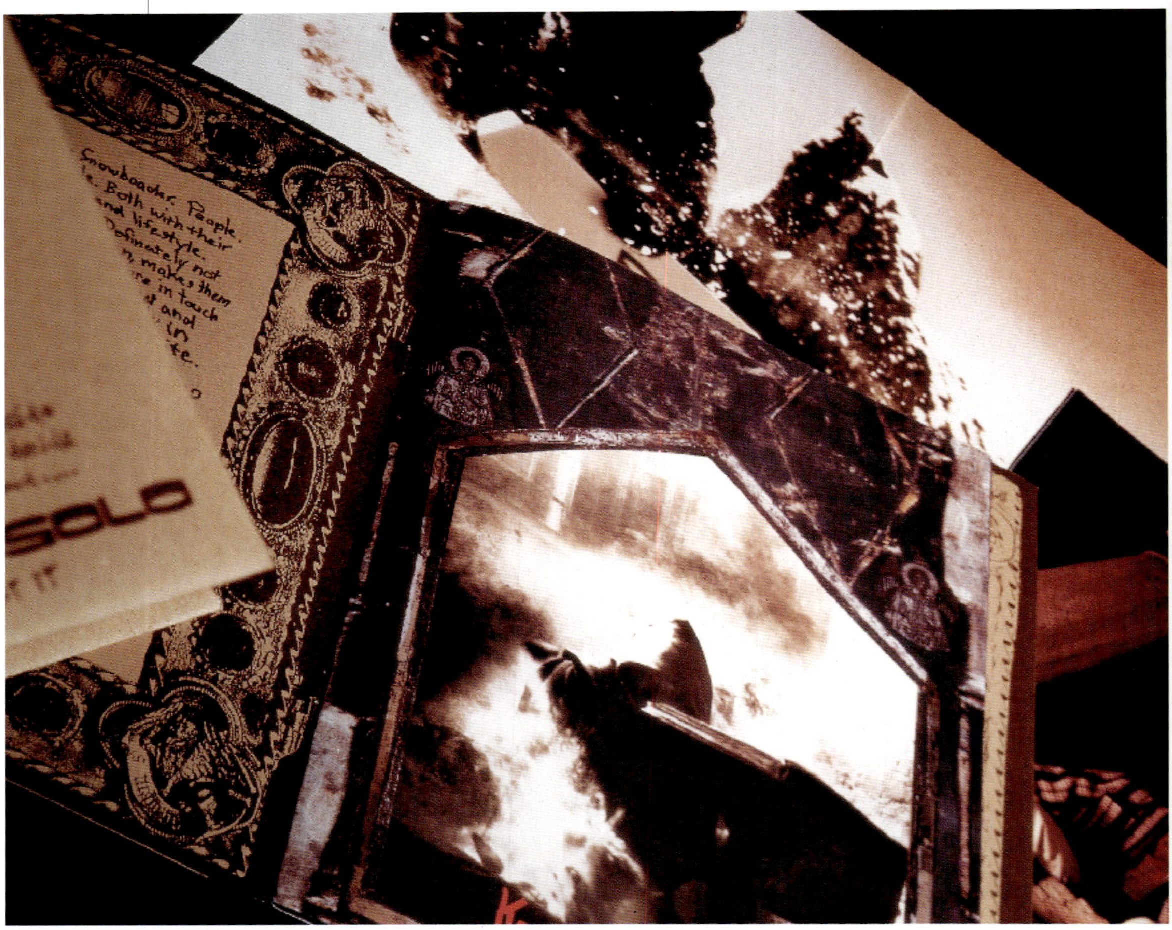

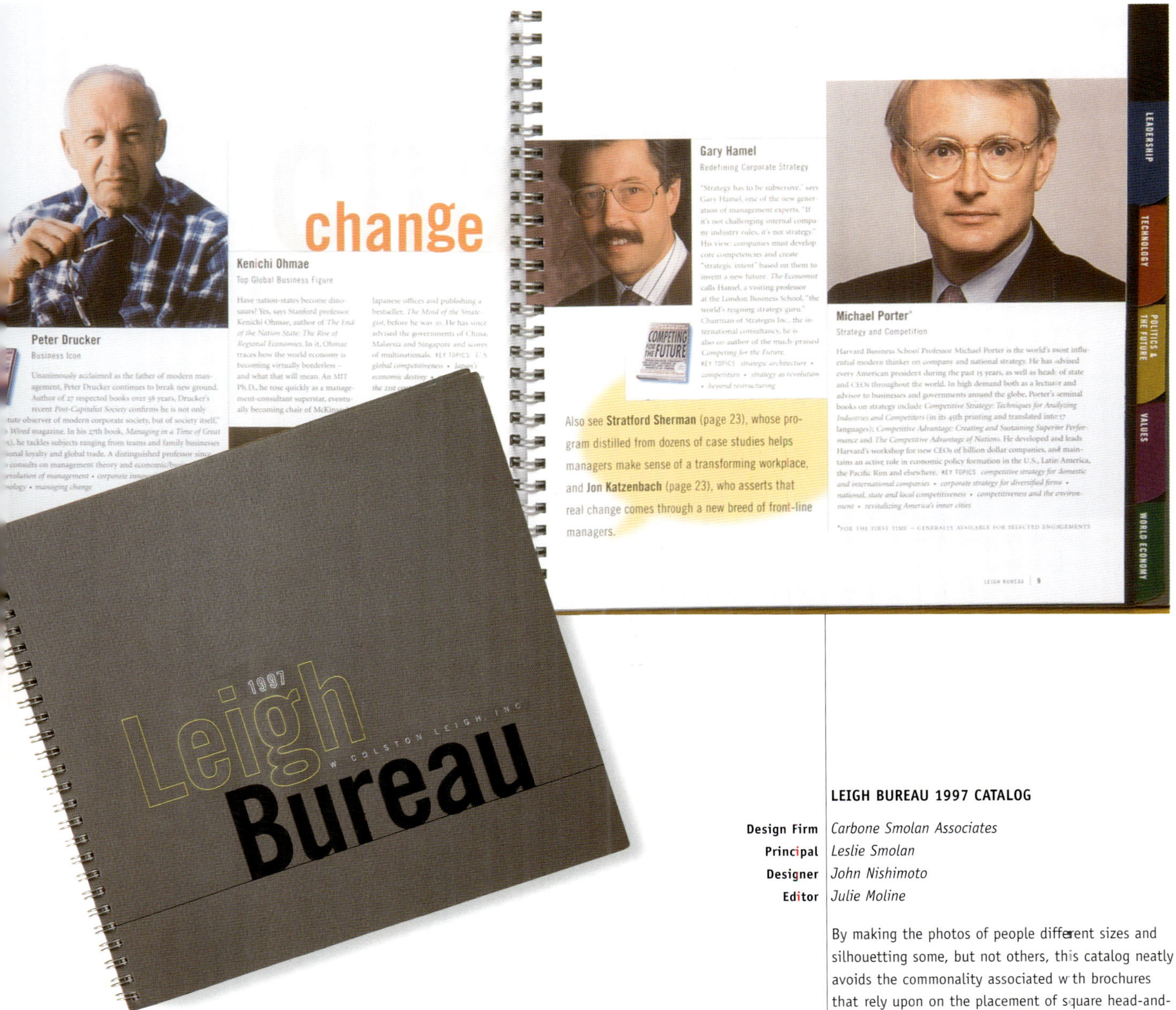


**LEIGH BUREAU 1997 CATALOG**

**Design Firm** *Carbone Smolan Associates*
**Principal** *Leslie Smolan*
**Designer** *John Nishimoto*
**Editor** *Julie Moline*

By making the photos of people different sizes and silhouetting some, but not others, this catalog neatly avoids the commonality associated with brochures that rely upon on the placement of square head-and-shoulders shots.

**Design Firm** *Gyro Interactive*
**Designer** *Wayne Rankins*
**Producer** *John Swales*
**Systems Integrator** *John Swales*

Integrating photography with digital color in an animated, interactive environment can be tricky, but in this CD-ROM for the Museum of Victoria, the photos are so expertly synthesized into the overall design that any appearance as an awkward add-on is avoided.

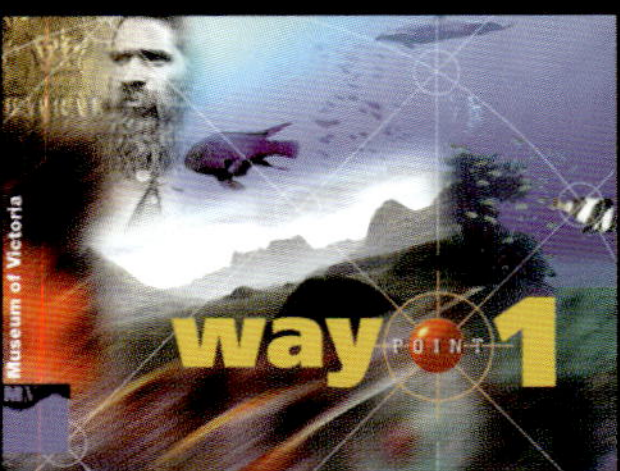

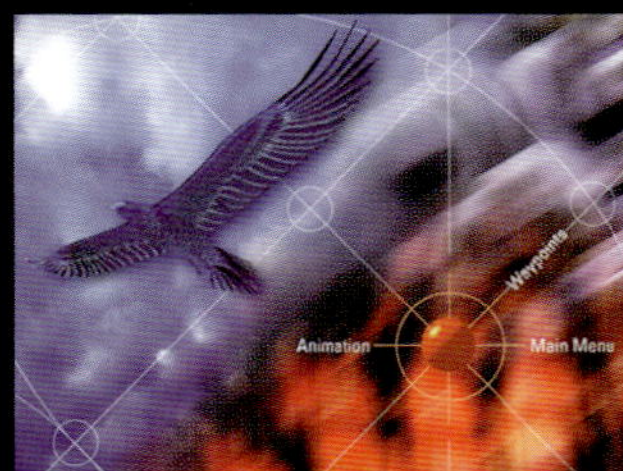

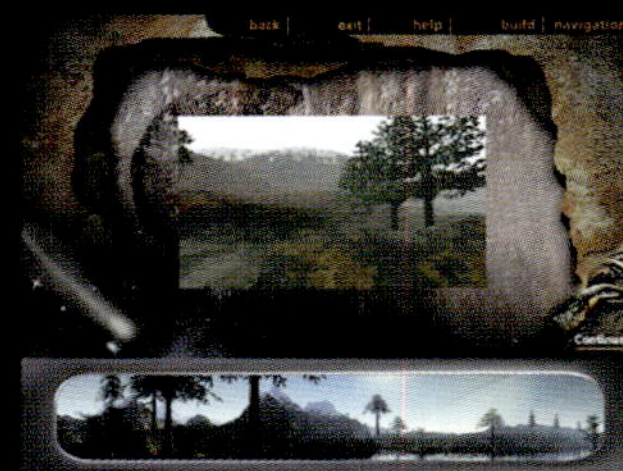
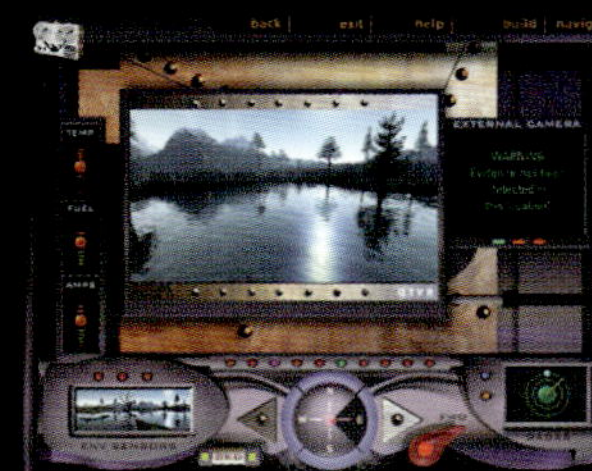
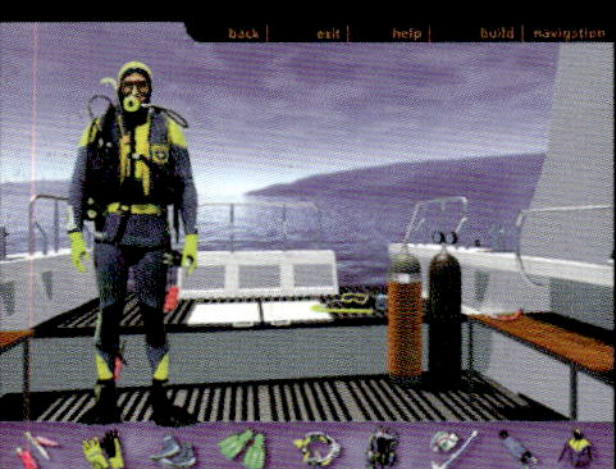
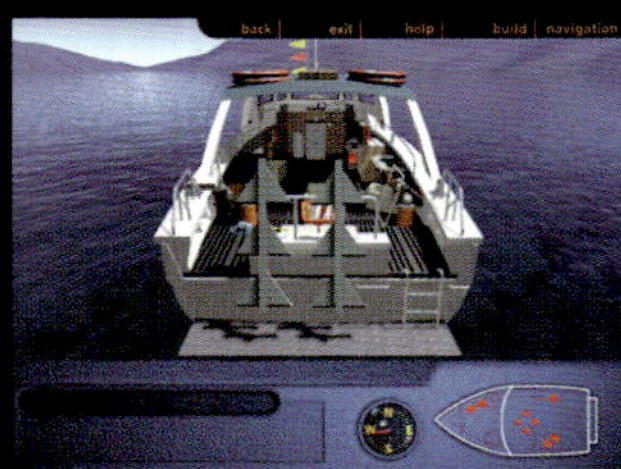
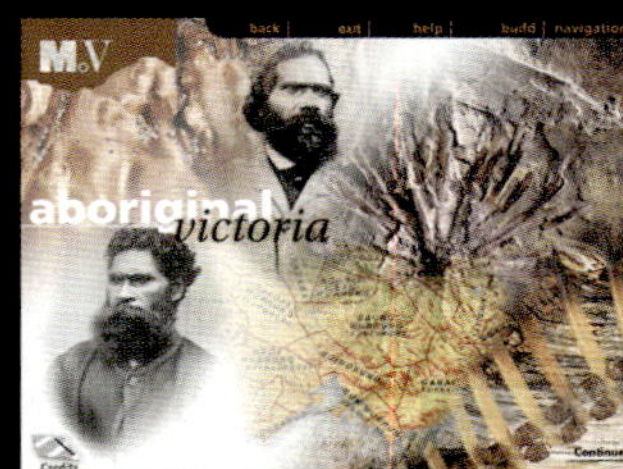

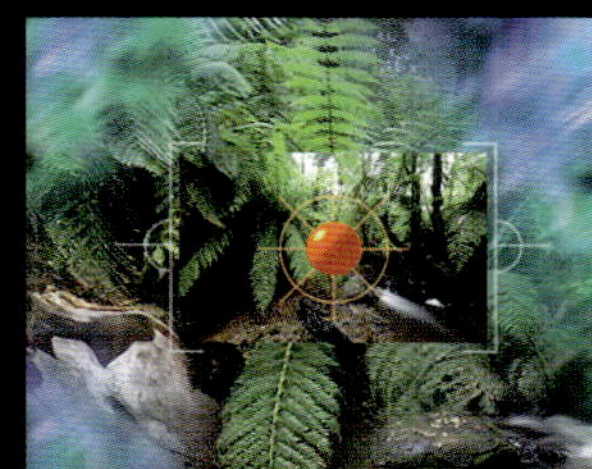
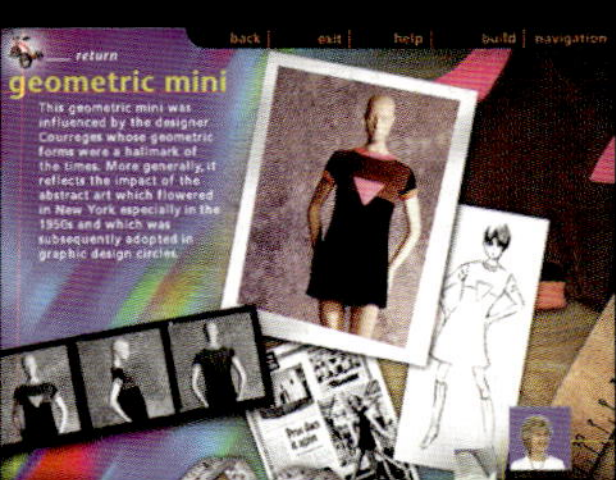

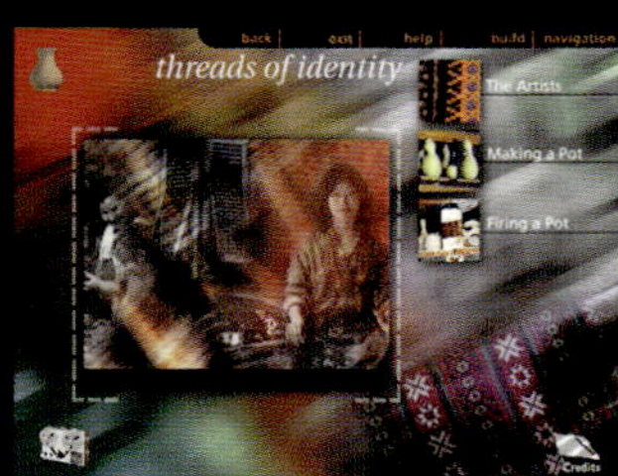

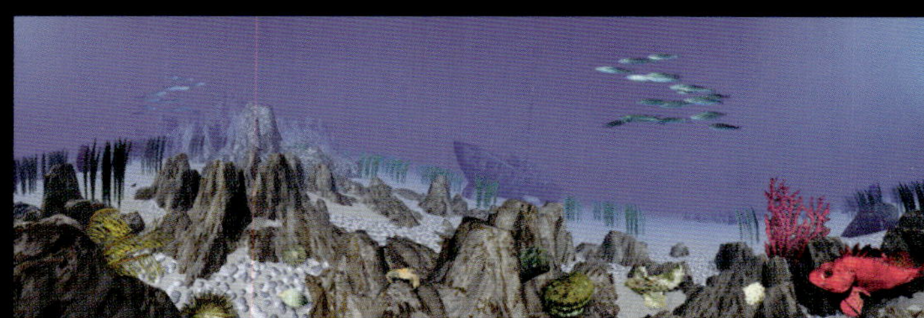
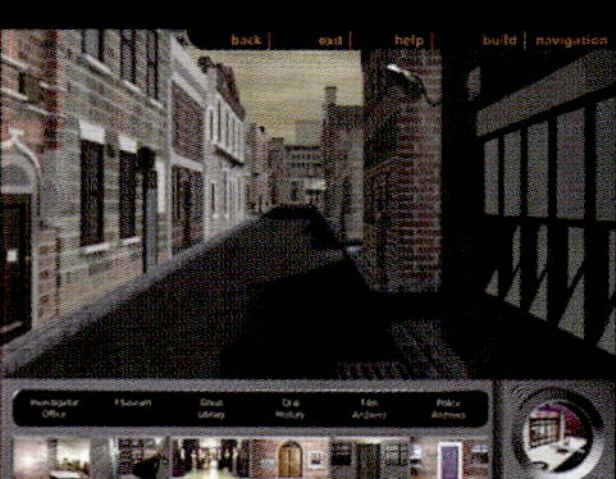
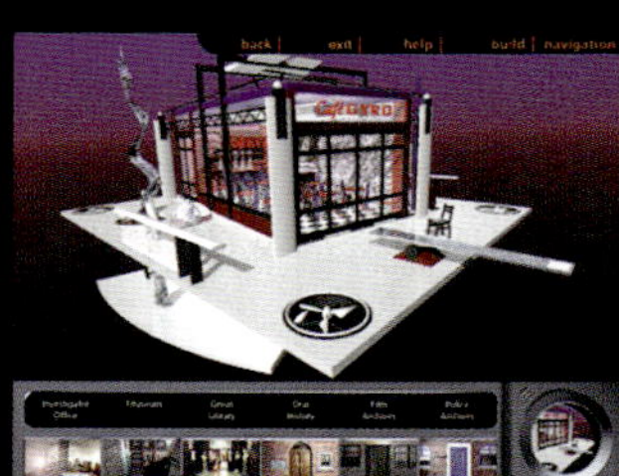
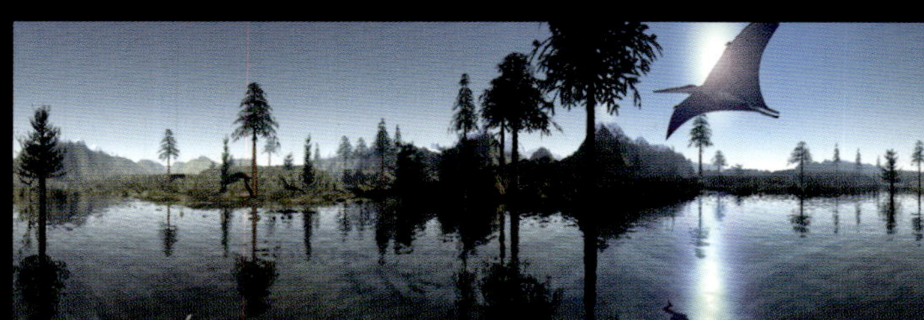

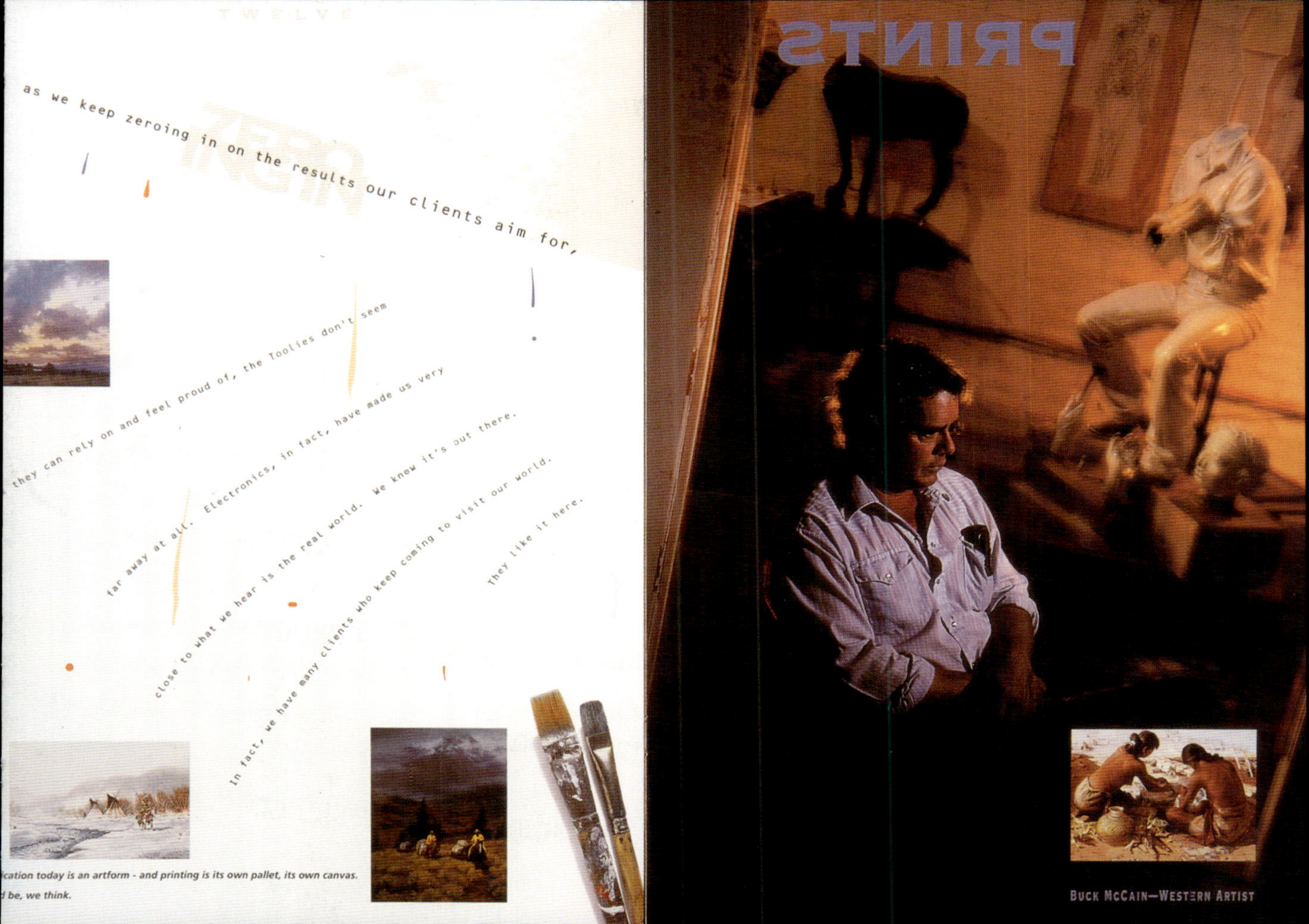


**ARIZONA LITHOGRAPHERS BROCHURE**

**Design Firm** *Boelts Brothers Associates*
**Designers** *Eric Boelts, Jackson Boelts, Kerry Stratford*
**Copywriter** *Sara Harrell*
**Photographer** *Steven Meckler*

Photographs of western landscapes dot the white space in this brochure for an Arizona-based printer and provide a lead-in to the facing page's full-bleed, deeply saturated, mood-setting shot that while contemporary, is also evocative of the old west.

## CENTRAAL MUSEUM, UTRECHT, 1996 ANNUAL REPORT

**Design Firm** *Wild Plakken*
**Designer** *Lies Ros*
**Photographers** *Ernst Moritz, Jasper Wiedeman, Hans Wilschut*

Photographs of museum interiors can appear static, but the angles in which the photos were shot, welcome the reader to tour its vast corridors. Moreover, by printing the full-color photo pages smaller than the text pages, readers naturally gravitate to them.

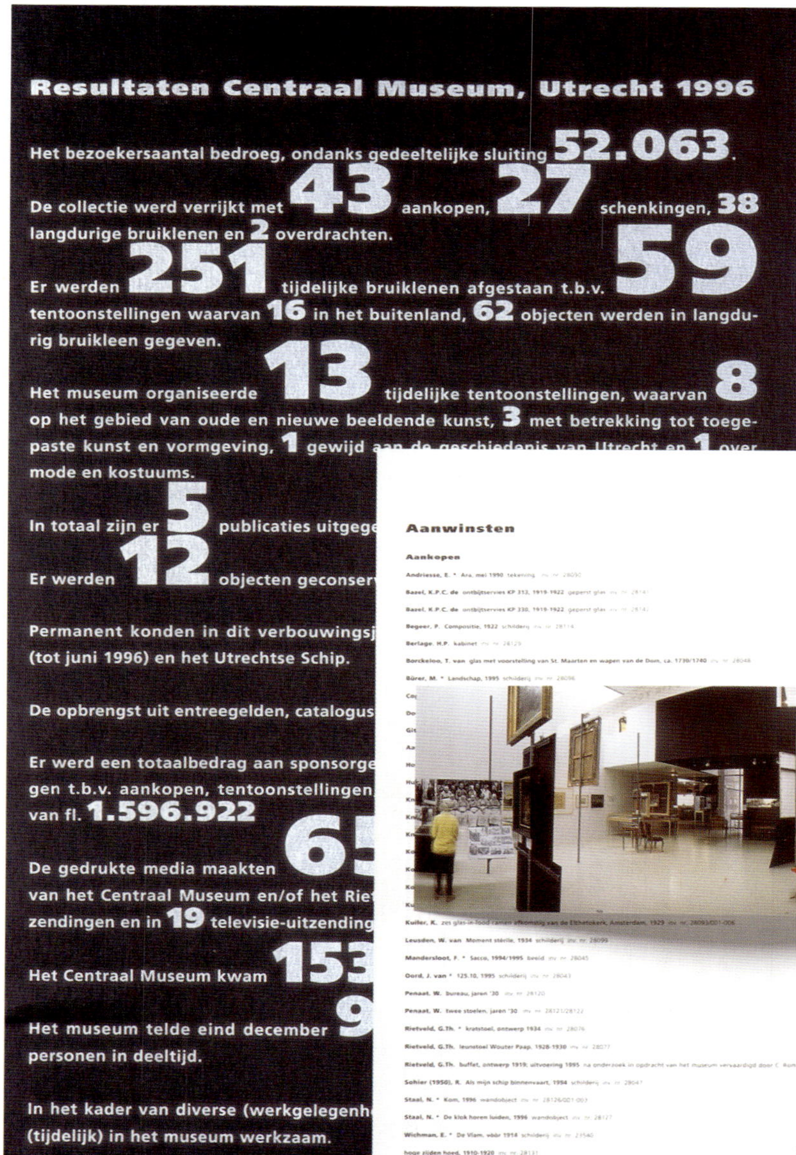
**Resultaten Centraal Museum, Utrecht 1996**

Het bezoekersaantal bedroeg, ondanks gedeeltelijke sluiting **52.063**.

De collectie werd verrijkt met **43** aankopen, **27** schenkingen, **38** langdurige bruiklenen en **2** overdrachten.

Er werden **251** tijdelijke bruiklenen afgestaan t.b.v. **59** tentoonstellingen waarvan **16** in het buitenland, **62** objecten werden in langdurig bruikleen gegeven.

Het museum organiseerde **13** tijdelijke tentoonstellingen, waarvan **8** op het gebied van oude en nieuwe beeldende kunst, **3** met betrekking tot toegepaste kunst en vormgeving, **1** gewijd aan de geschiedenis van Utrecht en **1** over mode en kostuums.

In totaal zijn er **5** publicaties uitgege

Er werden **12** objecten geconser

Permanent konden in dit verbouwingsj (tot juni 1996) en het Utrechtse Schip.

De opbrengst uit entreegelden, catalogus

Er werd een totaalbedrag aan sponsorge gen t.b.v. aankopen, tentoonstellingen van fl. **1.596.922**

De gedrukte media maakten **65** van het Centraal Museum en/of het Riet zendingen en in **19** televisie-uitzending

Het Centraal Museum kwam **153**

Het museum telde eind december **9** personen in deeltijd.

In het kader van diverse (werkgelegenh (tijdelijk) in het museum werkzaam.

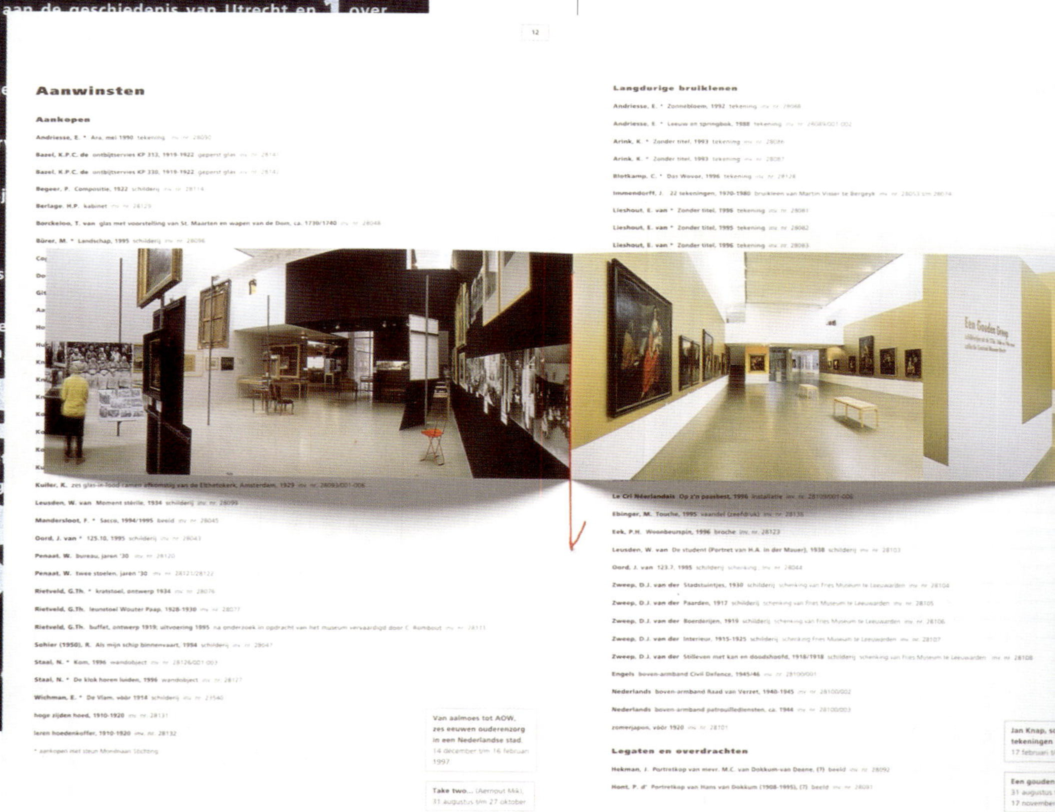
12

**Aanwinsten**

**Aankopen**

**Langdurige bruiklenen**

**Legaten en overdrachten**

Van aalmoes tot AOW, zes eeuwen ouderenzorg in een Nederlandse stad

Take two...

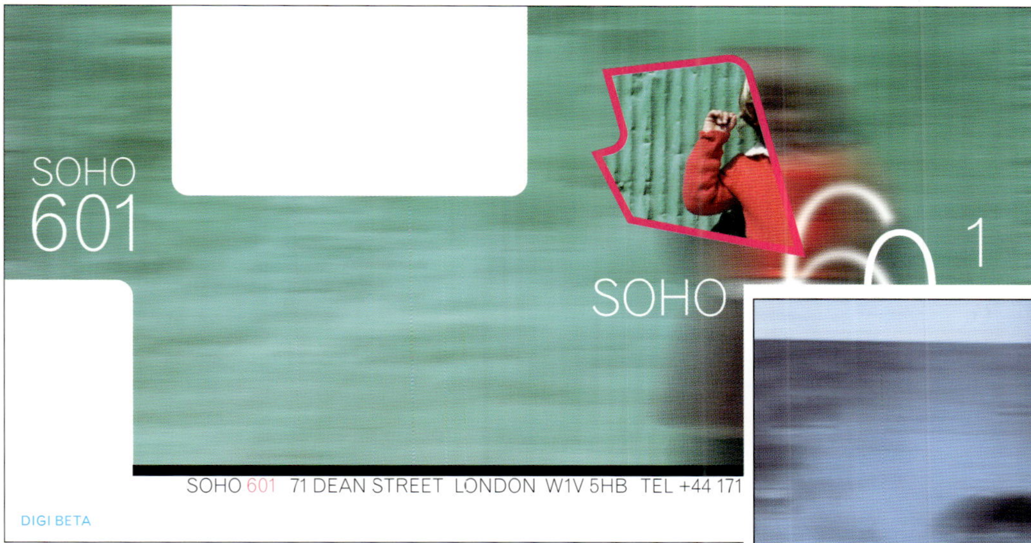


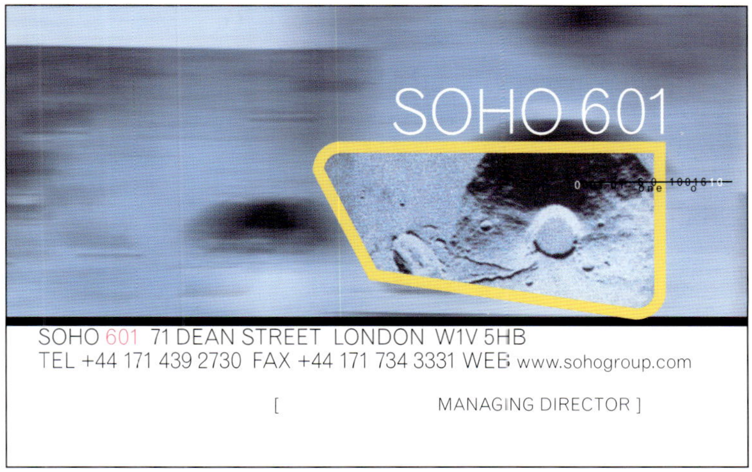


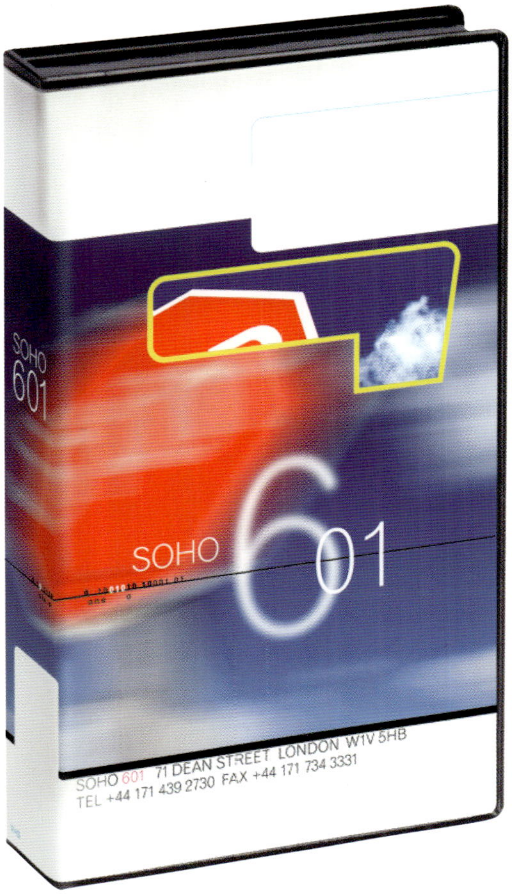


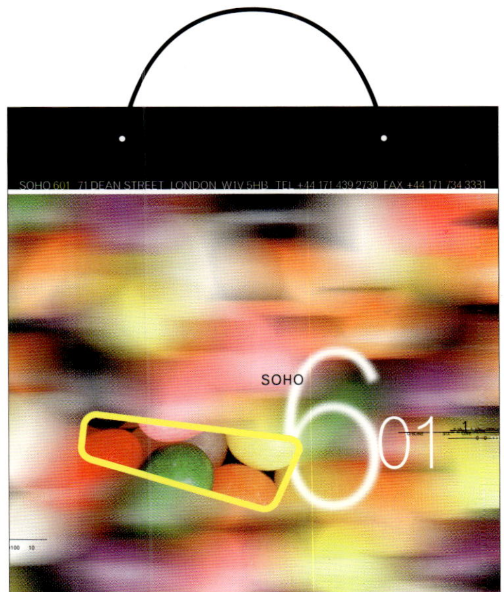


**SOHO 601 IDENTITY PROGRAM**

**Design Firm** *Why Not Associates*
**Designers** *Andy Altmann, Davis Ellis, Patrick Morrissey, Iain Cadby*
**Photographs** *PhotoDisc, Inc.*

A fun demonstration of photo manipulation is the cornerstone of this corporate-identity program for a digital post-production facility. Each image is unfocused except for one small, puzzle-sized piece—the graphic equivalent of a sound bite—that tells us exactly what Soho 601 does.

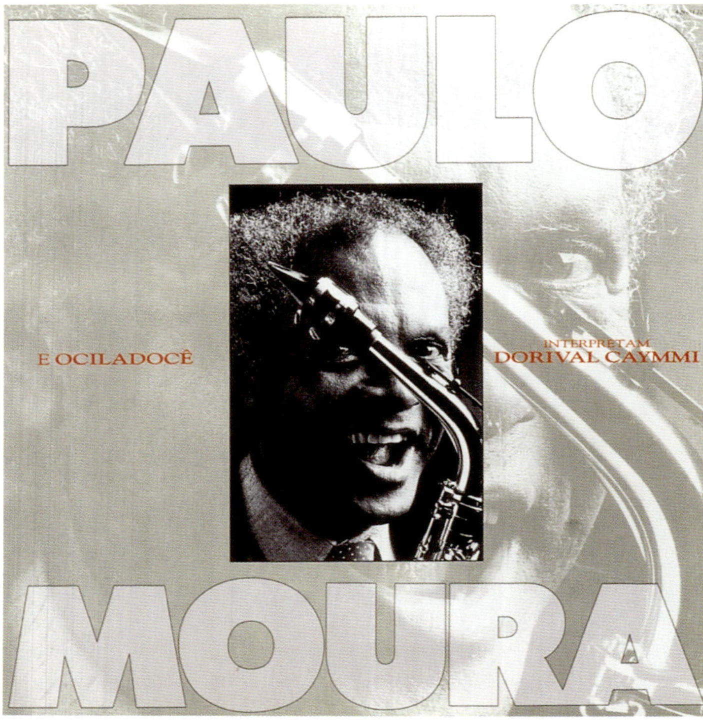


**CHORUS ESTUDIO LTDA. PAULO MOURA RECORD COVER**

**Design Firm** *Interface Designers*
**Art Director** *Sergio Liuzzi*
**Designer** *André Bonbonatti de Castro*
**Photographer** *Luiz Garrido*

Some may ask, "What's wrong with this photo?" while designers would exclaim, "Look what's right with this photo!" First, Moura stares directly at us. That, combined with the odd position of the saxophone, is more than a little unsettling. Lastly, enlarging and ghosting the portrait as the background makes this design memorable.

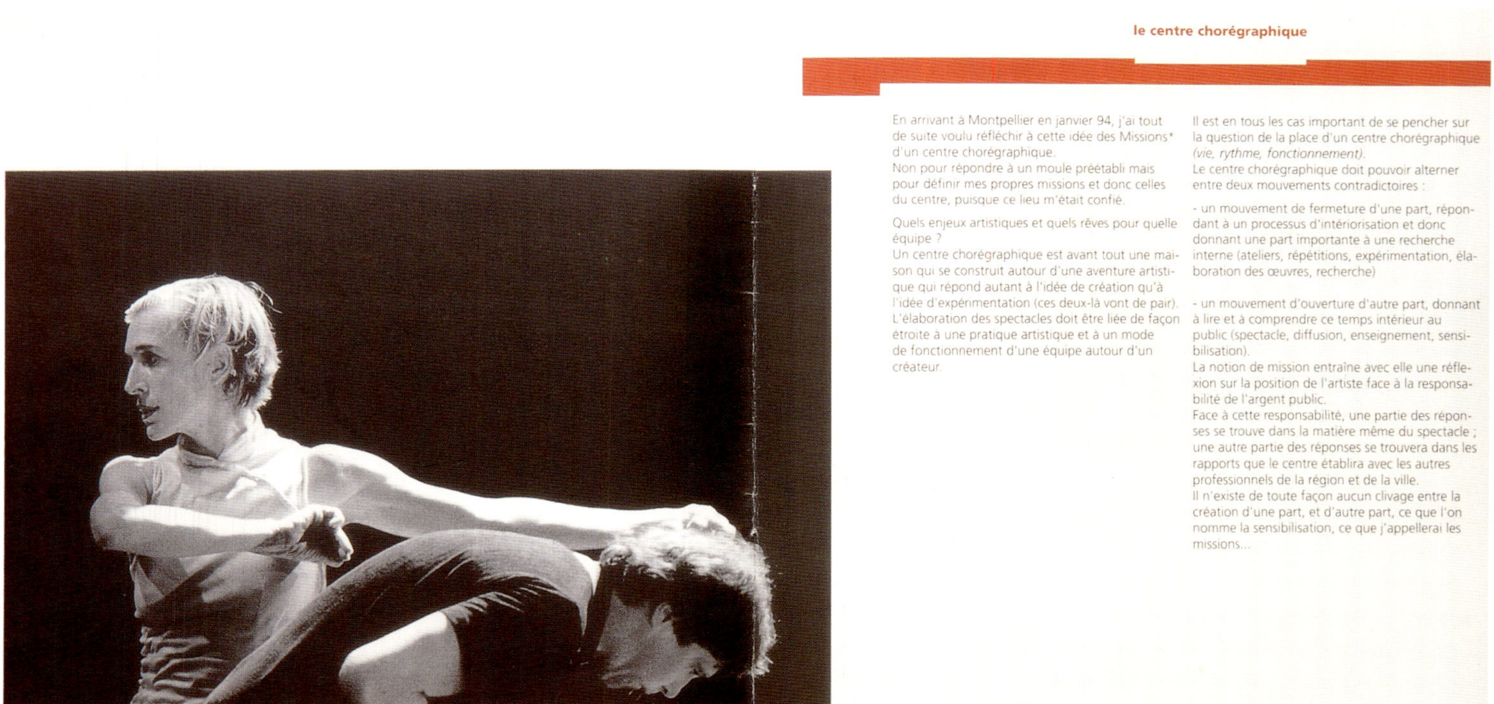

le centre chorégraphique

En arrivant à Montpellier en janvier 94, j'ai tout de suite voulu réfléchir à cette idée des Missions* d'un centre chorégraphique.
Non pour répondre à un moule préétabli mais pour définir mes propres missions et donc celles du centre, puisque ce lieu m'était confié.

Quels enjeux artistiques et quels rêves pour quelle équipe ?
Un centre chorégraphique est avant tout une maison qui se construit autour d'une aventure artistique qui répond autant à l'idée de création qu'à l'idée d'expérimentation (ces deux-là vont de pair).
L'élaboration des spectacles doit être liée de façon étroite à une pratique artistique et à un mode de fonctionnement d'une équipe autour d'un créateur.

Il est en tous les cas important de se pencher sur la question de la place d'un centre chorégraphique *(vie, rythme, fonctionnement).*
Le centre chorégraphique doit pouvoir alterner entre deux mouvements contradictoires :

- un mouvement de fermeture d'une part, répondant à un processus d'intériorisation et donc donnant une part importante à une recherche interne (ateliers, répétitions, expérimentation, élaboration des œuvres, recherche)

- un mouvement d'ouverture d'autre part, donnant à lire et à comprendre ce temps intérieur au public (spectacle, diffusion, enseignement, sensibilisation).

La notion de mission entraîne avec elle une réflexion sur la position de l'artiste face à la responsabilité de l'argent public.
Face à cette responsabilité, une partie des réponses se trouve dans la matière même du spectacle ; une autre partie des réponses se trouvera dans les rapports que le centre établira avec les autres professionnels de la région et de la ville.
Il n'existe de toute façon aucun clivage entre la création d'une part, et d'autre part, ce que l'on nomme la sensibilisation, ce que j'appellerai les missions...

**MATHILDE MONNIER DANCE COMPANY IDENTITY PROGRAM**

**Design Firm** *L Design*
**Designer** *Pippo Lionni*
**Photographer** *Marc Coudrais*

Black-and-white photography was used throughout this identity program to limit the majority of pieces to two-color printing. The shots are classically staged, perfectly complementing the wide-open layout.

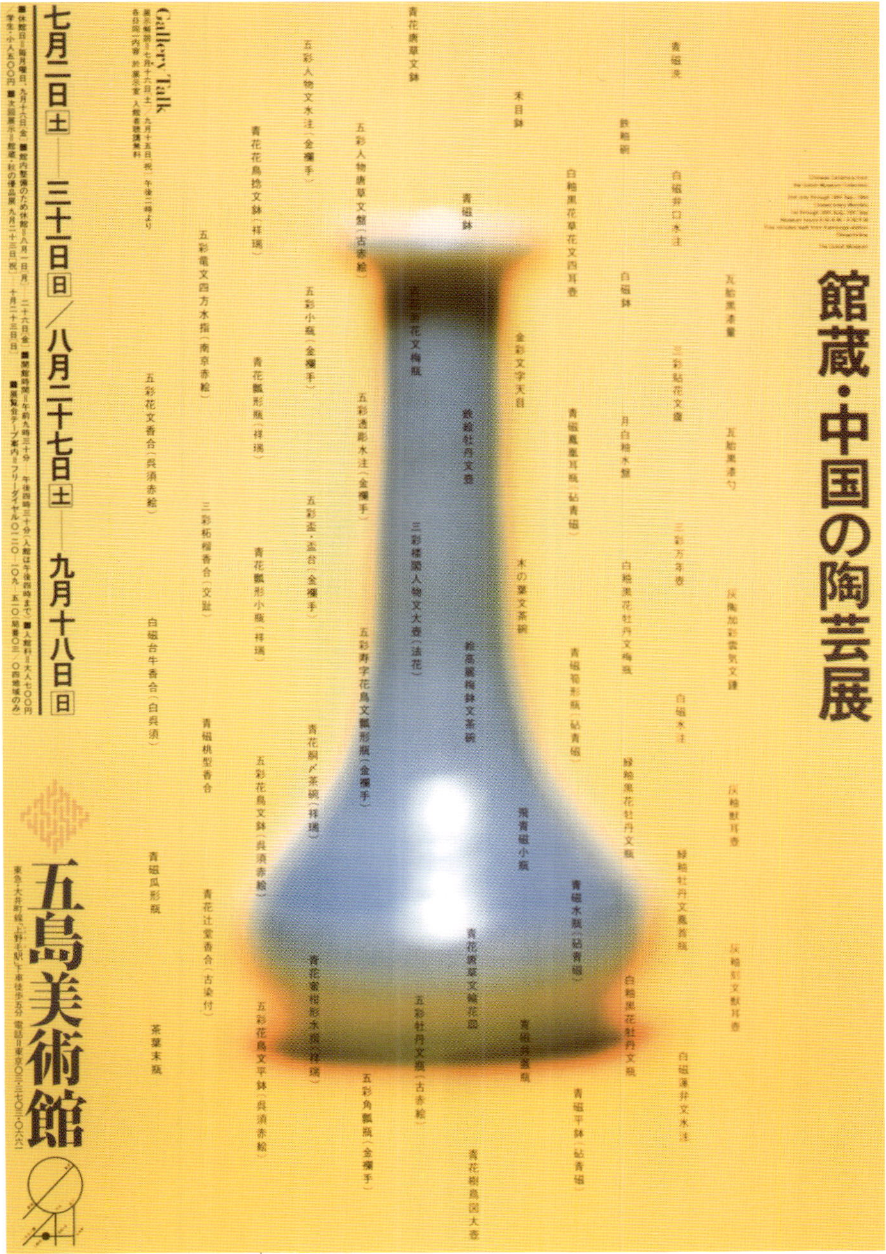


**THE GOTOH MUSEUM COLLECTION EXHIBITION POSTER**

**Design Firm** *UNO, Yasuyuki Design Studio Inc.*
**Designer** *Yasuyuki Uno*
**Photographer** *Yasuyuki Uno*

In a daring approach, the designer has blurred the photo of the very object the poster promotes. Nevertheless, the shot of the celadon vase is prominent and helps direct the eye to the copy, which lists the works being shown in the exhibit.

**MTV 1994 EUROPEAN MUSIC AWARDS PROGRAM**

| | |
|---|---|
| **Design Firm** | *John D. Berry Design* |
| **Art Director** | *John D. Berry* |
| **Typographer** | *John D. Berry* |
| **Copywriters** | *William Gibson, Bruce Sterling* |
| **Photographer** | *Patricia Quinn* |

It isn't the copy alone that conveys the cynicism of this MTV design, the photograph's message of material decay is equally clear. A foam slab, carved with four words was colored, photographed, and made into a photo CD before the layout was completed in Adobe PageMaker.

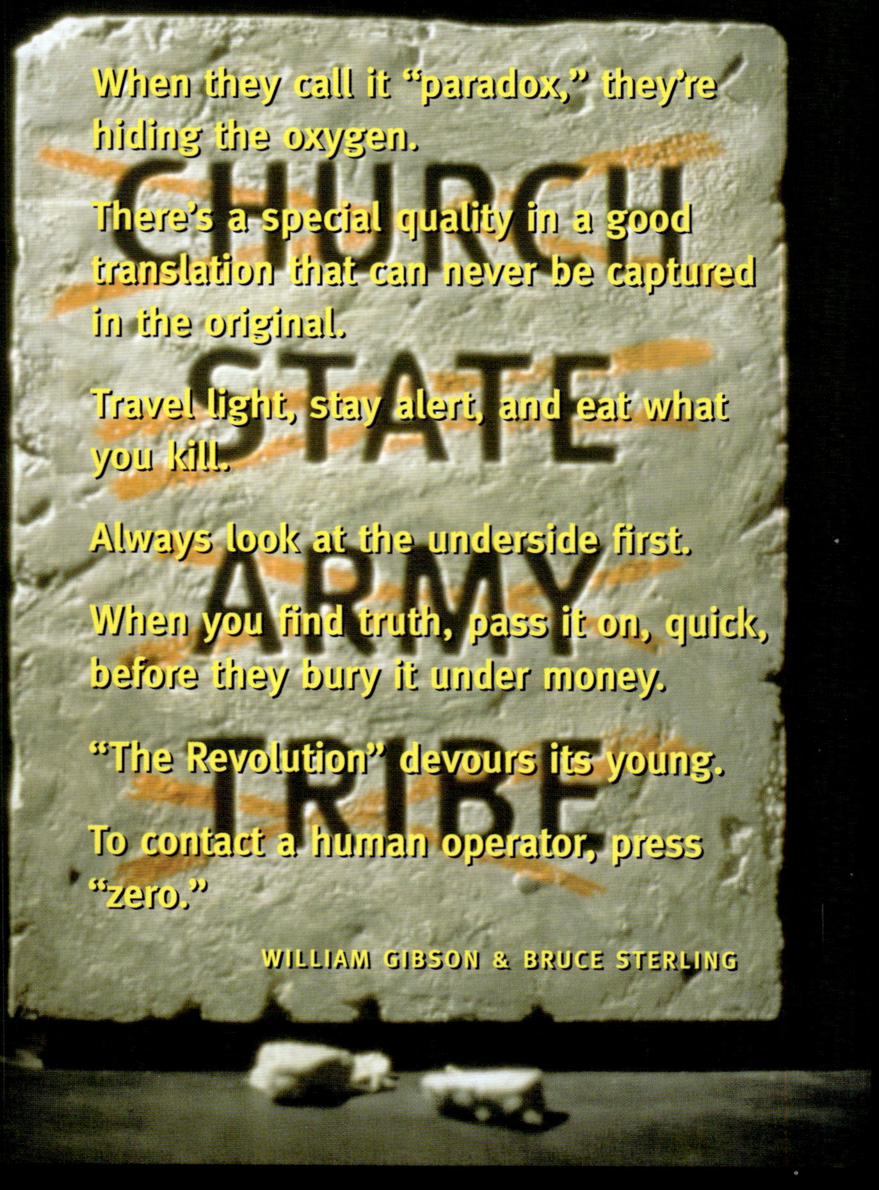

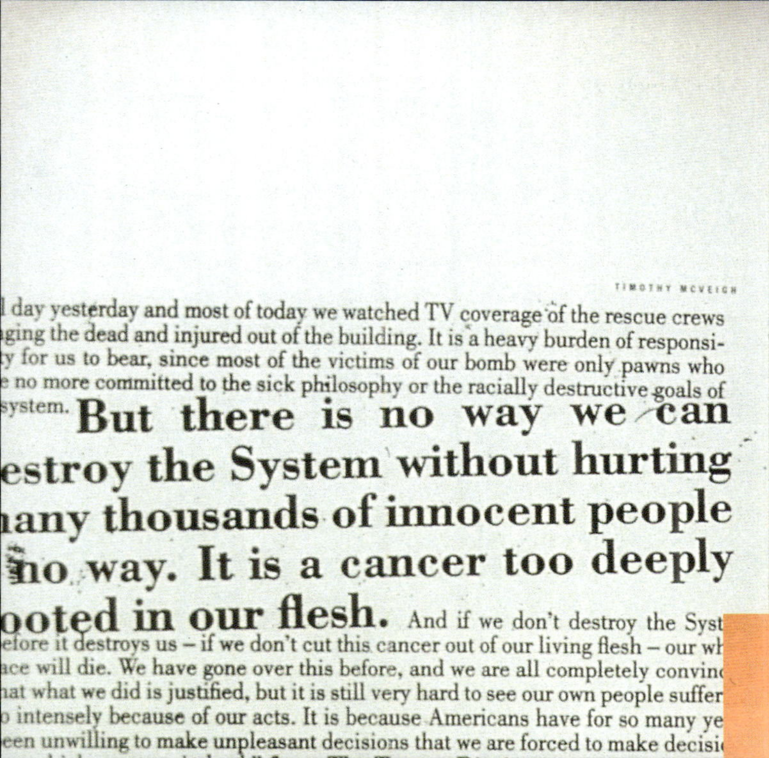

TIMOTHY MCVEIGH

l day yesterday and most of today we watched TV coverage of the rescue crews
ging the dead and injured out of the building. It is a heavy burden of responsi-
y for us to bear, since most of the victims of our bomb were only pawns who
e no more committed to the sick philosophy or the racially destructive goals of
system. **But there is no way we can
estroy the System without hurting
any thousands of innocent people
no way. It is a cancer too deeply
ooted in our flesh.** And if we don't destroy the Syst
efore it destroys us – if we don't cut this cancer out of our living flesh – our wh
ace will die. We have gone over this before, and we are all completely convin
at what we did is justified, but it is still very hard to see our own people suffer
intensely because of our acts. It is because Americans have for so many ye
een unwilling to make unpleasant decisions that we are forced to make decisi

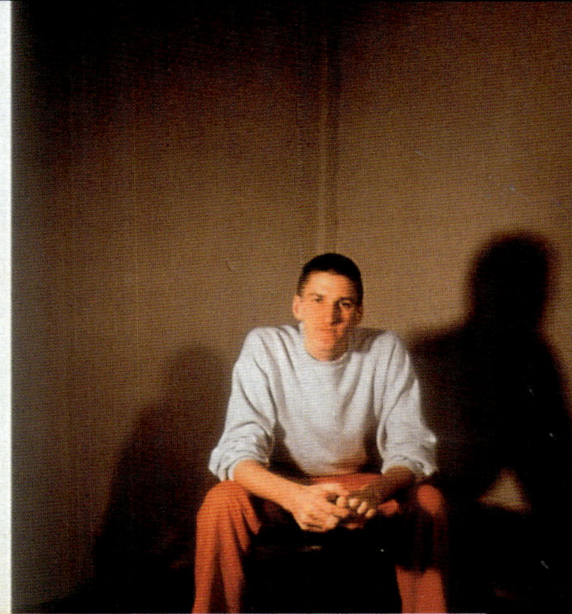

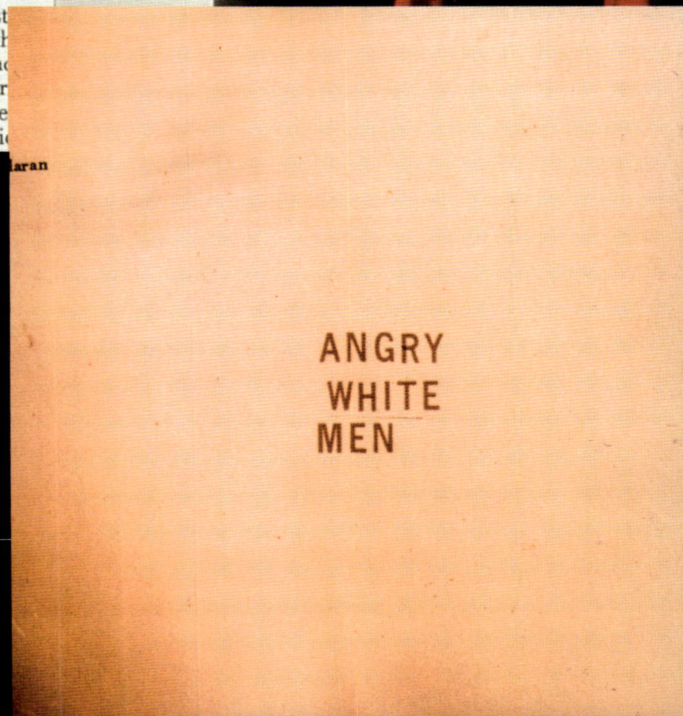


**ROBBIE McCLARAN'S *ANGRY WHITE MEN***

**Design Firm** *Johnson & Wolverton*
**Creative Directors** *Hal Wolverton, Alicia Johnson*
**Designers** *Robin Muir, Jeff Dooley*
**Photographer** *Robbie McClaran*
**Copywriter** *Rene Denfeld*

Robbie McClaran's book features his photographs of white male subjects on the political far right. Because he taps a controversial topic, the copy is presented in an objective, journalistic format. The photos, however, speak more loudly, clearly showing how isolated these men feel from

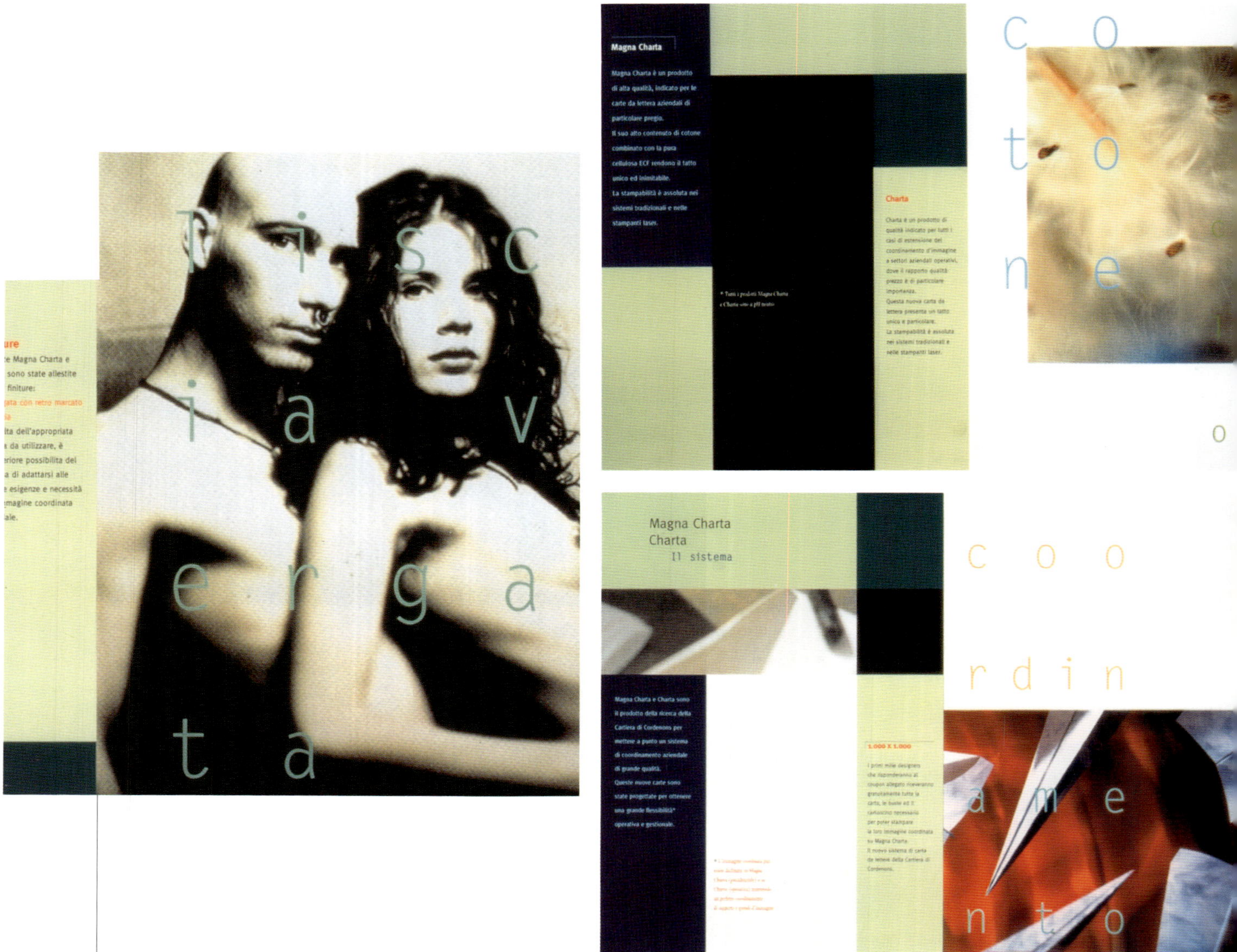


**CARTIERA DI CORDENONS BROCHURE**

**Design Firm** *Tangram Strategic Design*
**Designer** *Enrico Sempi*
**Photographers** *Various*

Despite the seemingly random placement of photos, text, and color blocks, this layout is comfortable and fresh. The content of the photos varies tremendously, yet without any apparent common thread—no one photo overpowers another.

**CHICAGO VOLUNTEER LEGAL SERVICES 1997 ANNUAL REPORT**

**Design Firm** *Froeter Design Company, Inc.*
**Art Director** *Tim Bruce*
**Designer** *Tim Bruce*
**Copywriters** *Lee M. Witte, Margaret C. Benson*
**Photographer** *Tony Armour*

In this three-color annual report, translucent title pages, reminiscent of doors in old office buildings, open to reveal the clients for whom Chicago Volunteer Legal Services exists. Their images, like the succinct title pages, are simple, candid, and straightforward.

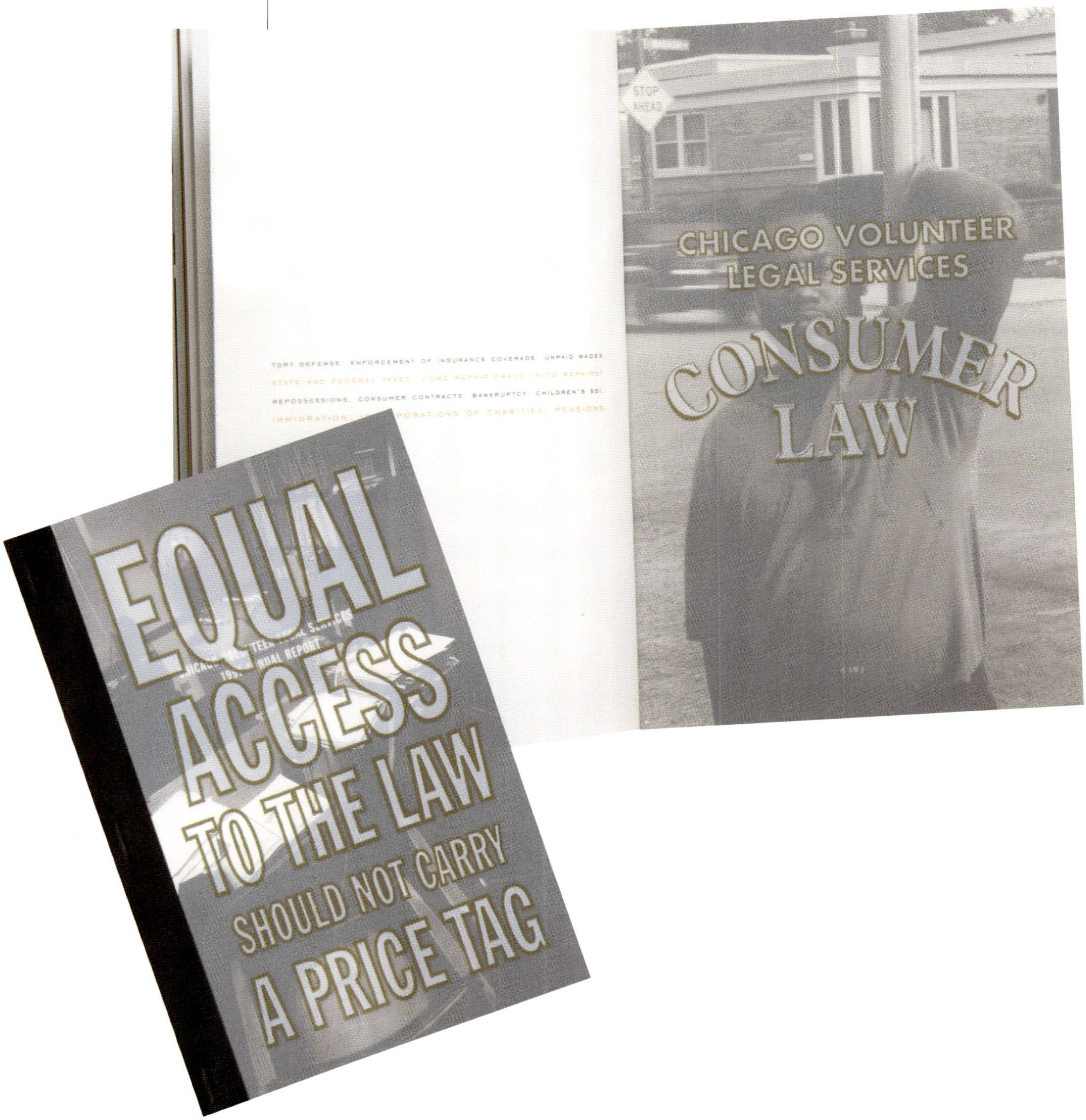

## SANYO SHOKAI CO. BURBERRY'S BLUE LABEL POSTER

**Design Firm** *Toda Office*
**Designer** *Seiju Toda*

This design breaks with tradition in the unlikely pairing of the young, urban fashion photo with Burberry's of London, an established clothing line known for its tweeds and trench coats. By giving the photo and logo equal prominence, it becomes clear that Burberry's is exploring new territory.

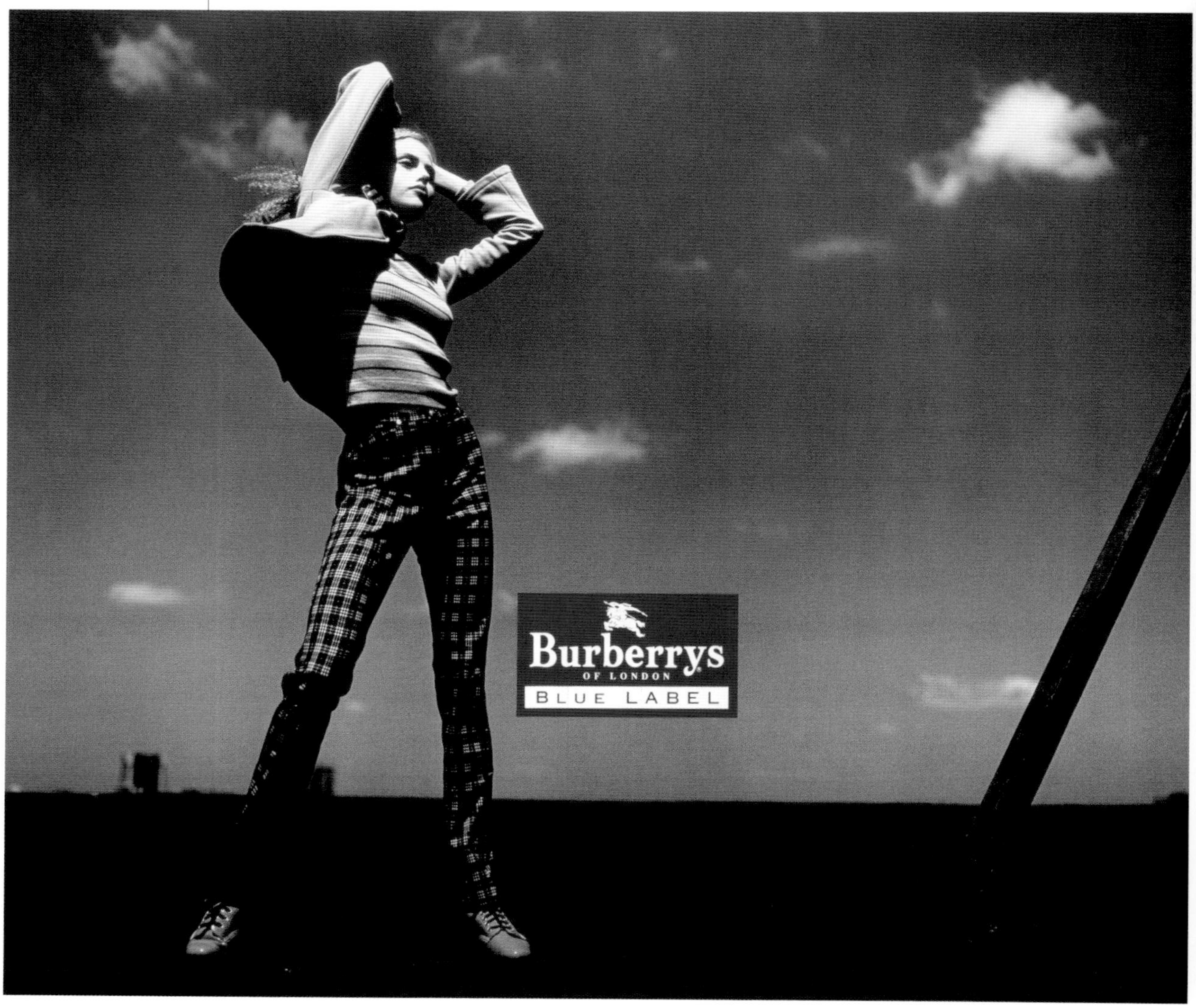

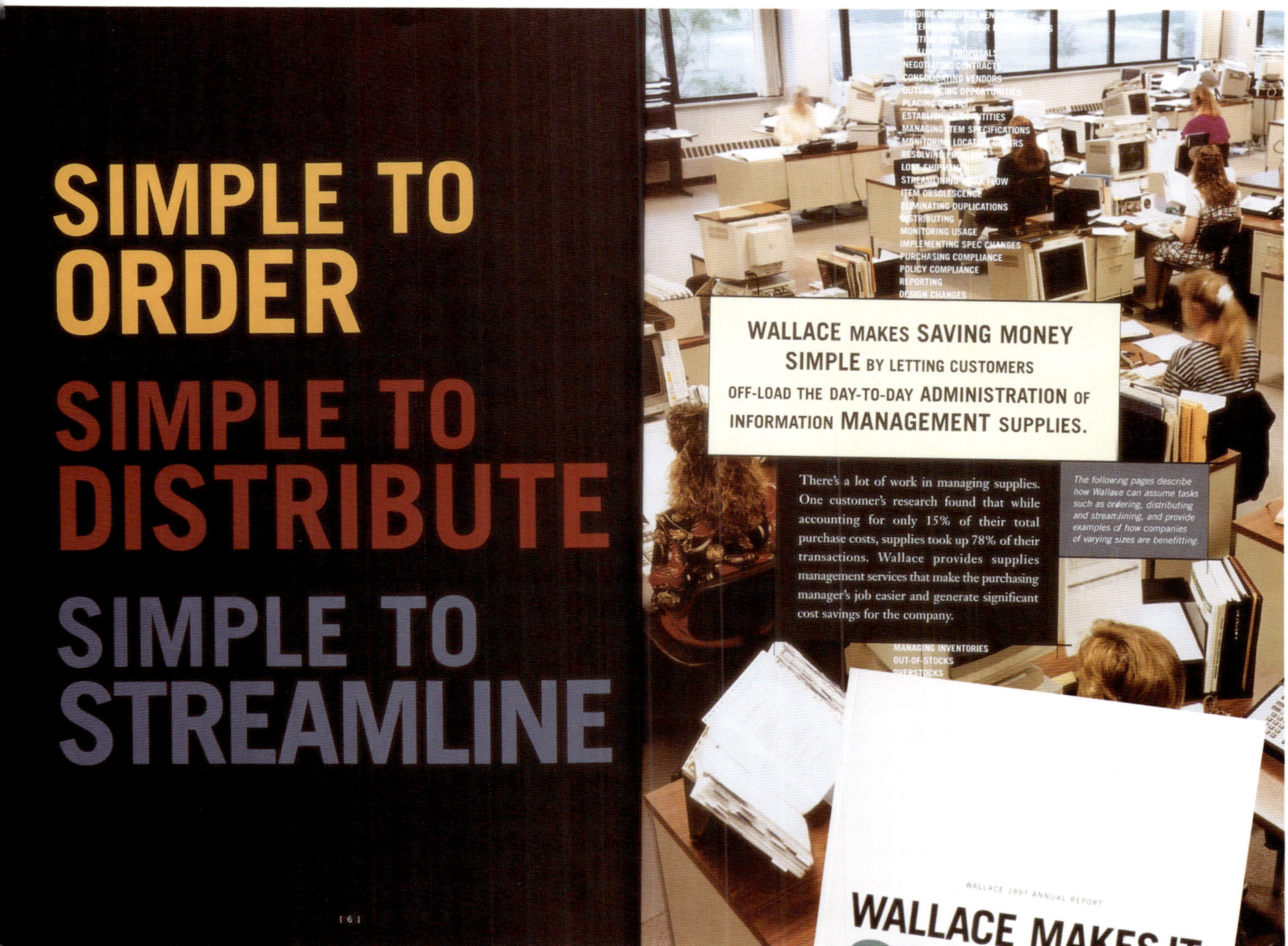


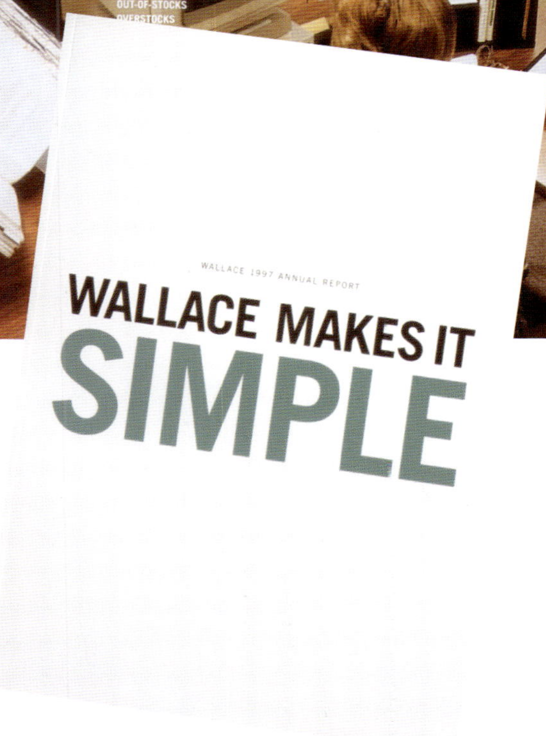


**WALLACE COMPUTER SERVICES, INC. 1997 ANNUAL REPORT**

**Design Firm** *Froeter Design Company Inc.*
**Art Directors** *Tim Bruce, Chris Froeter*
**Designer** *Tim Bruce*
**Copywriter** *Brad Samson*
**Photographer** *Tony Armour*

The photo of the crowded, cluttered office screams chaos. Fortunately, Wallace Computer Services offers simple solutions that can calm chaotic situations. The typeface and the layout work together to convey this message in direct contrast to the photography.

**UNITED NATIONS HIGH COMMISSIONER FOR REFUGEES WEB SITE**
**www.unhcr.ch**

**Design Firm** *Ignition, Inc.*
**Creative Director** *Ray Kristof*
**Project Director** *Amy Satran*
**Designer** *Amy Satran*
**Photographers** *United Nations High Commissioner for Refugees Photo Archive*

With a directive to design this site to work with minimal computer equipment, images were chosen that would work as duotones and in silhouettes and posterized palettes for low-bandwidth viewing. The design seems to have benefited from the streamlining without sacrificing quality.

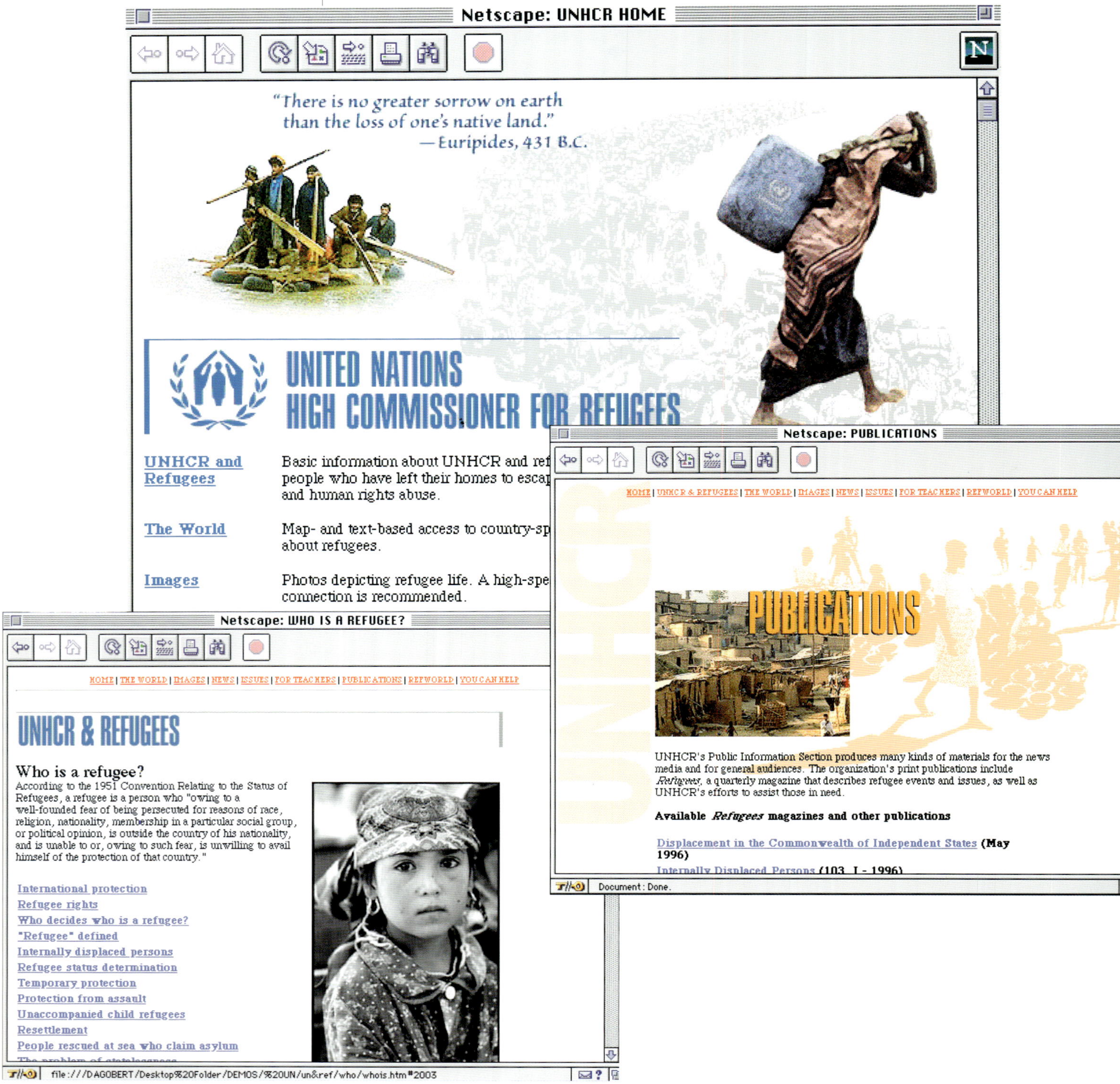

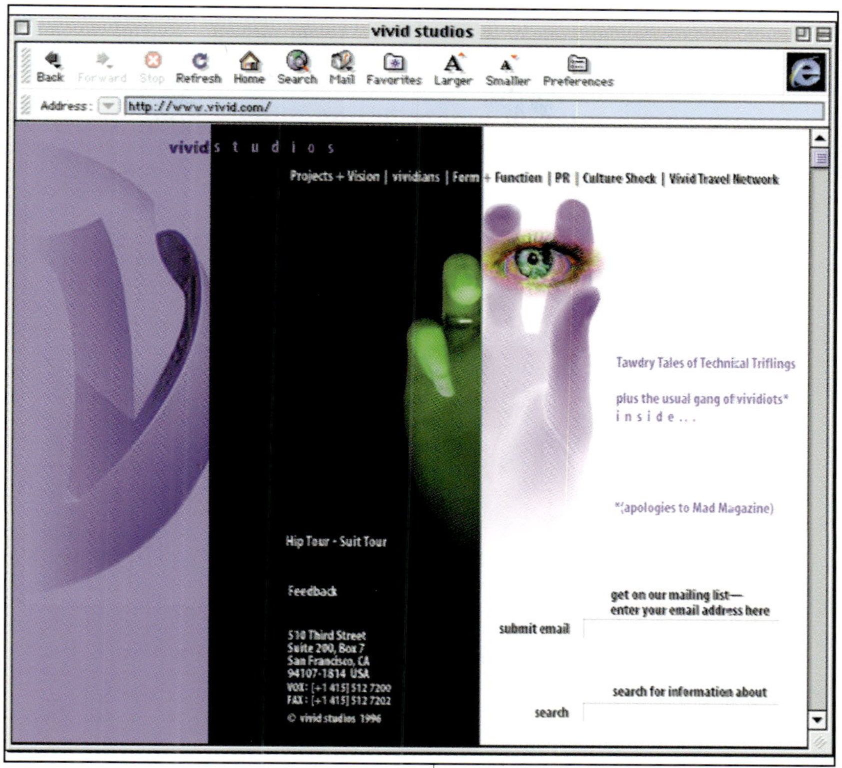


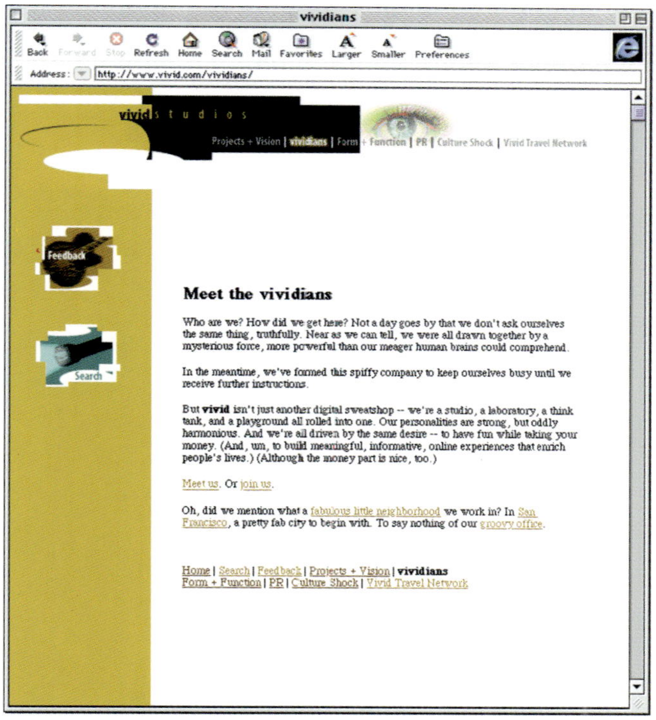


**VIVID STUDIOS WEB SITE**
**www.vivid.com**

| | |
|---|---|
| Design Firm | *Vivid Studios* |
| Creative Director | *Nathan Shedroff* |
| Designers | *Jeff Davis, Nathan Shedroff, Maurice Tani* |
| Copywriter | *Drue Miller* |
| Photographers | *Brian Bell, Chuck Gothard, Marsha Plot* |
| Programmers | *Paul Guth, Nat Johnson* |

The photography on this site is imaginative, abstract, and haunting. Especially uncanny is how the ever-alert eye gives us the feeling that Big Brother is watching.

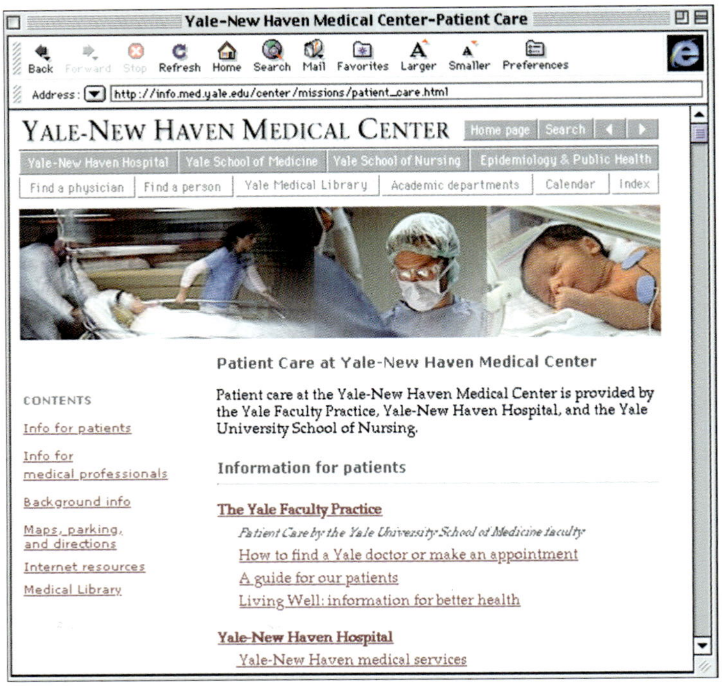


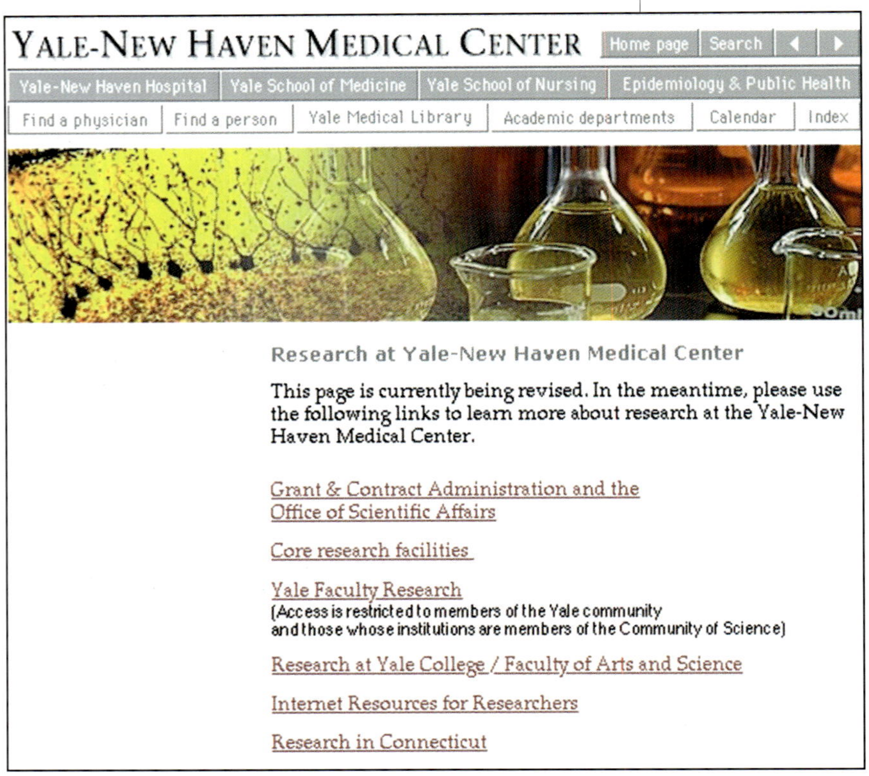


**YALE-NEW HAVEN MEDICAL CENTER WEB SITE**
**info.med.yale.edu/index.html**

| | |
|---|---|
| **Design Firm** | *Yale University Center for Advanced Instructional Media* |
| **Designer** | *Patrick J. Lynch* |
| **Illustrator** | *Patrick J. Lynch* |
| **Photographs** | *Yale University Biomedical Communications* |
| **Programmer** | *Sean Jackson* |

Rather than scattering several photos across a Web page, the Yale-New Haven Medical Center site builds multiple photographic images into bars that span the width of each page and work as the primary graphic element.

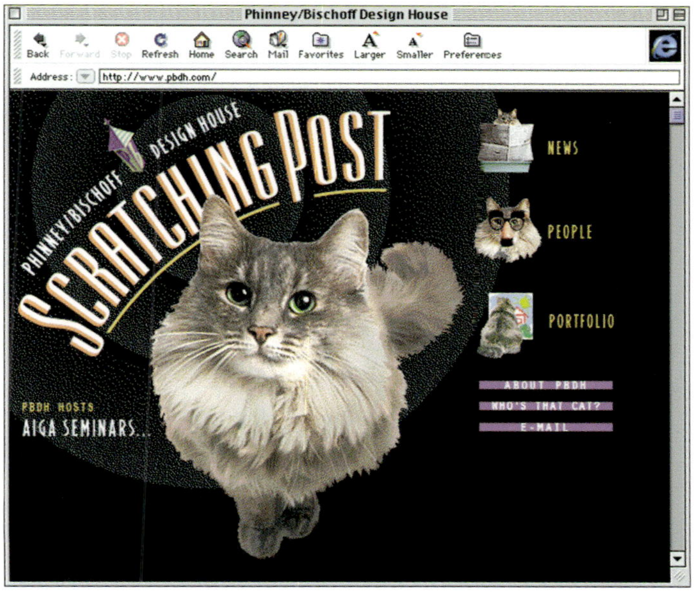


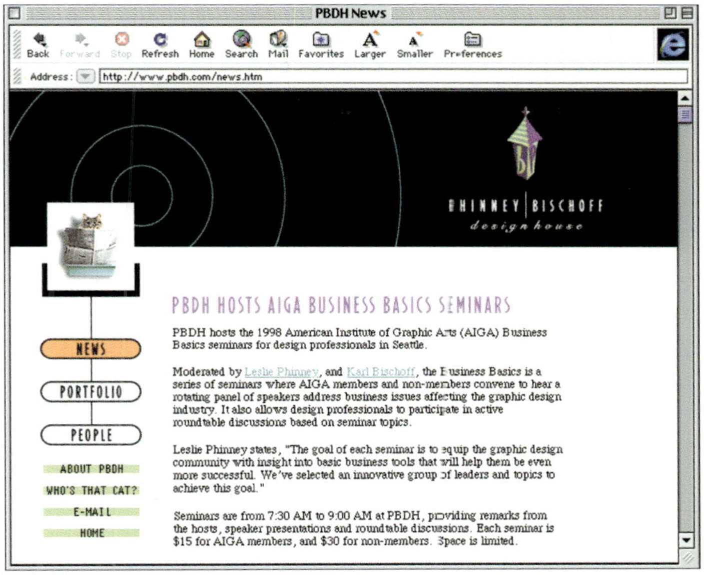


**PHINNEY/BISCHOFF DESIGN HOUSE, INC. WEB SITE**
**www.pbdh.com**

**Design Firm** *Phinney/Bischoff Design House, Inc.*
**Creative Directors** *Leslie Phinney, Karl Bischoff*
**Designer** *Neil Robertson*
**Illustrator** *Neil Robertson*
**Photographer** *Karl Bishoff*
**Programmers** *Neil Robertson, Scotty Carreiro*

Photography that is offbeat and unexpected makes this site noteworthy, while giving the potential client plenty of insight into the firm's creative style through an online portfolio.

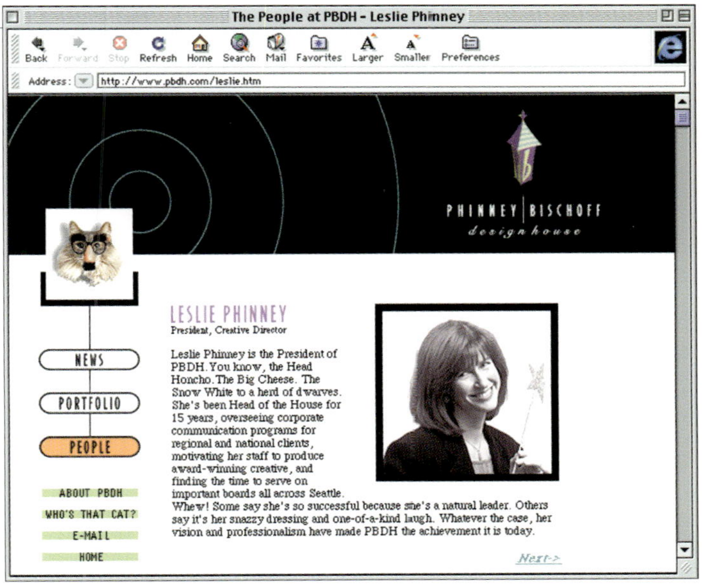

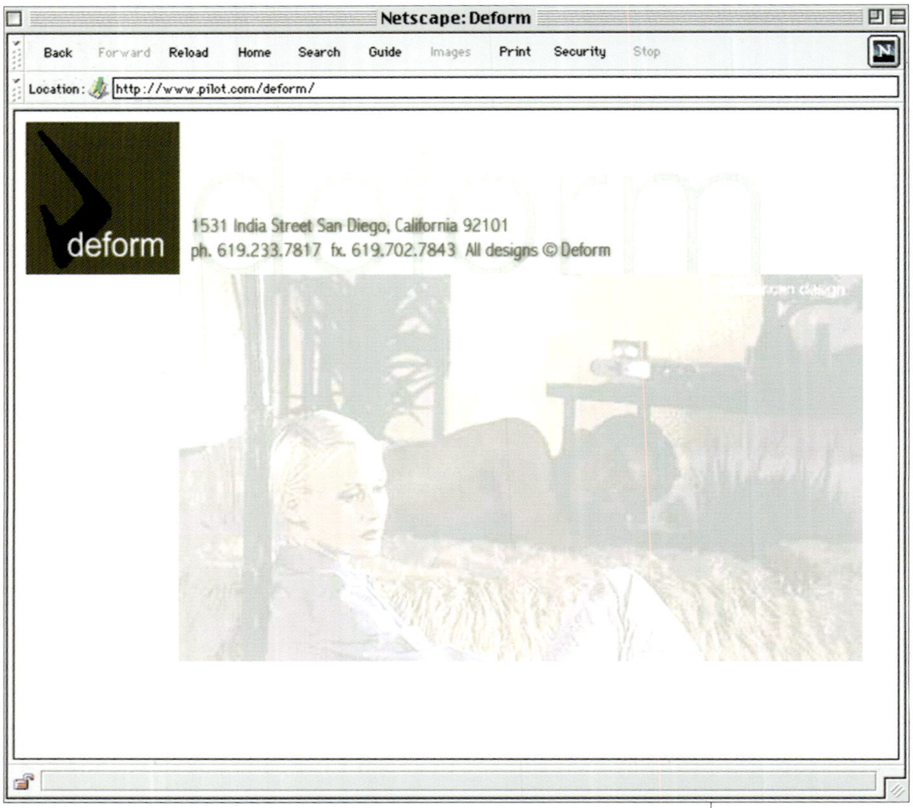


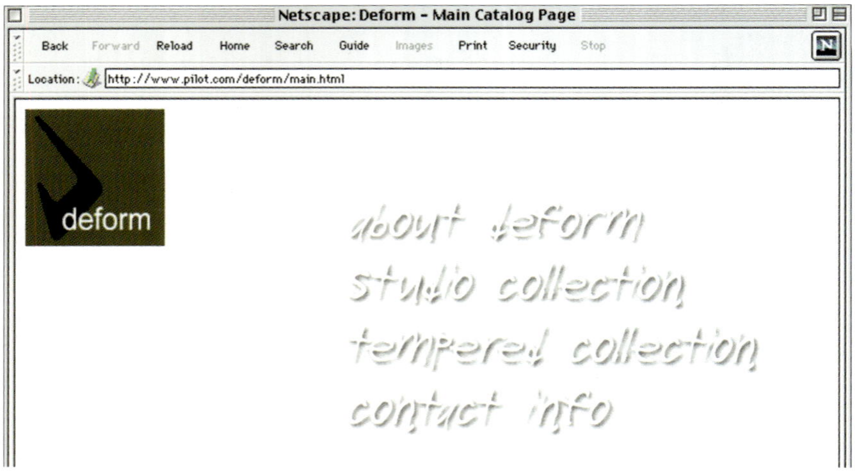


**DEFORM WEB SITE**
**www.pilot.com/deform**

| | |
|---|---|
| **Design Firm** | *Computer Diversion* |
| **All Design** | *Randal Antler* |
| **Photographer** | *David Harrison* |

While many Web sites shout, this one whispers. The photography is pale, faded to a gauzy image that make for a dream-like mural. Yet, despite its quiet approach, the message comes across clearly, even when white typ is used on a white background.

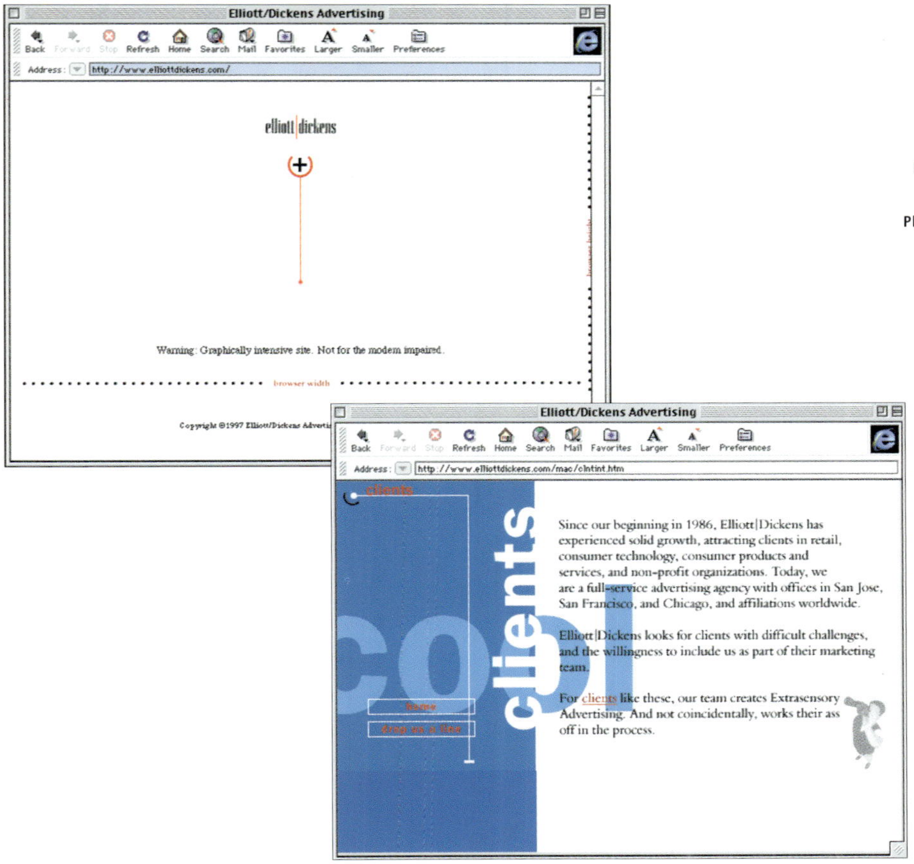


## ELLIOTT/DICKENS WEB SITE

**www.elliottdickens.com**

| | |
|---|---|
| **Design Firm** | *Elliott/Dickens* |
| **Designers** | *Percy Wang, Dave Cook, Cardinal O'Neill, Chris Tiernan* |
| **Photographer** | *Jack Christiansen* |
| **Producers** | *Ted Ganchiff, Andy Laing* |

We are accustomed to printed promotions using an in-your-face marketing approach, but to date, the Web has been more conservative, until this site, that is. Instead of using thumb-nail images of the principles, we get to meet them up close—very close.

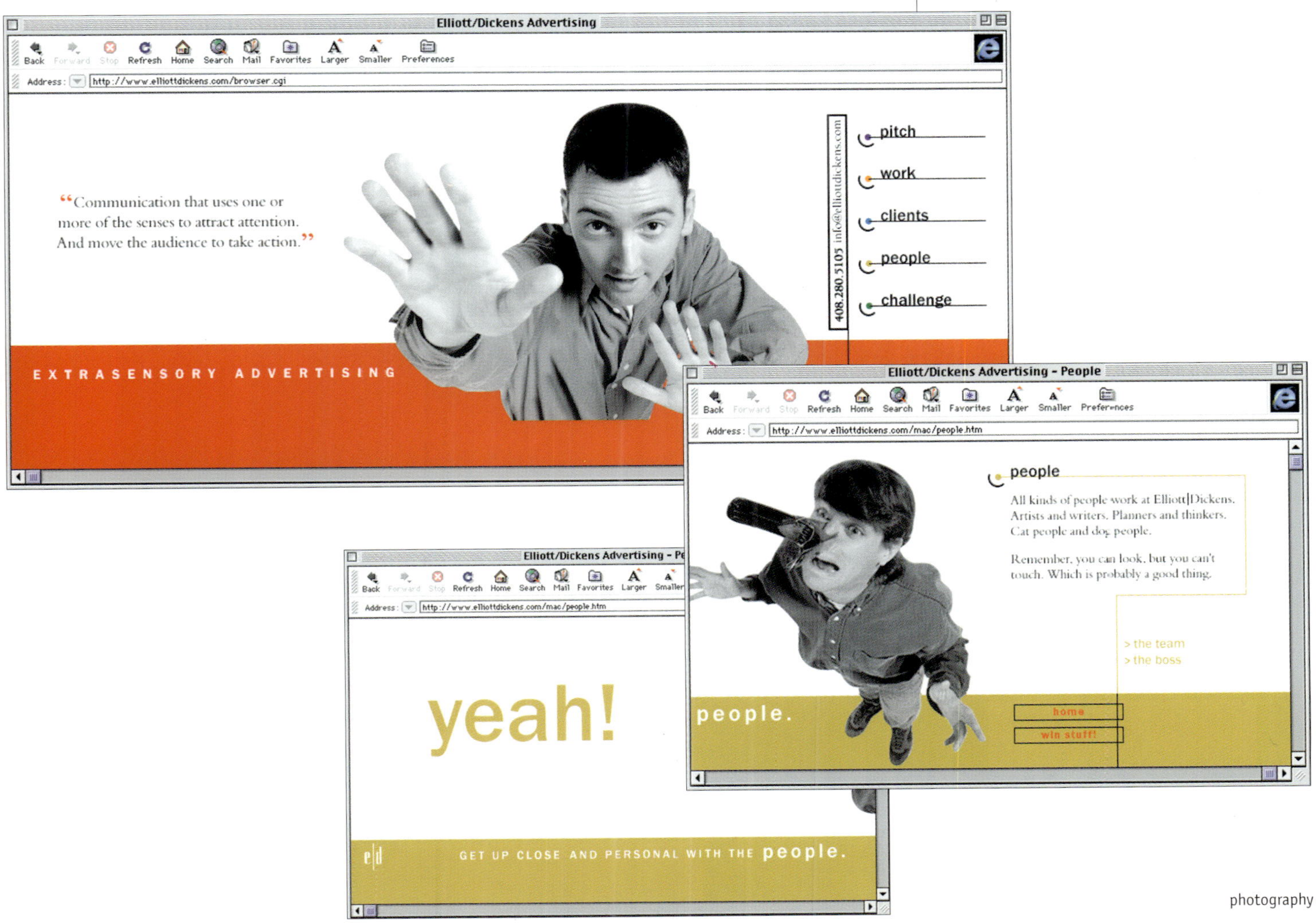

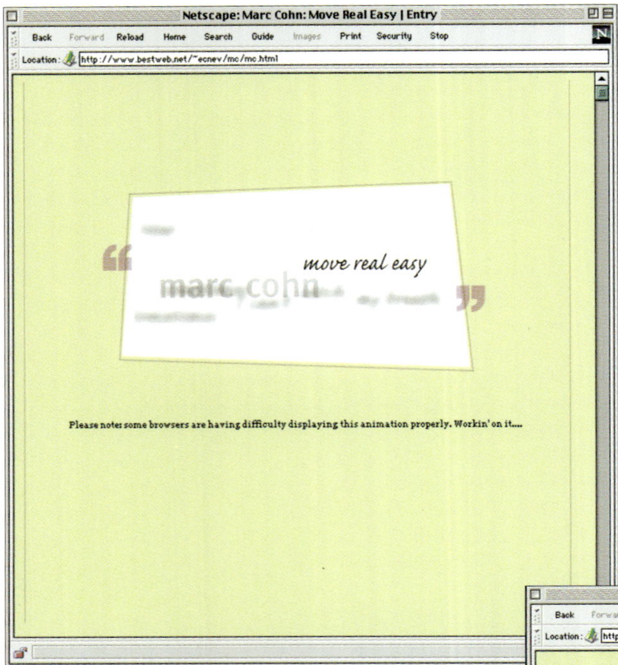


**MARC COHN *MOVE REAL EASY* WEB SITE**
**www.bestweb.net/~ecnev/mc/mc.html**

**Design Firm** *One Art Design*
**All Design** *Eric C. Nevin*

The title of the featured CD, *Move Real Easy*, sums up the photographic theme of Cohn's Web site. Some images are in focus, but unusually cropped, while others are screened back with mood-enhancing special effects.

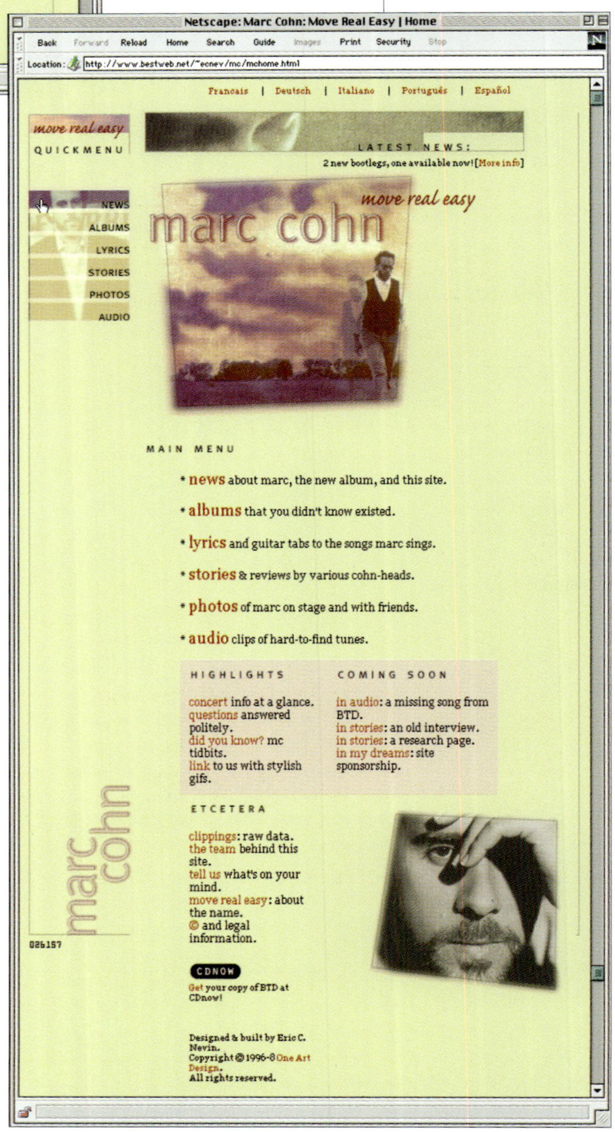

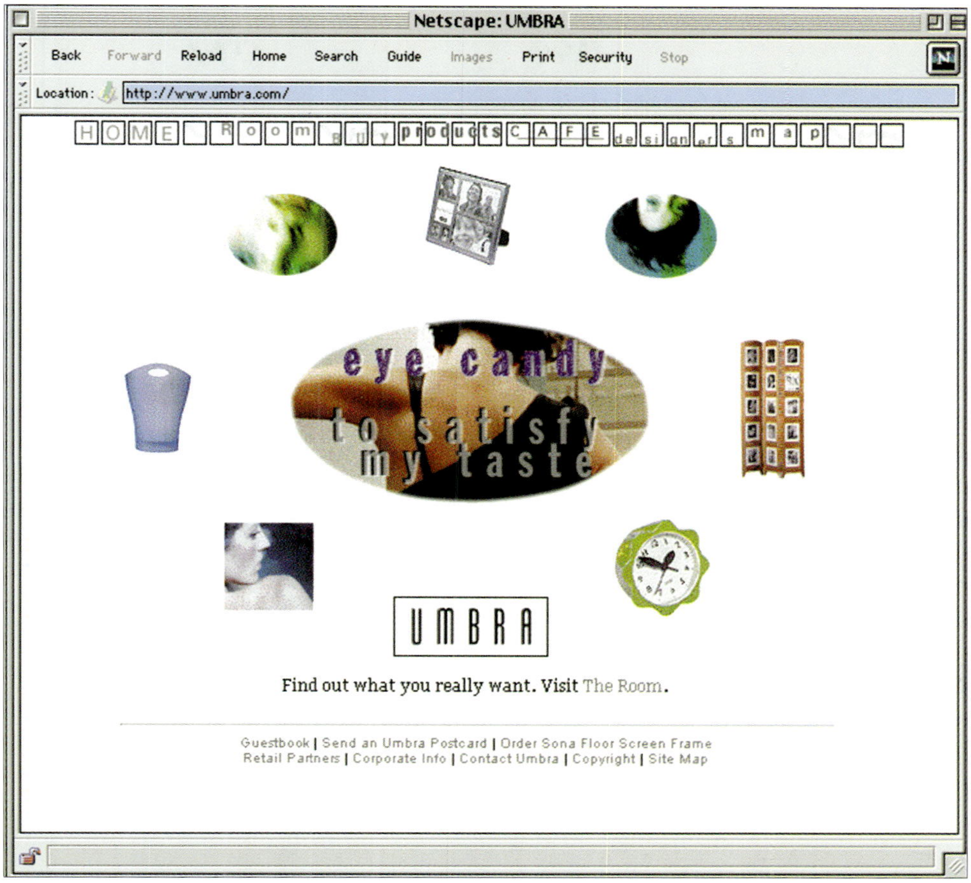


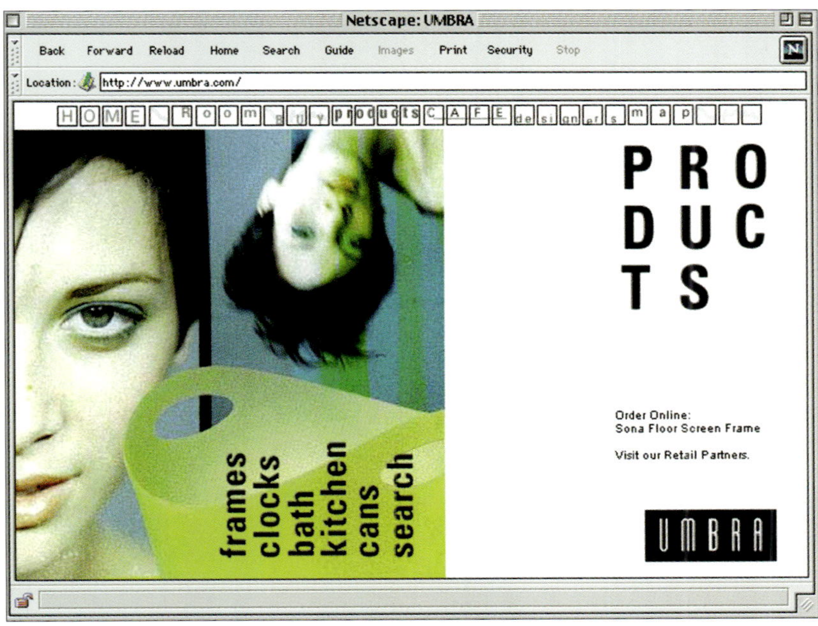


**UMBRA WEB SITE**
**www.umbra.com**

| | |
|---|---|
| **Design Firm** | *The James Gang* |
| **Creative Director** | *Mires Design* |
| **Designers** | *Bill James, Franke James* |
| **Illustrator** | *Franke James* |
| **Photographer** | *Franke James* |
| **Programmer** | *Bill James* |

Special photographic effects are used extensively on this Web site where images are unfocused, placed upside down, and cropped to reveal only what the designer wants us to see.

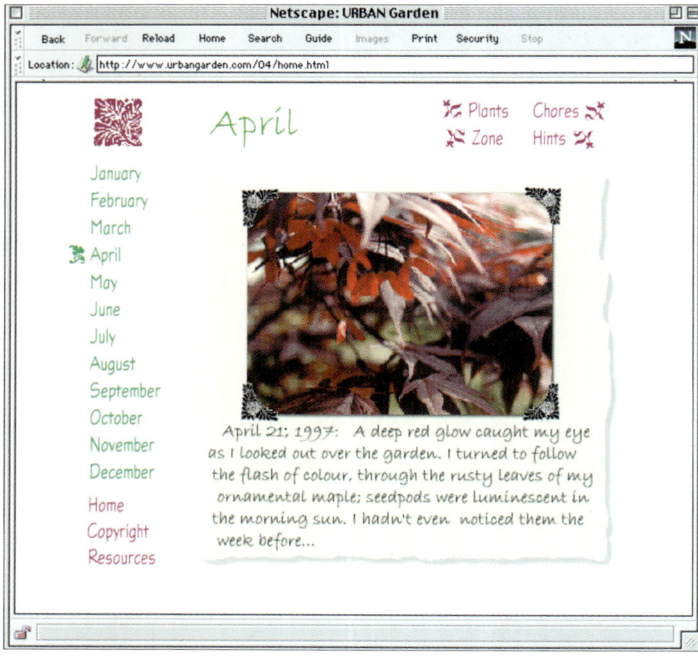


**URBAN GARDEN WEB SITE**
**www.urbangarden.com/index.html**

**Design Firm** *Buzz Solutions*
**All Design** *Deanna Beat*

The photography at this garden spot on the Web is integrated into the design so seamlessly that rather than looking like horticultural specimens, the photos appear as snapshots held in place by computer dingbats in a gardener's treasured journal.

**BLUE MARLIN WEB SITE**
**www.bluemarlincorp.com/home.html**

**Design Firm** *Atlas Web Design*
**Art Directors** *Francoise Sejourne, Blue Marlin*
**Designer** *Olivier Laude*
**Photographer** *Joe Budd*
**Programmer** *Michael Macrone*

The vintage look of this site is due primarily to the artful use and placement of photography that mixes and matches classic black-and-white with sepia-toned images.

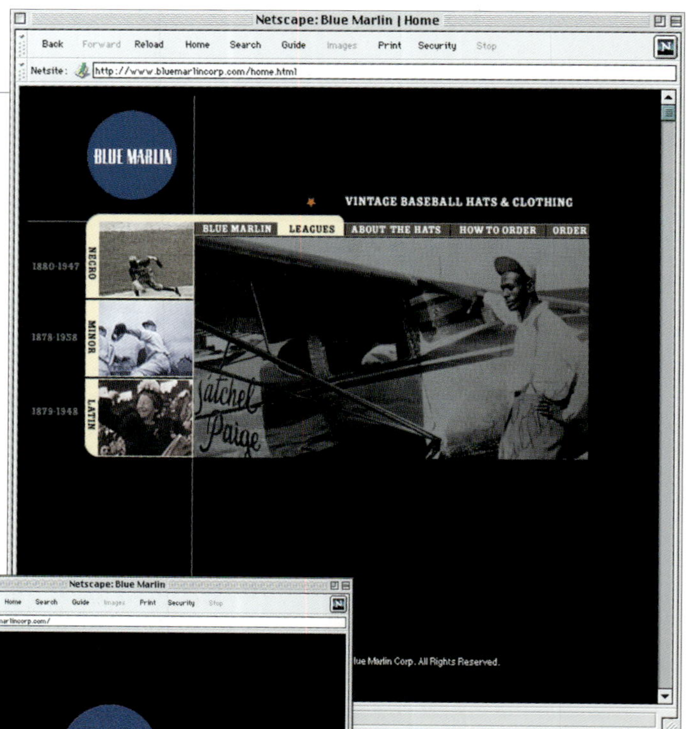


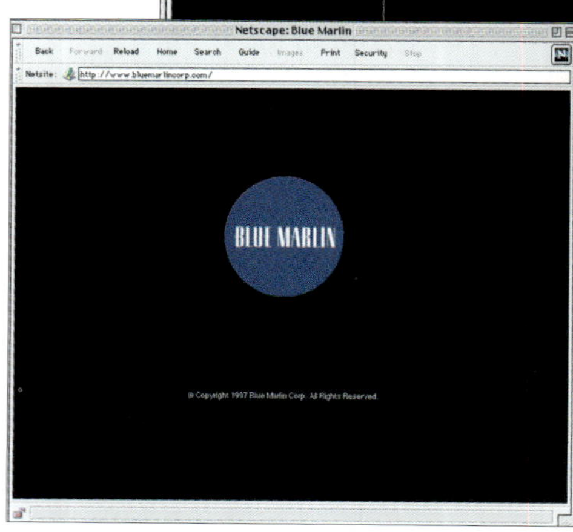

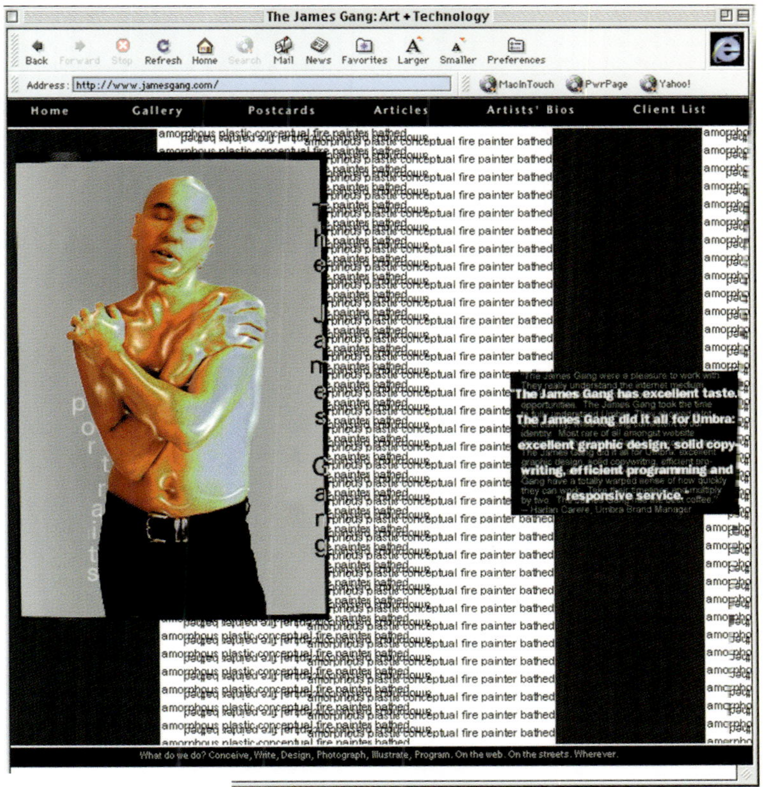


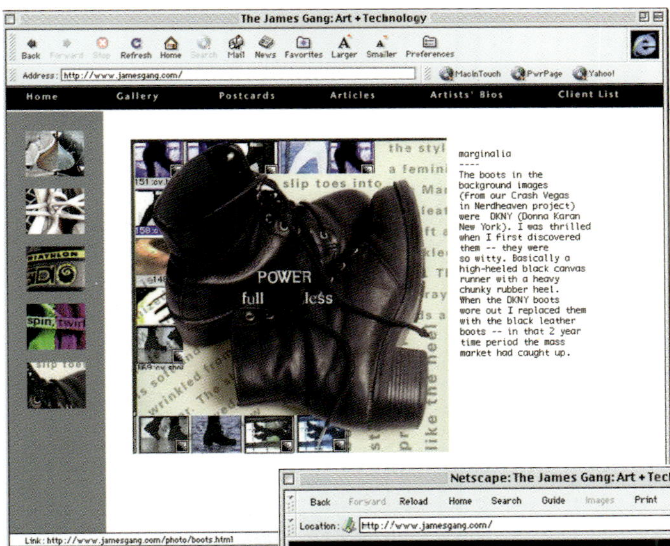


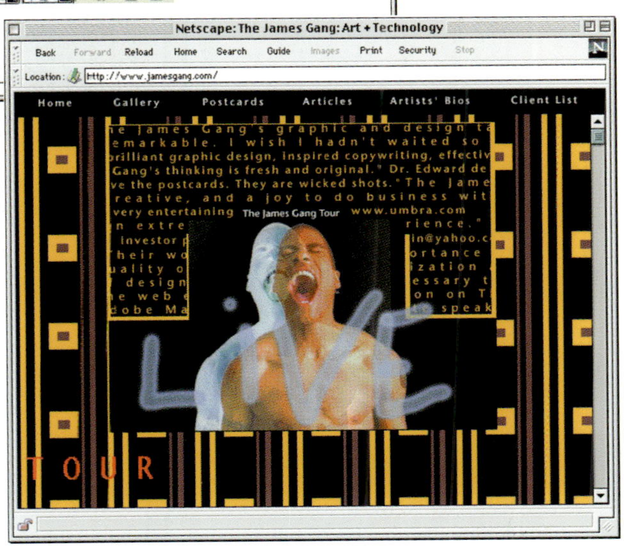


**THE JAMES GANG WEB SITE**
**www.jamesgang.com**

| | |
|---|---|
| **Design Firm** | *The James Gang: Art + Technology* |
| **Designers** | *Franke James, Bill James* |
| **Illustrator** | *Franke James* |
| **Photographer** | *Franke James* |
| **Programmer** | *Bill James* |
| **Model** | *Ronnae (Ford Models)* |

The James Gang makes good use of simply staged prop shots, but with model shots they really excel. By imposing the model's negative image behind the color version, his voice seems to literally reverberate from the home page.

**PRIVATE ART WEB SITE**
**www.private-art.com**

**Design Firm** *Enviromedia, Inc.*
**Designer** *Rebecca Pranger*
**Illustrator** *Rebecca Pranger*
**Programmer** *Larry Pranger*

Taking photos from various sources and giving them a uniform look can be an overwhelming challenge, but the designer sidestepped any problems by washing the photos with a khaki tint. This not only unifies all the images, but gives the site its wartime atmosphere as well.

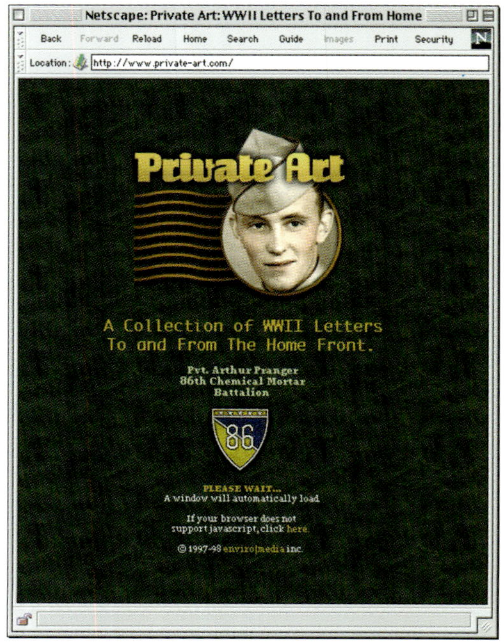


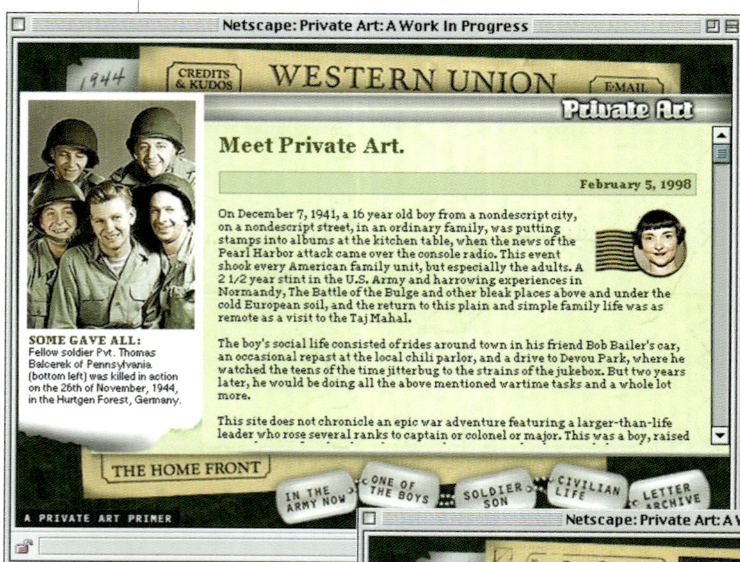


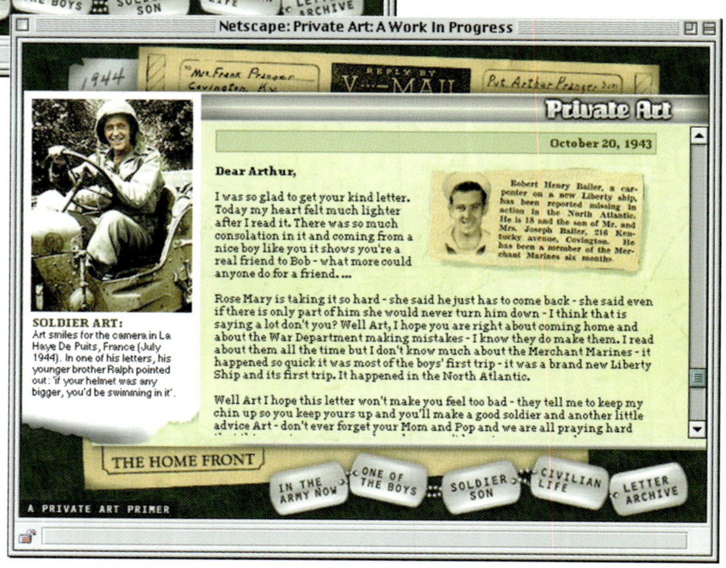

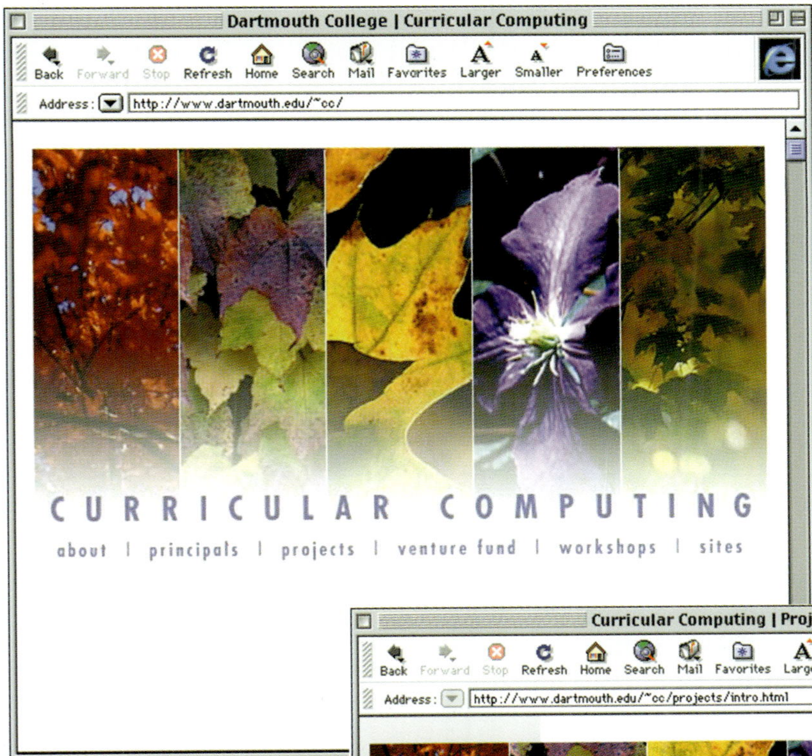


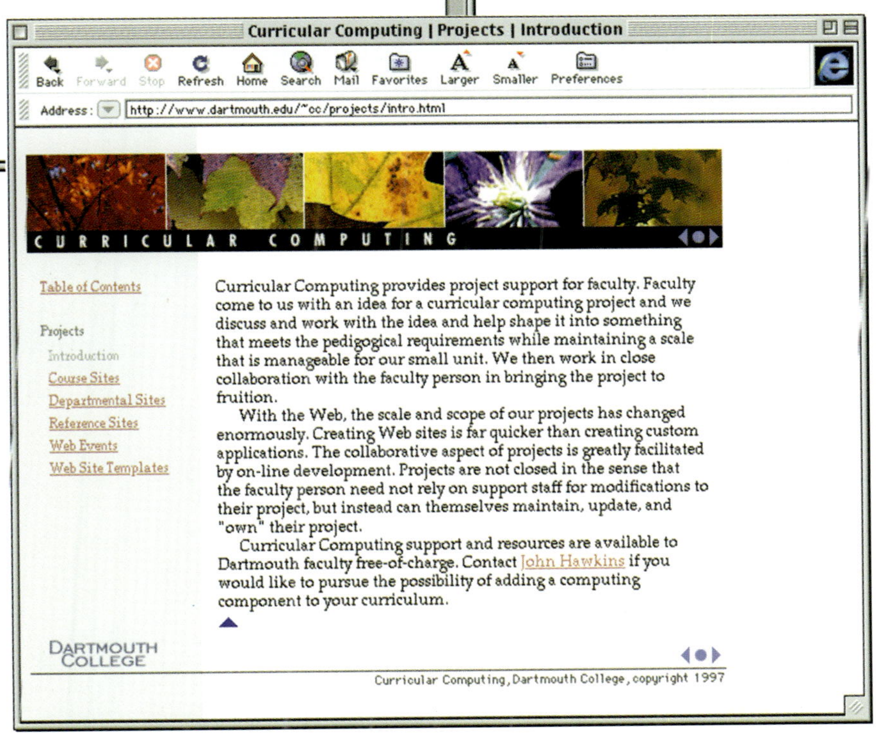


**CURRICULAR COMPUTING WEB SITE**
**www.dartmouth.edu/~cc**

**Design Firm** *Dartmouth College Curricular Computing*
**All Design** *Sarah Horton*
**Photographers** *PhotoDisc, Inc.*

Five dominant stock images, each a perfect complement to the other, are narrowly cropped and fade to nothingness as they give way to the title bar on the home page. Subsequent pages rely on the same images, recropped as thumbnails, that provide an overall cohesiveness and graphic appeal to an otherwise copy-intensive site.

**SOULFLARE WEB SITE**
**www.soulflare.com**

**Designer** *Lance Arthur*
**Programmer** *Lance Arthur*

The image of the hand and the ball in mid air against the black backdrop is simple, eerie, and mysterious, all of which beckons us to enter.

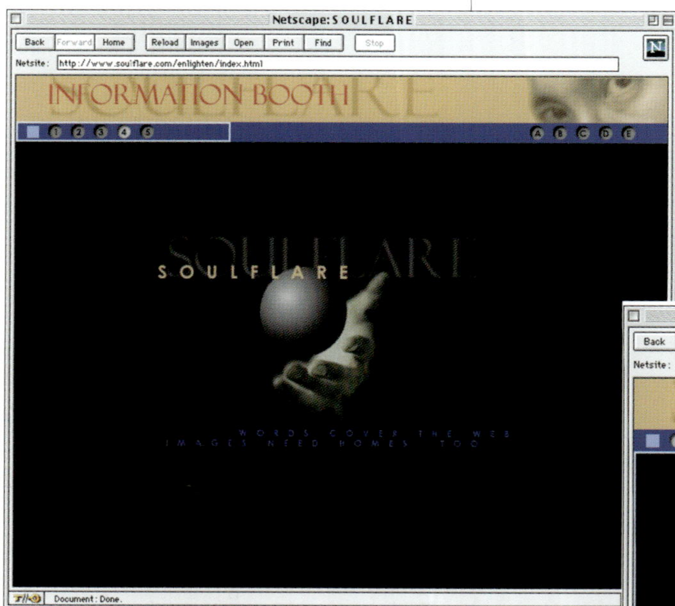


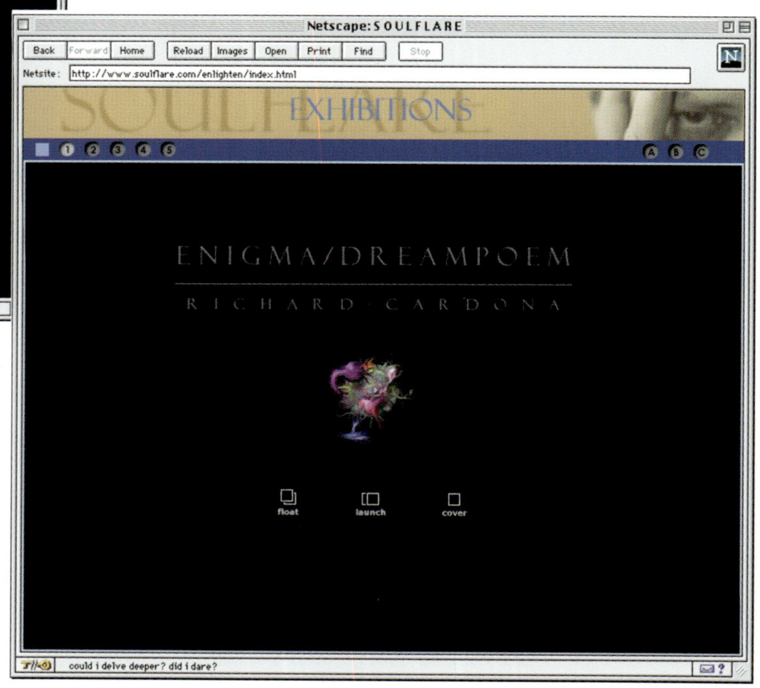


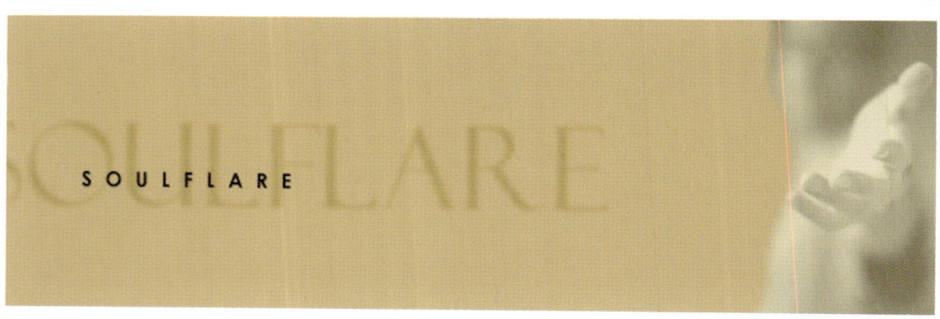

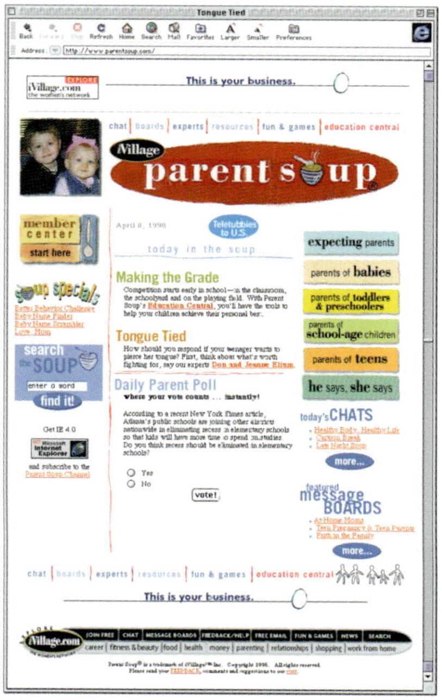


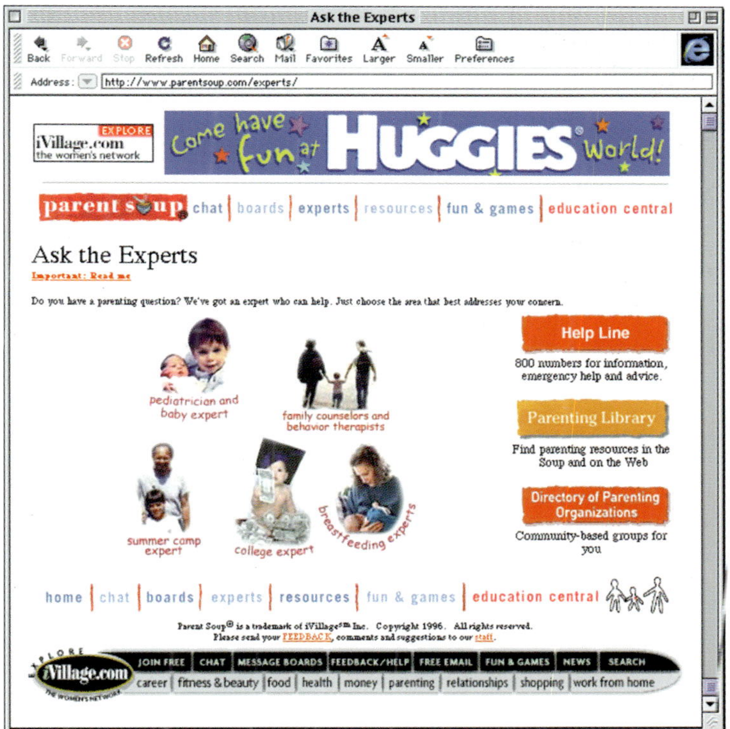


**PARENT SOUP WEB SITE**
**www.parentsoup.com**

| | |
|---|---|
| **Design Firm** | *Parent Soup* |
| **Designer** | *Christina Fredericks* |
| **Illustrator** | *Christina Fredericks* |
| **Programmers** | *Fay Ku, Tom Simpson* |

The photography at this site about kids, yet directed at adults, is endearing and humorous without being overly sappy. Particularly noteworthy are the photos that communicate their message without words, such as the graduation-capped baby sitting in a pile of paper money.

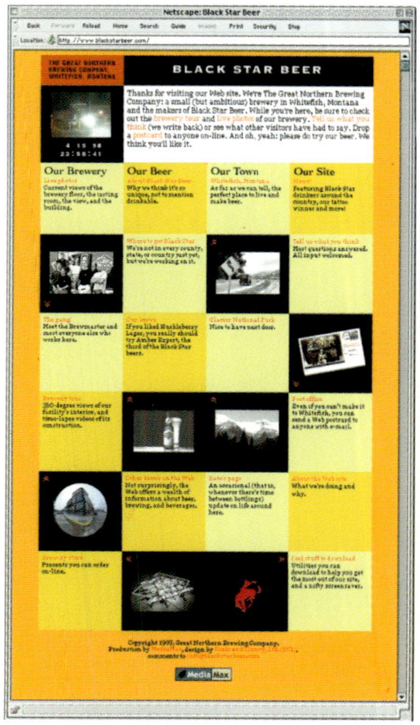

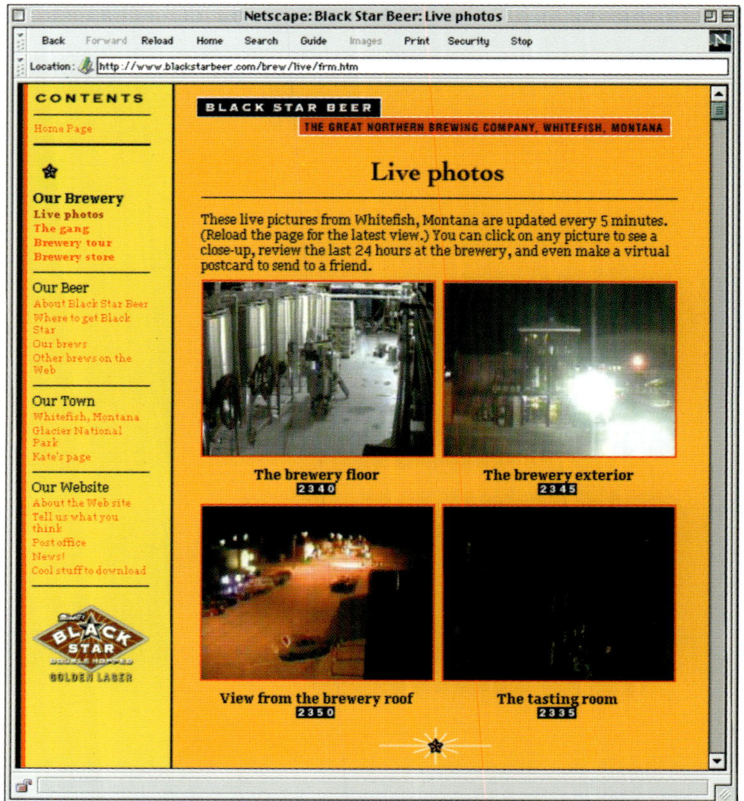


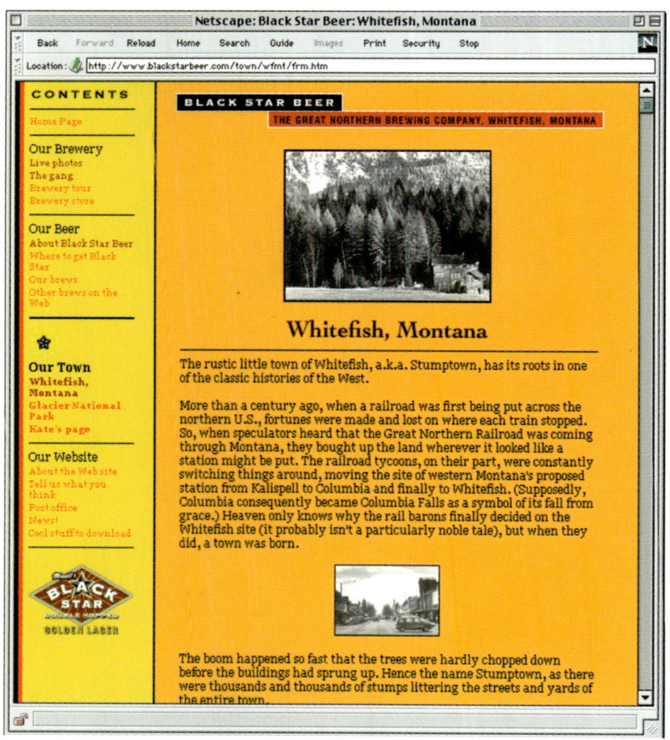


**BLACK STAR BEER WEB SITE**
**www.blackstarbeer.com**

| | |
|---|---|
| **Design Firm** | *DCL (Doris and Clancy, Ltd.)* |
| **Designers** | *Doris Mitsch, Clancy Nolan* |
| **Copywriters** | *Toby Barlow, Doris Mitsch, Kate Greenlee* |
| **Photographers** | *Doug Menuez, Mike Calabro, Amy R. Colson* |
| **Programmer** | *Mediamax* |

Manufacturers' Web sites with static photos and boilerplate copy requiring infrequent updates can become stale quickly. To encourage return visits, Black Star Beer keeps their site fresh and timely by updating live photos of the brewery every five minutes and allowing access to the images for use as virtual postcards.

**WE MAKE ART DOLLS AND AUTOMATA WEB SITE**
**www.home.earthlink.net/~chomedolls/cmcollector**

**Design Firm** *Chomick & Meder*
**All Design** *Chris Chomick*

The photography of the collector dolls at this site shows an incredible level of detail. Since collectors like to scrutinize their purchases before buying, this site gives them an eyeful with crisp, clear imagery.

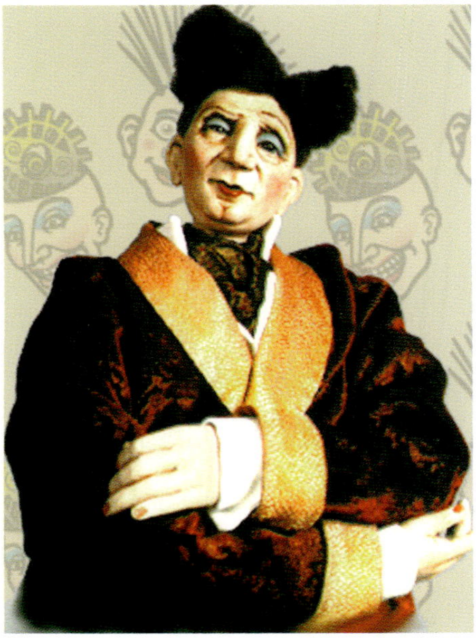

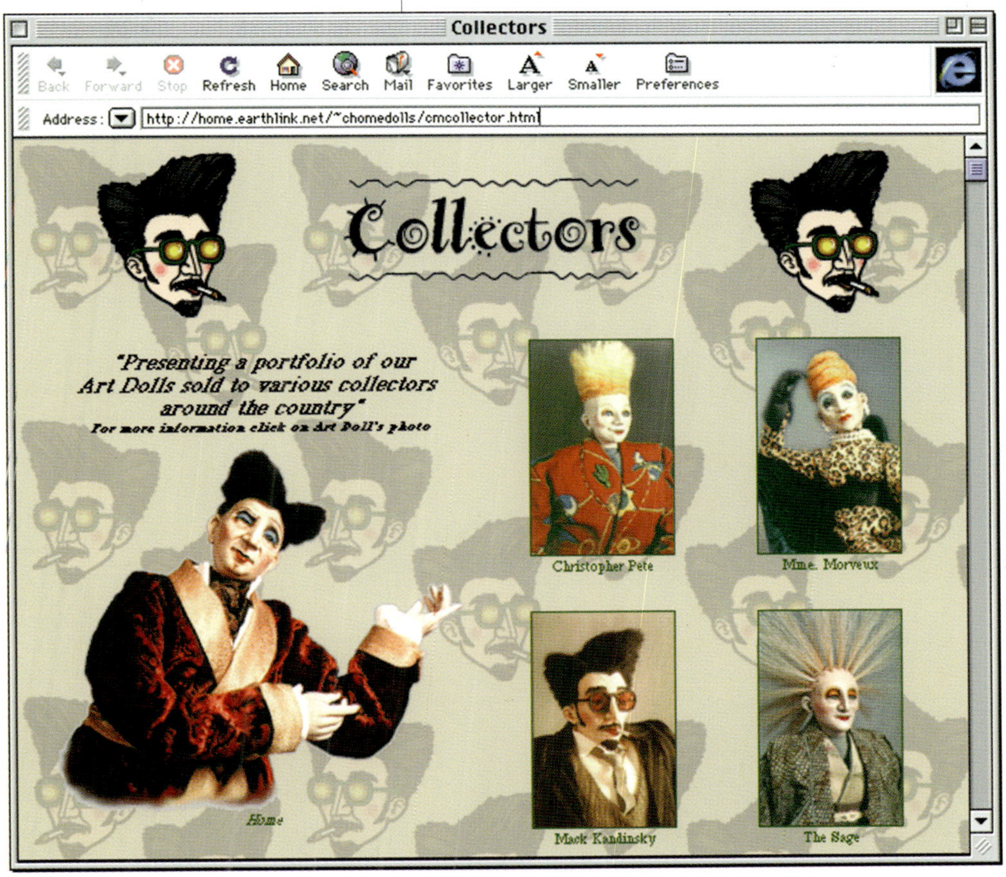

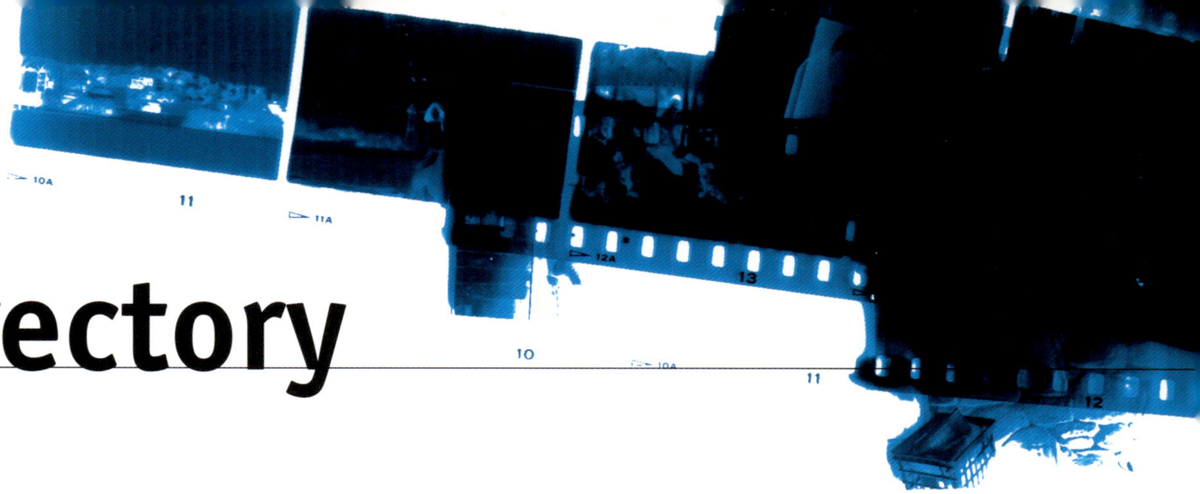

# directory

40 | *Adventure 16*
4620 Alvarado Canyon Drive
San Diego, CA 92120

90 | *Lance Arthur*
76 Lexington Street
Auburndale, MA 02166

58 | *Asylum, Inc.*
848 W. Eastman Street, Suite 206
Chicago, IL 60607

27 | *Atlantic Design Works*
24 Glenbrook Road
W. Hartford, CT 06107

40 | *Edward Behr*
*The Art of Eating*
P.O. Box 242
Peacham, VT 05862

52 | *Berni Design*
660 Steamboat Road
Greenwich, CT 06830

72 | *John D. Berry Design*
525 19th Avenue East
Seattle, WA 98112

86 | *Blue Marlin*
540 Florida Street
San Francisco, CA 94110

67 | *Boelts Brothers Associates*
345 E. University Boulevard
Tucson, AZ 85705

55 | *Bonita Pioneer Design & Packaging*
7333 SW Bonita Road
Portland, OR 97224

8 | *Boxer Design*
548 State Street
Brooklyn, NY 11217

6 | *Brooklyn Academy of Music*
30 Lafayette Avenue
Brooklyn, NY 11217

42, 43 | *Cahan & Associates*
818 Brannan Street
San Francisco, CA 94103

62, 65 | *Carbone Smolan Associates*
22 West 19th Street, 10th Floor
New York, NY 10011

49 | *Carré Noir*
82, bd. Des Batigrolles
75850 Paris
Cedex 17
France

93 | *Chomick & Meder*
5248-52nd Avenue North
St. Petersburg, FL 33709

32, 33 | *Christie's*
502 Park Avenue
New York, NY 10022

44, 45 | *City of Hope*
208 W. 8th Street
Los Angeles, CA 90014

89 | *Dartmouth College*
Kiewit Computation Center
Hanover, NH 03755

82 | *deform*
1531 India Street
San Diego, CA 92101

50 | *Design Guys*
119 Fourth Street, 400
Minneapolis, MN 55401

12 | *Design: M/W*
149 Wooster Street
New York, NY 10012

54 | *Elle In-House*
1633 Broadway, 44th Floor
New York, NY 10019

83 | *Elliott/Dickens*
97 S. Second Street, Suite 220
San Jose, CA 95113

29 | *eman communications design, inc.*
105 S. Narcissus Avenue, Suite 402
West Palm Beach, FL 33401

88 | *Enviromedia, Inc.*
617 Vine Street, Suite 1336
Cincinnati, OH 45202

49 | *Estee Lauder In-House Design*
767 5th Avenue, Floor 37
New York, NY 10153

75, 77 | *Froeter Design Company, Inc*
954 W. Washington
Chicago, IL 60607

28 | *G*
640 E. 15th Avenue, Apt. 206
Eugene, OR 97401

51, 53 | *Gee & Chung Design*
38 Bryant Street, Suite 100
San Francisco, CA 94105

22 | *Grafik Comm Ltd.*
1199 North Fairfax Street, Suite 700
Alexandria, VA 22314

92 | *The Great Northern Brewing Company*
2 Central Avenue
Whitefish, MT 59937

66 | *Gyro Interactive*
502 Albert Street
East Melbourne
Victoria 3002
Australia

41 | *H. J. Heinz Company*
P.O. Box 57
Pittsburgh, PA 15230

30, 31 | *Hal Apple Design & Communications, Inc.*
1112 Ocean Drive, Suite 203
Manhattan Beach, CA 90266

26 | *Hornall Anderson Design Works, Inc.*
1008 Western Avenue, Suite 600
Seattle, WA 98104

78 | *Ignition, Inc.*
870 Market Street
San Francisco, CA 94102

70 | *Interface Designers*
Rua Do Russell 300/702
Gloria 22210-010
Rio de Janeiro, Rio,
Brazil

91 | *iVillage/Parent Soup*
170 Fifth Avenue
New York, NY 10010

85, 87 | *The James Gang*
3080 Young Street, Suite 5044
Toronto Ontario M4N3N3
Canada

73 | *Johnson & Wolverton*
510 NW 19th Avenue
Portland, OR 97209

57 | *Kan & Lau Design Consultants*
28/F Great Smart Tower
230 Wanchai Road, Hong Kong

# P H O T O G R A P H Y

**24, 25** *Kiku Obata & Company*
5585 Pershing Avenue, Suite 240
St. Louis, MO 63112

**70** *L Design*
5 bis, rue des Haindriettes
75003 Paris
France

**46** *Larsen Design + Interactive*
7101 York Avenue South
Minneapolis, MN 55435

**9** *Lautman & Company*
Suite 700
1730 Rhode Island Avenue NW
Washington, D.C. 20036

**14** *Lorenc Design*
724 Longleaf Drive NE
Atlanta, GA 30342

**9** *Malchow Adams & Hussey*
1400 I Street, N.W., Suite 650
Washington, DC 20005

**16** *Maxima New Media*
2472 Broadway, Suite 195
New York, NY 10025

**64** *Media Artists Inc. s.r.l.*
Via G. Marconi 10/A
Albino BG
Italy

**63** *Minelli Design*
381 Congress Street
Boston, MA 02210

**13** *Stewart Monderer Design, Inc.*
10 Thacher Street, Suite 112
Boston, MA 02113

**10** *Moondog Studios, Inc.*
210-309 W. Cordova Street
Vancouver, British Columbia
Canada V6B1E5

**18, 19, 20, 21** *G. E. Neise Digital Communication*
1402 W. Superior #2
Chicago, IL 60622

**11** *Ocean Home Shopping Ltd.*
5 Pensbury Street
London SW84TL
United Kingdom

**84** *One Art Design*
P.O. Box 490
Briarcliff, NY 10510

**60** *Pentagram Design*
204 Fifth Avenue
New York, NY 10010

**81** *Phinney/Bischoff Design House, Inc.*
614 Boylstone
Seattle, WA 98102

**38, 39** *Princess Cruises*
10100 Santa Monica Boulevard
Los Angeles, CA 90068

**23** *Giorgio Rocco Communications*
Via Domenichino 27
Milan 20149
Italy

**54** *Saatchi & Saatchi Business Communications*
255 Woodcliff Drive
Fairport, NY 14450

**15** *Mike Salisbury Communications*
2200 Amapola Court
Torrance, CA 90501

**47** *Sibley Peteet Design*
2905 San Gabriel #300
Austin, TX 78705

**7** *Socio X*
245 East 60th Street, 2nd Floor
New York, NY 10022

**62, 74** *Tangram Strategic Design*
Via Negroni 2
28100 Novara
Italy

**76** *Toda Office*
#505 Azabu-Toriizaka Building
5-10-33 Roppongi
Minato-ku
Tokyo 106
Japan

**34, 35** *University Media Services*
California State University—Sacramento
6000 J Street
Sacramento, CA 95819

**71** *UNO, Yasuyuki Design Studio Inc.*
710, Casa Grande Miwa Building, 7-5-11 Roppongi
Minato-ku
Tokyo 106-0032
Japan

**86** *Urban Garden*
411-1106 Pacific Street
Vancouver British Columbia
Canada

**79** *Vivid Studios*
510 3rd Street
San Francisco, CA 94107

**36, 37** *VSA Partners, Inc.*
542 South Dearborn, Suite 202
Chicago, IL 60605

**69** *Why Not Associates*
Studio 17
10–11 Archer Street
London WLV7HG
England

**68** *Wild Plakken*
Elandsstraat 149'
1016-RZ
Amsterdam, Netherlands

**80** *Yale University*
Center for Advanced Instructional Media
47 College Street
New Haven, CT 06511